# Strength Training for Women

Lori Incledon

**HUMAN
KINETICS**

**Library of Congress Cataloging-in-Publication Data**

Incledon, Lori.
 Strength training for women / Lori Incledon.
    p. cm.
Includes bibliographical references and index.
ISBN 0-7360-5223-2 (soft cover)
1. Weight training for women. 2. Exercise for women. 3. Physical fitness for women. 4.
 Muscle strength. I. Title.
 GV546.6.W64I63 2005
 613.7'1'082--dc22

                                    2004014047

ISBN: 0-7360-5223-2

The Web addresses cited in this text were current as of October 18, 2004, unless otherwise noted.

**Acquisitions Editor:** Edward McNeely; **Developmental Editor:** Julie Rhoda; **Assistant Editor:** Carla Zych; **Copyeditor:** Kathy Knight Calder; **Proofreader**: Anne Rogers; **Indexer**: Nan N. Budgett; **Permission Manager:** Toni Harte; **Graphic Designer:** Nancy Rasmus; **Graphic Artist:** Francine Hamerski; **Photo Manager:** Dan Wendt; **Cover Designer:** Keith Blomberg; **Photographer (cover):** K. Vey/Jumpfoto; **Photographer (interior):** Dan Wendt except where otherwise noted; **Art Manager:** Kareema McLendon; **Illustrator:** Jason McAlexander; **Printer:** Versa Press

We thank Gold's Gym in Champaign, Illinois, for providing the location for the photo shoot for this book.

Human Kinetics books are available at special discounts for bulk purchase. Special editions or book excerpts can also be created to specification. For details, contact the Special Sales Manager at Human Kinetics.

Printed in the United States of America    10 9 8 7 6 5 4 3 2 1

**Human Kinetics**
Web site: www.HumanKinetics.com

*United States:* Human Kinetics
P.O. Box 5076
Champaign, IL 61825-5076
800-747-4457
e-mail: humank@hkusa.com

*Canada:* Human Kinetics
475 Devonshire Road Unit 100
Windsor, ON N8Y 2L5
800-465-7301 (in Canada only)
e-mail: orders@hkcanada.com

*Europe:* Human Kinetics
107 Bradford Road
Stanningley
Leeds LS28 6AT, United Kingdom
+44 (0) 113 255 5665
e-mail: hk@hkeurope.com

*Australia:* Human Kinetics
57A Price Avenue
Lower Mitcham, South Australia 5062
08 8277 1555
e-mail: liaw@hkaustralia.com

*New Zealand:* Human Kinetics
Division of Sports Distributors NZ Ltd.
P.O. Box 300 226 Albany
North Shore City
Auckland
0064 9 448 1207
e-mail: blairc@hknewz.com

*This book is dedicated to all the wonderful women who
have graced my life with their friendship, humor, and love.
Your strength is my strength.*

# Contents

# Part III  Movements and Muscles

# Acknowledgments

Thanks to Edward McNeely, who did a fantastic job of helping me develop the outline and scope of this book. Thanks to Julie Rhoda, who artfully and skillfully brought this book together and saw it through the home stretch while enduring the stress of both her first pregnancy and my wedding.

Much appreciation to the photo shoot crew of Dan Wendt, Carla Zych, Nicole McBean, and Yvette Dorian. I'd spend a late Saturday night with you anytime!

Special thanks to the entire Human Kinetics staff for their invaluable help in producing this book.

I gratefully thank all of my parents and all of my friends, who were always a source of constant encouragement and support.

To my amazing and brilliant husband Tom, who has given me the inspiration, motivation, and confidence to succeed: Thank you for your professional help and your love.

# Introduction

Are you spending hours in the gym without seeming to make any progress? Are you one of hundreds of women who crave more information on strengthening and balancing the body through strength training than the trainers at the gym or any fitness magazine can give you? If you think that you've tried it all on your way to being in the best possible shape you can be, think again. This book will take you to the next level if you are already strength training and will hopefully convert you to strength training if you are not. I've designed it especially to show you the benefits and pleasures of this great way to train your body.

Throughout this book you will learn not only the *hows* of strength training, to satisfy your body, but also the *whys*, to satisfy your mind so that you become well versed in the benefits of strength training. Then you can eloquently explain to your girlfriend how you lost 20 pounds with the help of a solid strength-training program, whereas she may still be trying to lose pounds exclusively by sweating up a storm on the stair machine.

In the beginning of the book you will read about the evolution and progression of women's fitness and training. You'll see where we have been, where we are, and where we are heading. You'll read about exercise trends and fads and about proven knowledge from a research perspective. Because I list and describe all of the benefits of strength training, you'll discover why it is one of the most beneficial and valuable types of exercise you can do. If you have questions about muscularity and strength (having either too much or too little), you will find answers here. If you are concerned about fat loss, you will learn why and how strength training (compared to most types of cardiovascular endurance exercise) is the best way to cut fat and increase your metabolism.

In part II you'll learn everything you ever wanted to know about physical fitness but didn't have the time to ask. This section highlights strength training and explains it in detail. Find out about the different kinds of training that exist and how you can incorporate them into your strength-training routine. You will also gain information on nutrition, both for general health and for specific conditions like training and competition. In the last chapter you'll get tips for designing your own program. Ready-made routines are there for you to try. You'll find specific routines for beginning, intermediate, and advanced trainers as well as a bone-building program.

Part III wraps it all up with detailed descriptions of the major strength exercises, the muscles they primarily work, and the effects of these exercises on your body. You'll even discover some new exercises that you may never have heard of, to help you add variety to your strength-training workouts. The last chapter describes a training regimen for weightlifting, powerlifting, and strongwoman competitions. If you are an intermediate to advanced strength trainer who is looking for new ideas or who wants to make sense of all of the information out there, this book will be your salvation. But don't despair if it is all new to you, because this easy-to-understand book will introduce you to a whole new way of thinking and lead you down the fitness path to a better body!

# Exercise Finder

# Part I

# Designing Women

# Becoming Fashionably Strong

We've ridden a roller coaster of ideas over the years about women's training. We've gone from doctors' forbidding women to engage in physical activity because they were too delicate, to doctors' warning of the dangers of not enough activity. When women first started to exercise and engage in athletic endeavors, some ridiculed them for being too masculine. As the popular advertisement said, "You've come a long way, baby!" Or have we? Some attitudes and preconceived notions about women's training still exist—perhaps you unknowingly harbor some of them.

So hang on to your leotard while we whip through some history on women's strength training to find out how it has evolved into the most recent practices backed by the latest research. You'll learn about all the benefits that strength training has to offer women, such as improving quality of life and possibly even prolonging it. You'll discover how to reprogram your attitude on muscularity and truly become the strong and fit woman you were meant to be.

## Strength Training Origins and Evolution

Strength training is in no way a modern invention. Pictures on Egyptian tombs show the lifting of bags filled with sand along with stone swinging and throwing, which were also popular in the early histories of Germany, Scotland, and Spain. Men's weightlifting competitions date back to early Greek civilization, which originated the games that became the modern Olympics. Of course, these pioneers didn't have the sophisticated equipment that we have today or the research on training and physiology to back up the exercises, but they did have the most important thing—the desire to lift something heavy for fun, sport, and physical health.

As weightlifters began to make their own equipment instead of using Mother Nature's gifts, we gained more modern inventions. For example, dumbbells originated in the 1700s when a rod was placed between two church bells. When the clapper was removed from the bells, they became silent, or dumb—hence the word *dumbbell*. Indian clubs—which resemble bowling pins—and kettlebells, which are cast-iron balls with a handle attached, were popular in the early 1800s. As the 19th century progressed, so did weight-training equipment in the form of pulleys, air pressure devices, and multistations. Strongmen performing at contests and exhibitions were the primary users of weight equipment at this time. Amateur weightlifting became a sanctioned event at the Olympics in 1896, although there were no female athletes. Women's weightlifting didn't become a sanctioned Olympic sport until 2000.

By the early 1900s, weight training had progressed significantly with the invention of the adjustable, plate-loaded barbell. Training with weights became more popular because it was much easier to change the weight on the barbells. But weight training really gained momentum when sports coaches began to see it as an excellent addition to their athletic and physical education programs. Bodybuilding soon followed on the sandy shores of Muscle Beach in Venice, California. Both men and women participated in physique shows, weightlifting competitions, and acrobatics demonstrations. When the Nautilus variable resistance cam machines hit the market in the 1970s, resistance training really took off, especially for women. The machines were less intimidating than free weights and allowed people to lift light weights easily—perfect for the woman who was just starting out. The creator of Nautilus, Arthur Jones, preached a philosophy of training that virtually gave people a road map and instructions for the use of his machines. He proposed a 20-minute workout three times a week that included 1 set of 8 to 12 repetitions for each Nautilus machine. Many people are still following his recommendations today.

The Nautilus machines inspired a fitness revolution, and many different companies burst on the market with their own types of selectorized resistance machines. Health clubs multiplied and prospered. The aerobics revolution began in the 1970s and flourished throughout the 1980s. Women who had previously been training with weights were now jumping and stepping in huge proportions in the confines of the aerobics room rather than venturing out to the weight floor. The late 1980s saw the introduction of plate-loaded machines, a hybrid of selectorized equipment and actual free weights. The first of these machines, Hammer Strength, focused on entire body movements (rather than targeting specific body parts) and had independent arms. The machines felt natural and smooth and actually led to a resurgence of lifting free weights. Women started flocking back into the weight room, many possibly as a result of injuries from high-impact aerobics. It was also becoming apparent, through research and anecdotal reports, that resistance training produced a huge benefit for those who participated in sports. There probably isn't any serious athlete or sports team today that doesn't augment training with weights.

As you can see, training with weights wasn't always a popular activity for women—to some extent, it still isn't. While men were lifting weights in the first Olympics, women had foot races in their own separate Olympics, called the Games of Hera. Female strength training was not promoted in the early years of civilization, primarily because women did all of their physical activity farming in the fields, cooking, cleaning, and taking care of the children. Consider how much work these everyday jobs actually required before there were grocery stores, microwaves, vacuum cleaners, and babysitters. Women weren't concerned about staying in shape, because they were in shape—and exhausted! As the Renaissance approached, it became even less popular for women to strength train because the focus was on culture, and fencing became a popular sport for men and women. Fencing wasn't promoted for health or fitness, but for self-defense and perfection of skill and technique. This emphasis is quite contrary to today's trends, in which martial arts are turned into aerobics classes for the sole purpose of exercise. Finally, the ideal female physique of the Renaissance period was soft and well rounded; having muscles was correlated with being poor and working in the fields.

The times were slowly changing. Although social norms discouraged vigorous exercise for women during the Victorian era, they promoted exercising with light weights and sticks to improve posture and body symmetry. The notion in America was that women shouldn't exercise in the same way that men did, because men and women were fundamentally different. Women should exercise only to make themselves more attractive to men, to make childbirth easier, and to make themselves strong so that their sons would be strong.

As the 19th century progressed, a style of German gymnastics was introduced to American women that included weightlifting and vigorous body-weight exercises on parallel bars. Women performed chin-ups, dips, and one-leg squats, and they swung from triangles that hung from the ceiling. But the tide turned from this high-intensity training to low-intensity calisthenics when American society didn't approve of women gaining muscularity and having callused hands. The new calisthenics of the 1800s sounds eerily familiar to the aerobics classes of today. Calisthenics were movements set to music and done in a group with perhaps light dumbbells, wooden or iron canes, or Indian clubs. Later in the century, calisthenics progressed to more dynamic exercise, and women's schools often included them in physical education programs. By the end of the 19th century women started lifting heavier weights. In 1892 the journal *Physical Education* (a publication of the YMCA) devoted an entire issue to women, saying that women needed physical strength and endurance.

Strength training for women really took off in the 1930s and 1940s with the advent of Muscle Beach in Venice, California, and with Bob Hoffman's *Strength and Health* magazine, which emphasized weight training for athletic improvement. His magazine featured female athletes and the women of Muscle Beach. In the mid- to late 1950s, it was clear that strength training was positively enhancing athletes' performances, and many professional and Olympic female athletes tried to add strength training to their routines. Unfortunately, because the weights were primarily located in men's training rooms, women often did not have access to the equipment.

The access issue changed in 1972 when congress passed Title IX. This legislation stated that "no person in the United States shall, on the basis of sex, be excluded from participation in, be denied the benefits of, or be subject to discrimination under any education program or activities receiving Federal financial assistance." It essentially opened the doors of the weight rooms to women. When President Nixon signed the act, about 24,000 women were involved in intercollegiate sports and about 300,000 were involved in high school sports. Today more than 100,000 women participate in intercollegiate athletics and more than 2.4 million high school girls play high school sports. The majority of these athletes are strength training.

## Strength Training Today

We've seen exercise trends come, and we've seen them go. We've even seen some come back into vogue. Yesterday's ideas have come full circle, freshened up with today's research and knowledge. Today's strength training involves functional, metabolic, and weight training. Once you've learned about these methods, you can incorporate them into your own program suited specifically to your goals.

**Functional training** is definitely the newest buzzword for strengthening the body. We first heard of functional training when athletes began to incorporate sports movements into their exercise programs, rather than just training individual body parts as a bodybuilder does. Strength coaches and trainers developed exercises that mimicked the movement patterns required for a particular sport and added weights, elastic bands, and other devices. Because athletes were training for the ultimate function in their sports, the term functional training was coined. Now functional training has come to mean function not only in sports, but also in activities of daily living. If you need balance and strength to reach down and pick up a heavy bag of groceries while holding a child in one arm, you can functionally train for that by holding a medicine ball in one arm while doing a lunge to reach for a dumbbell with the other hand. Functional training now runs the gamut from specific exercises that mimic sports movements to exercises that mimic life movements. You'll find out more about functional training in chapter 4 and about why it is really just your specific exercise program with a specific goal.

**Metabolic training** in a strict scientific sense means training an athlete's body at particular work and rest intervals that closely mimic those the athlete encounters during her sport. The word *metabolism* is usually found in the dictionary of women's dirty words. Some of us say we have a fast metabolism and can't put on weight, but most of us say our metabolism is so slow that if we even look at a cookie, we put on weight. The truth of the matter is that metabolism is really what you make of it. Your body's metabolism is the amount of energy your body requires to live—whether you sit on the couch or climb a mountain.

Most sports include high-intensity, high-effort periods that are followed by low-intensity intervals or even total rest periods. For example, in tennis the work interval occurs during actual movement of the ball, when players are serving or volleying. In between such actions, when a player is walking back to the service line and preparing for the next volley, he is in a rest interval. The player is also in a rest interval between games and sets. When athletes are trained with the work-to-rest intervals that mirror their sport, their sport performance is maximized. Scientists discovered that such training came at a huge metabolic cost to the body. In other words, it burned a ton of calories! They also discovered that metabolic training actually put on muscle, which increased the body's metabolic rate. Thus, we now have a form of metabolic training called interval training that is becoming popular in our gyms. An athlete follows a bout of high-intensity exercise with a period of lower-intensity exercise, and the pairing is repeated for a certain amount of time in order to increase metabolism. Look for more information and sample metabolic training programs in chapter 7.

**Weight training** is one area that used to be labeled *men only*, but that women are now venturing into. Weight training creates buffed bodies. Men have known this for years, but women are just starting to get the message. And whereas women had previously gravitated only to the selectorized type of weight machines, they are now exploring the world of lifting free weights for strength training. Weight training is fun; you can do it with or without a partner, and it produces benefits that more women are discovering. Depending on your goals, you can weight train for muscular hypertrophy, endurance, strength, or power (as further described in chapter 4). You can certainly augment functional and metabolic training programs with weights, but using weights is not the focus in these programs as it is in dedicated weight-training programs. You'll find a beginner, an intermediate, and an advanced weight-training program in chapter 7. If you want to compete in a strength sport, chapter 13 will help you out.

# Benefits of Strength Training for Women

Strength training benefits women greatly, possibly even more than it benefits men. Men already have the advantage of producing large amounts of testosterone (much greater amounts than women), a hormone that allows them to have strong muscles and keep their body fat low.

Anatomically speaking, girls are usually about two years ahead of boys when it comes to bone ossification. Girls' estrogen levels cause the growth plates in their bones to close more quickly than they do in boys. So although girls may be taller than boys for a few years of adolescence, the girls' bones stop growing and the boys soon catch up and surpass the girls. On the average, girls' bones are completely formed by the time they are 18, as opposed to boys' bones, which can continue to grow until they are 21. Higher amounts of human growth hormone account for the larger, heavier, and taller frames of men. At the end of the growing stages, men tend to be about five inches taller than women. Men also have larger, longer, and denser bones than women. Their shoulders are broader relative to their hips, whereas women have broader hips relative to their shoulders. These bone characteristics allow men to have much more muscular tissue as a whole on their limbs, especially in the upper body.

Another difference between men and women that makes strength training even more beneficial for women is fat—probably our least favorite three-letter word. Both men and women must have some fat to live, which is called essential fat. Essential fat is present inside vital organs such as the heart, and it is found in most of the central nervous system and bone marrow. Women also have sex-specific essential fat in their breasts and in their pelvic, buttock, and thigh regions. Such fat is only found on women, specifically for hormonal functions and childbearing. We need this fat to produce estrogen and stay the beautiful women that we are. We also need the fat that surrounds our reproductive system, just in case we want to have a baby. But even if we don't want to procreate, it is extremely difficult to get rid of sex-specific fat—it is genetically programmed into our bodies, and is nature's way of supporting the survival of human beings.

We usually want to lose the storage fat, but some of this fat is important too. Some storage fat provides energy reserves, and some protects our internal organs and bones. Surprisingly, men and women have very close relative percentages of storage fat, but the sex-specific essential fat makes the difference between the amount of fat men and women have. Women also have more fat trapped between their muscle fibers than men do. We can change this amount slightly, but not a great deal. Physiologically, then, nature intends women to be a little more rounded, a little bit softer, and a little bit smaller than men. We can do our best to decrease nonessential body fat and get as lean as possible, but a little fat will always need to remain.

Men often have the advantage of being more active throughout their growing years. Girls are more likely to be sedentary and are often taught to play in ways that are less active, whereas boys are more likely to be encouraged to be outside running, jumping, and wrestling. Although hopefully the ways in which girls and boys are encouraged to play are changing, many women have already grown up with this mind-set and haven't experienced as much physical activity as many men.

© Photo Network

We have seen that women possess a very specific genetic makeup that differentiates us from men and from any other organism. Our two X chromosomes give us certain genetic traits that simply won't allow gender confusion. On average, a woman's body structure is smaller than a man's, so she will have difficulty ever becoming as large. Women also have lower levels of testosterone, the anabolic hormone that contributes to increased muscle mass (see chapter 2). Rather than causing big and bulky muscles, weight training actually promotes changes in body composition that most women find favorable (such as decreased fat, tighter musculature, and increased strength), without their restricting calories. So maybe strength training really is the Holy Grail of fitness and exercise for women. Think about

Women can experience the myriad physical and psychological benefits of strength training without worrying about becoming overly muscular.

all of the benefits that strength training produces. From a health and longevity aspect, strength training can increase bone density, improve the immune system, and decrease or reverse the effects of aging. Also, as anyone who has ever lifted a weight in her life knows, strength training can elevate your mood, give you confidence, and just plain perk you up.

## Increased Strength

Imagine living your life with more energy and strength to perform all of your daily tasks. You don't need help carrying out the garbage, lifting the heavy boxes at work, moving the couch in the family room, or running around with the kids. This isn't just a pipe dream. Strength training can help you perform all of these activities with ease. Women can increase their strength if the training intensity and duration are sufficient, and even retain that strength when they aren't able to work out for a while.

What about the popular notion that women are weak and can never be as strong as men? Pound for pound, it is extremely difficult for women to be as strong as men. Relatively speaking, however, women can achieve the same strength. Men are stronger because they generally have more muscular tissue than women (mostly because they are larger organisms altogether). But if you compare small samples of muscular tissue taken from a man and a woman, they do not differ in strength. So there is no reason that a woman cannot get as strong as she possibly can, within her genetic potential.

## Increased Muscle Mass and Decreased Body Fat

Through strength training, muscles get larger, or hypertrophy. This increased muscle mass has many advantages for women. First of all, it gives women a sexy, sculpted, and tight body like that of an elite athlete, instead of the skinny, scrawny, and starved body of a runway model. Second, increased muscular size leads to increased muscular strength. Third, the more muscle you have on your body, the higher your metabolic rate. The higher your metabolic rate, the more calories you burn throughout the day. Muscle itself is highly metabolic—it requires a lot of calories not only to function, but also to merely exist. That's why it seems as if men can eat anything that they want to and never gain an ounce, whereas we are counting the calories in our carrot sticks in fear that they may turn up on our thighs later in the day.

Women often carry on long bouts of cardiovascular endurance exercise in the hope of burning calories and subsequently losing fat. The truth, however, is that cardiovascular endurance exercise alone does not selectively burn fat off of your body. People probably got the idea that cardio burned fat because in the case of highly trained endurance athletes who do one- or two-hour endurance workouts on a regular basis, the body uses fat as a primary fuel source. This process doesn't necessarily happen for those of us who are not highly trained or who don't engage in regular, steady endurance activities longer than 60 to 90 minutes. Slow, steady cardiovascular endurance exercise can burn a certain number of calories per session, but those calories mostly (especially for exercise lasting less than an hour) come from carbohydrate sources and not fat.

It doesn't really matter what source the calorie comes from, because a calorie is just a calorie and the burning of fuel sources mixes and varies. You can't tell your body that you want to burn only fat, just as you can't tell your body to reduce only the fat on your thighs. If that were the case, every woman on the stair machine would have legs of steel. So how does strength training help to decrease body fat? Since a calorie is just a calorie, the more calories you burn, the more likely you are to lose body fat. And guess what? Strength training is a high-intensity exercise that requires a ton of calories. Also, don't forget that when you strength train regularly you increase your muscle mass, which increases your metabolism, leading to more calorie burning throughout the day.

## Increased Bone Density

Weight-bearing physical activity like walking, jogging, and strength training has a positive effect on bone mineral density by mechanically loading the skeleton, as scientific research shows. Research studies support the idea that resistance exercise increases bone mineral density in pre- and postmenopausal and elderly women. Since osteoporosis is a serious health threat to women, it makes sense to attempt to prevent it by making our bones as strong and as healthy as possible throughout life. Because peak bone mineral density is reached in late adolescence, prior to this period is the ideal time for women to start a strength-training program to possibly delay osteoporosis. However, you are never too old to start strength training to increase your bone mineralization. Bones that are strong can handle more stress and are less likely to fracture. The National Osteoporosis Foundation's *Physician's Guide to Prevention and Treatment of Osteoporosis* (1998) recommends regular weight-bearing and muscle-strengthening exercise, both for osteoporosis prevention and overall health. The guide states that not only can this type of exercise improve agility, strength, and balance (thus reducing the risk of falls), but it may also yield a modest increase in bone density. Strength training is a valuable tool in the prevention of osteoporosis and fractures.

The most important fact that women need to realize about starting resistance training to prevent osteoporosis is that lifting only with weight-training machines doesn't cut it. Research on the benefits of Nautilus machines for bone mineral density suggests that women can obtain better results by lifting free weights. Other research has shown that after 20 weeks of training on Universal-type machines, women improved their muscular strength and defined their bodies, yet did not increase bone mineral density. So, choose free weights whenever possible. You'll find that almost all of the exercises and programs in this book focus on free weights for this benefit and others. Chapter 7 details all of the benefits of using free weights, and after reading chapter 2, you will become an expert on osteoporosis.

## Improved Immune Function

One of the best ways to stay healthy throughout your lifetime is to adhere to a regular exercise routine. Anecdotal reports and scientific research are increasingly showing that moderate training boosts immune function and may even prevent cancer. You can define regular exercise as any activity you do outside of your normal everyday functions. You can strength train, walk, or play softball, as long as you incorporate it into your lifestyle so that it becomes almost a daily habit. Such activities produce health benefits for many reasons. Regular exercise usually decreases body fat, which is strongly associated with certain cancers, mainly colon cancer. In addition, regular exercise increases bowel movements, which can also decrease the risk of colon cancer. Regular exercise decreases the body's susceptibility to environmentally found estrogens, which can increase the risk for breast cancer. Research has suggested that physical inactivity reduces insulin sensitivity, which leads to a friendly environment for disease.

Regular, moderate exercise can also boost the body's natural immunity. Realize, however, that excessive exercise has virtually the opposite effect on the body's immune system. Repeated bouts of high-intensity or endurance exercise without rest and recuperation periods may be more detrimental to the immune system and a person's health status than being a couch potato. Clearly, having a well-structured and organized plan for your fitness goals is the best way to stay healthy.

## Reversed Effects of Aging

You may have seen stooped-over women in the grocery store who must use the grocery basket as a rolling walker to get around the aisles. Their upper backs have been rounded for so many years that now they can barely lift up their heads. No one wants to end up looking stooped or experiencing the pain that arises from that condition.

One of the best ways to prevent and even reverse these effects of aging is to strength train. Everyone talks about how important it is to have excellent cardiovascular health, and that is true. However, having the heart of a marathon runner doesn't do any good for a 70-year-old woman who is so weak she can't even get off the couch, let alone run. If you have ever been close to such elderly people, you know how their weakness handicaps them. As we age, we lose muscle fiber and bone density. If we strength train when we are younger and maintain that training philosophy throughout our lives, we may never experience those effects of aging.

Numerous research studies have proven that resistance training in elderly women is safe and increases muscular size and strength. Resistance exercise in the elderly population improves function, which can lead to more independent living. The high level of disability and falls in the elderly may be due to their low muscular strength. Because training with weights increases muscular size, muscular strength, and bone density, older women who weight train can experience all of these benefits. Being stronger, with larger muscles, at an older age delays some of the natural aging processes like muscle loss, bone loss, decreased metabolic rate, and decreased energy and activity levels. Practically speaking, older adults who weight train may have an easier time with their daily activities, lengthen their years of independent living, and experience fewer chronic diseases.

## Improved Mood and Increased Confidence

I may be preaching to the choir for those of you who already train with weights, but just the act of training and completing a workout makes you feel good. Lifting weights in particular gives you more self-confidence. Don't just take my word for it. Numerous studies have been done on the subject, and they all arrive at the same conclusion—choose physical activity over inactivity any day to prevent depression and elevate your mood. In general, people who are inactive are twice as likely to have depression symptoms as more active people. A report from the U.S. surgeon general in 1996 stated that the consensus of people who are physically active is that they have an enhanced mood, higher self-esteem, greater confidence in their ability to perform tasks requiring physical activity, and better cognitive functioning than people who are sedentary or less physically fit.

The jury still seems to be out on exactly why and how exercise elevates mood. There are many theories, but it is likely a combination of events that promote the positive effects. Some psychological theories are that exercise leads to increased self-mastery or self-efficacy, that it provides social interaction and support, that it provides a form of meditation, that it provides a form of distraction from negative thoughts or behaviors, or that it is a pleasant activity and positively reinforces itself. Some physiological theories are the thermogenic theory, that the increased body temperature from exercise decreases muscular tension; the endorphin theory, that the body releases endogenous opiates during exercise; and the monoamine neurotransmitter theory, that the body releases increased levels of norepinephrine and serotonin during exercise. There is little evidence on the endorphin theory, and researchers are leaning toward a combination of psychological theories with the neurotransmitter theory. Some researchers think that exercise may help the brain cope better with stress or that it gives the body a way to deal more appropriately with stress. Regardless of the whys, adding a strength-training program can positively influence the way you feel.

## Improved Quality of Life

All of this evidence may make the conclusion a no-brainer, but let's sum it up. If you are strong enough to complete all of your daily tasks with ease, if you have a lean body with strong bones, if you're healthy and cancer free, if you stay young and active even when you're old, and if you're always in a good mood and have a high opinion of yourself, then your life has got to be good. Strength training can definitely improve your quality of life. Once you've started lifting your first weights, you may never go back.

# Stronger, Not Bigger

Even after reading about all of the wonderful benefits that strength training can have for women, some women still fear that it will make them overly muscular. Unfortunately, the popular media have reinforced a negative image of very muscular women. When most people think of strength training, they may picture the excessively muscled women who compete in professional bodybuilding contests—the extreme results of strength training. Women who compete in any sporting event, whether bodybuilding, weightlifting, powerlifting, or softball, are often at the edge of the spectrum when it comes to what is healthy. These competitors sometimes do things that average people wouldn't consider doing, such as training extremely aggressively many times a day, putting their social lives on hold for the sake of their sport, and experimenting with drugs to further their careers. So when you see that exaggerated muscularity on some female athletes, recognize that these women are not the norm and are indeed the exception, and that they are likely doing something in their training that is over and above what most people would do.

Why does it seem that when you start an exercise program, particularly a high-intensity weightlifting one, you puff up right away? You definitely aren't imagining your body getting bigger, although it may be something of an optical illusion. When you begin a weight-training program, your body realizes how hard you are working now (compared to your previous workout of, say, sitting on the couch and popping bonbons in your mouth), and stores carbohydrate to use for fuel. Carbohydrate sources are largely filled with water, and new exercisers often see a small weight gain and an increase in their muscular size from this water. What is actually happening is very similar to the bloating you experience in your monthly cycle—it's just in your muscles and not confined to your abdomen. It's not new muscular tissue; rather, your muscles are a little swollen with water. Who wants that? No one, I am sure, and it might not happen to you. The good news is that the bloating is a temporary condition, and as soon as your body knows you are serious about your weight-training program, it will regulate itself and not store excess amounts of carbohydrate that can lead to that puffy look. If you stay on a consistent weight-training program for at least a month, you will notice that the bloated look decreases and find that the sculpted look is just around the corner. If you stay hydrated throughout your workout and your entire day, water will be readily available to your muscles and your body will need to store less carbohydrate to make water.

# Building
a Better Body

Y ou've decided to take the plunge and devote yourself to achieving a better body. But like being physically fit, having a better body means something unique for each person. Not only do people have different ideas about what it means to have a better body, but they also have different genetic makeups and body structures that predispose them to having a certain body build. That is not to say you can't alter your build, but you have to be realistic with the hand that Mother Nature has dealt you. If you come from a family of short, curvy women, it is unlikely you'll ever achieve the look of a runway fashion model, no matter how hard you exercise. However, there are some universal truths about the way that our bodies react to exercise, specifically to training with weights. Internally and externally, resistance training will show obvious benefits.

When you train with weights all of your body's systems are affected in some way, and these systems overlap and connect. To build a better body you must understand how weight training influences the body so that you can understand the benefits that training with free weights provides.

## Nervous System Adaptations

Your body is filled with intricate spiderwebs of nerves that connect every part of your body to the primary nerve center, the spinal cord, and the brain. Every nerve has a different job to do. The nerves that control muscles are called motor nerves. The smallest part of the motor nerve is a single cell called a motor neuron. The neuron has many nerve fibers that branch out to provide nerve impulses to individual muscle fibers. The area of innervation is called the neuromuscular junction (the place where the nerve and muscle join). Although each muscle fiber only has one neuromuscular junction, the motor neuron can innervate hundreds of fibers. The motor neuron and the fibers it innervates are collectively called a motor unit (see figure 2.1). When the motor neuron is stimulated, all of that motor unit's muscle fibers will contract.

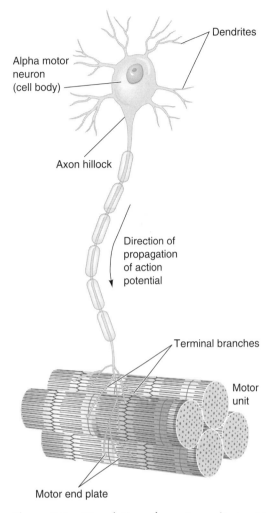

Alpha motor neuron (cell body)

Dendrites

Axon hillock

Direction of propagation of action potential

Terminal branches

Motor unit

Motor end plate

**Figure 2.1** Stimulation of a motor unit causes its muscle fibers to contract.

Reprinted, by permission, from J.H. Wilmore and D.L. Costill, 2004, *Physiology of sport and exercise*, 3rd ed. (Champaign, IL: Human Kinetics), 40.

The trick to strength training effectively is to get the most motor units working at one time. The more motor units that are working, the more muscle fibers are contracting, the more force you can produce, and the more training benefits you see in terms of performance and aesthetics. During most daily activities, every motor unit in the muscle doesn't need to be recruited. It takes less muscular force to sit at a computer or drive in a car than it does to lift heavy weight or move a piece of furniture. If these lazy motor units aren't called on for duty very often, then it's a case of use it or lose it. When you introduce weight training, you are calling into action motor units that have never been taxed before. Now the muscle activates fully and becomes more efficient at doing everyday chores as well.

Most of the significant strength gains that you see when you first embark on a weight-training program are due to neural factors. Your nervous system is very good at adaptation. It listens to what you want your body to do and responds appropriately. When you begin training with weights or try any new sport or movement, your nervous system steps up to the plate and does everything in its power to allow you to accomplish the task at hand. It recruits more motor neurons, which in turn recruit more muscle fibers. The increase in fiber recruitment and neural coordination leads to strength gains, without the muscles actually getting bigger (hypertrophy). Even advanced weightlifters have been shown to increase their strength and power, without increasing muscle size, when they change their exercise programs. This phenomenon can only be the result of neural adaptations and increased recruitment.

# Bone Adaptations

When most of us see a hunchbacked elderly woman at the mall or on the street, we unconsciously pull our shoulders back and straighten our spines. We take our calcium pills and eat our yogurt dutifully in the hope that we won't one day end up like that old lady, too fragile and bent over to function as we would wish. Osteoporosis is an entirely preventable disease that is not only disfiguring and painful but can also lead to life-threatening situations. As women, we owe it to ourselves and to those we love to become well versed on the topic of bone health and what we can do to preserve it. Fortunately, strength training has an incredibly positive effect on our bones. It stimulates new bone growth so that our bones grow strong, and it is one of the most effective ways to avoid osteoporosis.

Imagine bone as a living and breathing tissue, just like your heart or lungs. Although we usually think of bone as being hard, it is really viscoelastic—sticky, gummy, filled with thick fluid, and bendable. Bone is constantly working, whether it's protecting internal organs, providing movement through joints and muscles, or acting as a reservoir of calcium. It gives your body its shape and allows white blood cells to flourish. It also is adept at reinventing itself, either through the ongoing natural process of remodeling, whereby it removes old bone cells and forms new ones, or through mechanotransduction, which is how bone cells respond to physical activity. Bone is composed of thousands of cells, some tightly packed and some loosely packed.

Osteoblasts are young bone cells that lay the groundwork for the osteocytes, which are mature cells. Osteoclasts are bone cells that remove old bone. Collagen is a protein that the osteoblasts manufacture and secrete to connect the cells together and form the strong geometric mazes of the bone matrix. Some of the collagen in the matrix mineralizes into salts like calcium, phosphate, magnesium, and sodium. Bone mineral density (BMD) is how dense your bones are, or how much mass they have. Researchers have now proven that peak bone mineral density is reached by late adolescence. After adolescence it is difficult to build more bone mass, but if we eat well and train correctly and in moderation, we can maintain our bone mass and prevent the bone loss than can result in fractures and osteoporosis. Osteoporosis occurs over time when the amount of bone broken down greatly exceeds the amount of bone replaced by new bone cells. At this point bone mineral density decreases, which decreases the bone mass. The results are bones that become more porous or brittle and have an increased risk of fracture.

A popular saying, "Form follows function," couldn't be truer than when describing bone. The most widely accepted theory on bone formation comes from German anatomist Julius Wolff's classical theory, called Wolff's law. He proposed that bone formed and changed formation depending on the force of muscular tension and the stress of gravity placed on it. Because bone is living tissue, it adapts to the stress placed on it and can increase and decrease in size as muscular tissue does. His theory led biomechanists to devise a load-deformation relationship for bone, in which load is defined as stress (force per unit area), and deformation is defined as strain (change of length). A stress-strain curve was developed to determine how much stress and strain is beneficial for a bone and how much is detrimental, resulting in bone loss and fracture.

When we consider the body's anatomy, we can understand why increasing muscular stress can increase bone tissue. Examine any place on the body where many muscles or particularly strong muscles attach to the bone and you will find bony protuberances. Just place your hand below your kneecap on the part of your leg that you always cut shaving and you'll understand. That bony protuberance is where your quadriceps or patella tendon attaches to the tibia. It develops when the quadriceps muscles contract through physical activity and the tendon pulls on its attachment to the bone. When a muscle places the right amount of stress on a bone, the bone grows to support the stress. Muscle also adds weight to the bone, and the bone responds by increasing its mass so that it can support the weight. Many studies have shown that bone density decreases when muscles atrophy (waste away) through inactivity and in weightless environments like bed rest and space travel. Many highly competitive swimmers have low bone densities similar to those of sedentary people because of the weightless environment of the pool water. Just remember that strong muscles performing work against gravity make strong bones, and weak muscles that don't challenge gravity make weak ones.

We know that moderate-impact loading—weight-bearing physical activity like walking, jogging, and jumping—has a positive effect on bone mineral density by mechanically loading and stressing the skeleton. As you walk, jog, or jump, you transport your entire body weight a certain distance against gravity, which produces an impact on your heel that travels up through your entire skeleton. Of course the most pronounced effect is in your heel, but the rest of your bones get some benefit too. With each heel strike (the moment at which your foot hits the ground) you are basically tearing down some bone tissue to remodel it and replace it. The body senses the cell deformation that comes from the impact, resorbs the damaged cells, and sends in new cells to replace the old.

Here's a warning for those of you who follow the more-is-better philosophy: When you perform activities that include a great amount of impact or heel strikes, then the greater their number and frequency, the more likely you are to decrease bone mass rather than increase it. Your body just can't produce enough new bone cells to replace the old ones. Bone physiology requires a delicate balance. For example, marathon runners are at risk for fractures and osteoporosis, given the high number of heel strikes required in training for and running a 26-mile race. They lose bone faster than their bodies can replace it. Although they may supplement with calcium or vitamin D, the body can't produce osteoblasts as quickly as the stress and strain of training for a marathon breaks down bone cells. Ballet dancers are also known for having fractures and osteoporosis for a number of reasons (including poor nutrition and low body weight), but a primary factor is overtraining. They perform thousands of heel strikes (or toe strikes) and allow themselves little to no rest. Bone simply needs more time to rebuild. Clearly you must err on the side of moderate walking, running, and jumping to stay ahead in the bone-density race (see table 2.1).

When you think of impact-loading, weight-bearing activity, you usually think of typical cardiovascular endurance exercises like walking, jogging, and jumping, because they emphasize impact loading and weight bearing in the traditional sense. But did you know that the National Osteoporosis Foundation's *Physician's Guide to Prevention and Treatment of Osteoporosis* (1998) recommends regular muscle-strengthening exercise, both for osteoporosis prevention and for general health? Why is strength training so good for your bones and overall health? Because you typically do it standing (or otherwise bearing your own body weight) while also holding additional weights. Strength training also causes a stress to be applied to bone, and if the stress is significant enough, the bone becomes strained. When the bone is strained, the fluid within the bone moves around in a ripple effect, communicating with all of the cells. The fluid provides nutrition to the bone cells and information that a stress has occurred and must be repaired. Intracellular calcium is released to help the existing osteoblasts rebuild, and secondary messengers stimulate new osteoblast formation. Therefore, strength training is a valuable tool to prevent osteoporosis and fractures.

The strength training that is best for preventing osteoporosis, however, specifically uses free weights instead of machines. Research about the benefits of strength training with machines for bone mineral density suggests that although women can improve their muscular strength and size with machines, they do not increase their bone mineral density. The primary reason for this outcome is that sitting in machines to strength train does not provide your body with the benefit of bearing the weight against gravity, as you do when using free weights. Furthermore, allowing the machine to assist and guide you throughout an exercise doesn't provide

### Table 2.1   Factors Affecting Bone Health

| Optimal Factors | Suboptimal Factors |
| --- | --- |
| Moderate impact loading exercise | Excessive impact loading exercise |
| Free weights | Weight machines |
| Muscle hypertrophy | Muscle atrophy |
| Moderate physical activity | Overtraining |
| Balanced diet | Eating disorders |
| Adequate nutritional status | Vitamin and mineral inadequacies/deficiencies |
| Regular menstruation | Amenorrhea |

enough stress and strain on the bone. You can think of strength training with free weights as a weight-bearing activity.

Not only does strain affect the building of bone, but also the magnitude of that strain, otherwise known as strain magnitude; and how fast this strain is applied and released, otherwise known as strain rate. For bone maintenance, the mechanostat theory states that a minimum effective strain (MES) is necessary. To increase bone tissue, however, the strain has to generate an overload. Thus activities that increase strain magnitude, like heavy strength training, increase your bone mass. The strain on the bone is significantly more than that produced by just standing around or doing normal daily activities. In addition to strain magnitude, it appears that strain rate and unusual strain patterns may play an even more important role than the number of strain cycles, or how often the activity is done. Performing free-weight exercises vigorously in different planes (as in some functional training programs) and jumping instead of running increase both strain rate and magnitude, which is the most beneficial combination for bone building. Check out the section titled Bone-Building Program in chapter 7.

## Connective Tissue Adaptations

How is the heel bone connected to the shin bone, and the shin bone connected to the thigh bone, as the popular song goes? The connective tissues in our body hold bone to bone (ligaments), muscle to bone (tendons), and muscle to muscle (fasciae). Tendons and ligaments are composed of parallel strands of collagen fibers tightly bundled together. Fasciae are like spiderwebs that hold layers of muscle fibers together and join at the end of the muscle to form a tendon.

Cartilage is a special type of connective tissue. Although it does help to make the connection between bones and muscles more solid and stable, its primary functions are to provide a smooth surface for joint movement and to absorb shock. The shiny hyaline cartilage at the ends of our long bones (check out the end of a drumstick) allows the bones on either side of the joint to glide smoothly during movement. The shock absorbers provide a cushion in areas where greater effects of weight bearing are seen, such as the intervertebral discs found between each of our vertebrae or the meniscus found in our knees.

The tendons, ligaments, and fasciae, like the bones, respond favorably to physical activity and need more stress and strain than just daily life provides. Long, slow endurance training allows damaged collagen to be exactly replaced with new collagen, yielding a net zero equation. But high-intensity strength training increases the amount of collagen and makes these connective tissues even thicker and stronger. Think about the example given earlier of the patella tendon pulling on the bone. The tendon responds to the muscular contractions during a strength-training session and adds more collagen to handle the stress. As the muscle hypertrophies and gets stronger, the tendon must also increase size and strength in order to hold on to the bone.

Conclusive evidence shows that cartilage needs joint mobility and physical activity—specifically of the weight-bearing variety—to stay healthy. As a joint moves through its range of motion, it lubricates and nourishes the cartilage with synovial fluid. The fluid not only feeds the cartilage, but also facilitates the joint's smooth movement. You can think of it as extra-virgin olive oil for your joints. In the knee it is easy to see the effects of weight bearing on cartilage. The cartilage is thicker where the bone bears the most weight. Since strength training incorporates both joint movement and weight bearing, it is beneficial for cartilage health. And because cartilage is viscoelastic like bone, it distributes the stress of heavy loads well and returns to the same shape when the load is removed.

# Endocrine System Adaptations

Whenever we get that "hormonal" feeling during the month, we can thank our endocrine system. The endocrine system consists of glands and organs that secrete hormones into the blood to arrive at a target cell. Hormones are signaling messengers that give information regarding the body's current status and signal an action. They control and keep in balance numerous physiological processes in our bodies, like stress responses, reproduction, growth and development, and metabolism. The primary responsibility of the endocrine system is to regulate hormone levels and keep the body in homeostasis (balance). Because the nervous system is also intricately involved in homeostasis and endocrine function, many scientists refer to the two systems as the neuroendocrine system.

When you add exercise to your daily routine, your hormones have to adjust to keep your body in homeostasis. Hormones control your body both acutely (during the exercise session) and chronically (long after the actual exercise session is over). They regulate your body fluids, help your body adapt to the stress of exercise, and influence skeletal muscle.

## Fluid Regulation

How does your body cool itself down while you heat it up in the gym? How can you give it all you've got without your blood pressure threatening to explode your head off? You can thank your hormones for your fluid-regulation mechanism during exercise. In fact, your body is mostly made up of water, so when you start to exercise and challenge the body's delicate water balance, it may be a matter of life or death. This principle is true not only for any type of exercise but also for life in general. There are many ways to get dehydrated—simply not drinking water, not eating carbohydrate, being in Arizona during the summer, or lying out at the beach. The principle is especially true for weight training, however, because when the muscle fiber's sarcolemma (protective sheath) is stressed, it becomes more permeable and allows things like water and nutrients to travel in and out. Luckily, the endocrine system directs body tissues to give up water and shift it around where needed. It can go into the muscles, move into the blood, or be released as sweat to cool you down.

Of course you can always help the endocrine system maintain your body's water supply by drinking plenty of water before, during, and after exercise, and all day long. Some women think that drinking a lot of water will make them bloated, but in fact the opposite is true. Drinking a lot of water actually helps the endocrine system maintain the body's water levels and leads to less retention of water and bloating. When the body knows that it will always have a steady amount of water available, it doesn't need to store it. Some women are good at keeping themselves hydrated during cardiovascular endurance sessions, but are less so during strength-training sessions. Remember that water during any form of physical activity is essential. And if you are strength training with 100 percent effort, you'll want that water just as much as you would if you were running on the treadmill.

## Exercise As a Stressor

Sometimes your hormones might not seem to help you much in the psychological stress department, but they can help your body adapt to physiological stress. Researchers generally believe that the body goes through three stages when confronted with a stressor—in this case, exercise. The first phase is shock, represented in weight training as the delayed-onset muscle soreness you feel for several days after starting a new exercise or routine. In this phase your performance may actually decrease because of the soreness. The second phase is adaptation, which occurs as the body adapts to a particular training stimulus and starts to show improvement. The third phase is staleness, in which the body has already adapted to the exercise and is not showing further improvement. For example, if you have never bench pressed before, you will make significant progress when beginning this exercise. However, you will notice after a period of routinely performing this exercise that your gains will be smaller than they were in the beginning—that you've hit a plateau. The reason is that your body has adapted to the exercise with the benefit of your hormones and (as I mention earlier in this chapter) your nervous system. Now you either need to add weight, change the number of repetitions and sets, change the rest periods between sets, perform totally different exercises, change workout days, move the order of the exercises, or vary the exercise (for example, perform an incline bench press instead of a flat bench press) in order to again see performance benefits.

## Anabolic Hormones and Muscle

The hormones that influence muscular growth are known as anabolic hormones. With a little help from some thyroid hormones, these hormones (like testosterone, growth hormone, insulin, and insulin-like growth factor) help build all kinds of body tissue. They also block catabolic hormones, such as cortisol and progesterone, which destroy muscular tissue. As I discuss in chapter 1, testosterone and growth hormone rise when men train with weights. Some studies have shown that weight training does not significantly increase testosterone in women, but it does increase the levels of growth hormone in the blood. Maybe this is one reason why women's muscles don't get as large as men's; they don't have that double shot of hormones. But even just a healthy level of growth hormone is useful to have around. Not only does it stimulate new tissue growth, but it also helps the body break down fat to use for energy and improves immune function.

# Immune Function Adaptations

The immune system is our body's defense against predators like infectious and malignant diseases. The white blood cells it produces are responsible for finding anything that could possibly harm the body and shutting it down. There are many ways to help our immune system do its job. From eating fresh fruits and vegetables to maintaining a regular and sufficient sleep pattern, we can assist our body's natural healing properties. Regular exercise also seems to be one of these assistants. Strength training can especially bolster our immune system by increasing the production of human growth hormone.

Although many studies have shown that exercise in general increases immune cells, understanding the exact link between the two, and the process that occurs, is in its infancy. Research models are difficult and complicated because of the interconnection of the immune system, endocrine system, and central nervous system—specifically, the manner in which psychological processes of the brain affect the body. New areas of science are emerging, like neuroendocrineimmunology and psychoneuroimmunology, to explain how the interaction of these body systems influences health. It is also difficult to determine whether it is a specific exercise program that benefits the immune system, or the fact that people who exercise lead healthier lives in general, or both.

Whatever the reasons, one thing is clear—you can't be a casual, once-in-a-while exerciser to get the full benefits of immune functioning. You have to engage in regular, moderate exercise sessions and make them a part of your daily routine. A recent study showed that positive immune effects don't occur until after eight weeks of exercising at a moderate intensity. However, when exercise is extremely heavy for prolonged periods and a person becomes the victim of overtraining, immune function decreases and susceptibility to infection increases. Moderation, therefore, is also a key.

# Cardiovascular System Adaptations

You might think that weight training has no effect on the cardiovascular system—that you actually have to get on the step machine or run a couple of miles to do cardiovascular work. If you believe that, you are not the only one who does. This belief started in the 1980s with Dr. Ken "the Father of Aerobics" Cooper, who expounded on the value of aerobics and claimed that having excellent cardiovascular conditioning was the key to total well-being. He recommended LSD (long slow distance) training and keeping the body in a so-called steady state. He did see the benefits of strength and flexibility exercises, but only as an adjunct to a good aerobic exercise program.

Now we know that anaerobic exercise (the type of exercise that employs short bursts of strength and power) has many of the same benefits that aerobic exercise has on the cardiovascular system. The cardiovascular system transports oxygen and nutrient-rich blood throughout the body and removes waste products like carbon dioxide. The heart is a muscle that contracts, expands, and hypertrophies as other muscles do when worked. Arteries and veins that carry blood throughout the body are elastic in nature, but can become inflexible with lack of use. So any kind of exercise, because it is exercise and not lying down on the couch, benefits the cardiovascular system. Blood pressure and heart rate go down because as the heart gets stronger, it also gets more efficient and able to pump out more blood per beat. Flexible and plaque-free arteries and veins help deliver the nutrients and get the wastes out more quickly. Consider also that those who exercise have a healthier and less stressful lifestyle that may contribute to these findings.

The body adapts significantly to aerobic conditioning, just as it adapts specifically to weight training. However, the terms *aerobic conditioning* and *cardiovascular training* really aren't interchangeable. Despite the difference, somewhere along the line we have muddled the terminology. It all goes back to what you want for your body and what goals you have. To run a marathon, you absolutely must train aerobically, and your cardiovascular system will show specific and beneficial adaptations to that type of exercise, but you won't be much good at sprinting. If you train with weights, your cardiovascular system will also show specific and beneficial adaptations to that type of training, but you won't be preparing that system to run a good marathon. In each case, your cardiovascular system is improving for a specific goal.

# Muscular Adaptations

When muscles are challenged by the lifting of weights, many physiological changes occur. A muscle can grow bigger, become more efficient, change its composition, and increase its strength and speed. The change depends on what kind of a weight-training program you embark on. Different training methods, even if they all involve weights, have their own unique effects on muscle. You'll read about this in more detail in chapter 5.

One of the primary adaptations that the body makes to weight training is muscular hypertrophy, an enlargement of the muscle fiber. When the muscle is stressed, the protective outside covering of the individual muscle fibers gets stretched. This stretching creates spaces where various materials, such as nutrients, can flow in and out. Weight training increases protein synthesis (the making of protein), and protein is food for muscle. The increase in protein synthesis creates larger muscle fibers. Other studies have shown that hyperplasia, the splitting of muscle fibers to make more muscle fibers, can take place as well. For our purposes, I refer to muscular enlargement as hypertrophy.

Unfortunately, hypertrophy doesn't take place immediately. In fact, as we've seen in chapter 1, the swelling that you get in the beginning of a weight-training program is not a muscle fiber adaptation, but increased water. Actual muscular hypertrophy takes more than 10 weeks to occur. The length of time required is all the more reason for having a written training schedule and sticking with it (which I discuss in chapter 7).

Muscle fibers adapt in other ways to weight training. Muscle is generally divided into Type I (slow-twitch) and Type II (fast-twitch) fibers. Type I fibers are fatigue resistant; they are used for cardiovascular and muscular endurance work. Type II fibers fatigue quickly, but are big, strong, and quick. They are used for strength and power work. Consequently, Type II fibers hypertrophy more than Type I fibers. Although fiber types will always be mixed throughout the body, aerobically trained muscles have a predominance of Type I fibers, whereas weight-trained muscles have a predominance of Type II fibers. One theory says that we are born with a set ratio of Type I to Type II fibers and that although you can change a certain portion of them through exercise, for the most part you are stuck

Real increase in muscle mass takes place over an extended period of time.

with what you have. This conjecture may be another explanation for why some women get large hypertrophy gains and others get less.

Another muscular adaptation to strength training is increased strength. Strength is the maximal amount of force a muscle or muscle group can generate at a specified velocity. Typically strength movements are slow compared to other movements because it takes time to generate maximal force. A neophyte embarking on a weight-training program typically sees huge strength gains in the first few weeks, because of an increased cooperation of the nervous and muscular systems. Such gains also occur when an advanced trainer changes up her exercise program. As we train with weights and progress in our programs by adding more weight, we will get stronger. Certain training methods can assist with our maximum strength gains. We discuss strength in detail in chapter 5.

Muscle can also become more powerful through weight training. Power is the ability to exert force at a high speed of movement. It requires a lighter resistance and higher velocities than does pure strength training. Someone who is powerful is both strong and quick. Strength and power are closely intertwined, especially in sports. In fact, few sports exist without power except, ironically enough, powerlifting. You'll learn more about these matters in chapter 5.

# DELAYED-ONSET MUSCLE SORENESS

If you have ever trained with weights before or especially if you are just starting out, you may (or soon will) know about the common phenomenon of delayed-onset muscle soreness (DOMS). DOMS is the scientific term for not being able to move the day of or the day after a weight-training session. You might have difficulty just getting out of bed, and all day long you'll be walking as if you just got off a horse (if you can walk at all). You might even regret ever setting foot in the gym. Why do muscles get so sore when you first embark on a weight-training program, or after long layoffs, new exercises, or heavy workouts? Experts continue to debate the exact whys and hows of muscle soreness, but theories abound.

DOMS affects muscular performance temporarily because of both a voluntary reduction of effort (since the muscles are too sore to move) and an actual loss of the muscle's ability to produce force. Many studies have shown that strenuous and unaccustomed exercise damages muscle cells. Some studies have shown that eccentric exercises, in which muscles lengthen as they exert a force (as when slowly lowering a weight), cause more muscular damage than concentric exercises that shorten the muscle (as when lifting a weight). The extent of injury seems to be related more to the change in muscular length than to the force generated by the muscle. The high tension associated with eccentric exercise disrupts the muscle cell membrane. Extracellular calcium then enters the muscle cell and disturbs the delicate balance of electrolytes. This process results in tissue damage that peaks about two days postexercise. When tissue damage occurs, inflammatory cells called neutrophils infiltrate the muscle and cause inflammation. More inflammatory cells called macrophages move in to clean up and remove the cellular debris. A second wave of macrophages then comes in to assist the repair procedure, along with stress proteins. Inflammation is a necessary process in the healing of tissue. As the inflammatory process runs its course, muscle fibers are repaired and become stronger. As the muscle becomes stronger, this process may even prevent subsequent damage.

A popular theory, now refuted, was that DOMS was caused by lactic acid that accumulated in muscles after strenuous exercise. Research has now shown that lactic acid dissipates quickly and that eccentric exercise produces less lactic acid than concentric exercise.

Scientists do not know the exact reason for the pain associated with DOMS, but many hypotheses try to explain the phenomenon. One theory is that inflamed and swollen muscle fibers press on pain receptors and alert the brain to register pain. Another theory suggests that the inflammatory cells (phagocytes) that come to clean up the damaged tissue further damage the tissue, which leads to pain. Still another theory surmises that the free radicals (molecules that are highly reactive and harmful in the body) produced by the inflammatory cells aggravate the already existing damage, causing pain. Most likely a combination of all these factors contributes to the pain of DOMS.

We know that DOMS results in pain and stiffness, loss of muscular strength, loss of the ability to generate force, and an increase in muscular fatigue. But a significant, overlooked fact is that the damage from DOMS prevents proteins that transport glycogen from entering the muscle. This phenomenon results in an impairment of glycogen resynthesis, which is crucial to muscle development. Glycogen is the energy the muscle uses to work and grow. When it is depleted after exercise, it is difficult for the muscle to heal and to store up energy for its next work assignment. Excessive eccentric exercise also impairs muscle pH regulation and cellular function.

Although the pain from DOMS may have something to do with inflammation, many studies have shown that common anti-inflammatory medications taken before and after eccentric exercise do not decrease that pain. It is possible that the soreness is not entirely related to the inflammation, or that the inflammation seen in DOMS is not the typical inflammation seen in other types of muscular injuries. Regardless, it seems that taking anti-inflammatory medications may be harmful to the healing process and possibly even delay it. The same advice goes for massage. Currently there is little scientific evidence that massage can help decrease pain or increase function after DOMS—likewise with ultrasound, electrical stimulation, and ice.

How can you avoid DOMS in your training program? The most important step you can take is to have a specific training plan and gradually acclimate to exercises and weights. Don't take up where you last started if you have been away from the gym for some time. Likewise, if you have never trained with weights, starting slowly with light weights is more appropriate for muscular and joint health than moving quickly with heavy weights. Make sure that you get sufficient rest and recovery time. Muscles can get slightly damaged from weight training, and there is always an eccentric component. Waiting at least 48 hours between weight sessions for the same muscle group, or until the pain is gone, is appropriate. Also, limit your use of prolonged eccentric contractions. If you make yourself so sore that you don't want to strength train anymore, you only succeed in demotivating yourself.

# Muscling Up Your Metabolism

# 3

Why do many people think that to lose body fat they must spend countless hours on the step machine, treadmill, or bicycle, while spending little or no time pumping iron? The latest news about fat loss may surprise you and allow you to stop running around in circles. It's time to update your workout program and redefine your fitness goals, using the best information—based on scientific research—about what makes you stronger, healthier, and more fit.

First, let's define some basic terms related to why strength training helps build muscle while reducing fat. The scientific term for weight is *mass*. The term *body composition* refers to dividing the body's mass into fat-free mass (FFM), fat mass (FM), and lean body mass (LBM).

FFM consists of the portion of muscle, bone, and organ weight that contains no fat. FM is total body fat, which includes essential fat and storage fat. As we discussed in chapter 1, the body requires essential fat to maintain normal physiological functions. It is found inside organs, bones, and nerves, and on women also in the breasts and around the reproductive organs. Some storage fat is necessary to protect both men's and women's internal organs from trauma and to provide the body with reserve fuel. The other type of storage fat is made up of unburned calories from Oreo cookies and Häagen-Dazs ice cream, and is not necessary for life (unless you're going through a relationship breakup!). When most of us say that we want to lose fat, it's that Oreo cookie storage fat that we want to lose.

A person's lean body mass (LBM) is the amount of FFM and some FM that is essential for life. When body composition measurements are taken, the results tell you your percentages of FM and LBM. When you decrease FM and increase LBM, your body composition improves favorably, and the body takes on a harder and more muscular appearance with less fat. Remember, though, that muscle is denser than fat, so when you gain muscle and lose fat you end up with a net zero equation. Therefore, increasing muscle won't likely increase your body circumference by much. However, most people who gain muscle and lose fat also increase their body's metabolism—thus increasing the rate at which they burn calories.

People who are overweight often claim that their body has a slow metabolism and that that's why they can't lose weight. They are wrong. The real reason they are gaining weight is that they are not active enough. Fat is biologically inactive tissue. In other words, it doesn't do anything except sit on the couch with the remote control and keep us warm. Muscle, on the other hand, is constantly at work, even at rest. It generates and gives off heat and requires energy (calories) to do these things.

When we are awake, our bodies need energy to perform all sorts of activities just to keep us alive. The amount of energy that our bodies need for normal physiological functioning while we are awake is called our basal metabolic rate (BMR). The resting metabolic rate (RMR) includes the BMR plus the amount of energy we use when we are sleeping and waking up from sleep. Our total body metabolism actually refers to our total daily energy expenditure (TDEE) and is a combination of the RMR, our physical activity, and the thermic effect of food (TEF).

Your body actually burns calories from the food that you eat through the processes of chewing, digestion, and absorption. The body uses approximately 5 to 10 percent of the total calories of the food you ingest to process that food, and this calorie use is the TEF. On average our TDEE is divided up into approximately 60 to 75 percent for RMR, 10 percent for TEF, and 15 to 30 percent for physical activity (see table 3.1). Although a certain percentage of our TDEE is genetically programmed, we do have direct control over some areas. For example, we can increase our physical activity simply by training longer, harder, or more days per week, and we can increase our RMR by adding more muscle to our bodies. Strength training is the best way to add more muscle to our bodies and increase our RMR.

Table 3.1   **Makeup of Your Total Daily Energy Expenditure (TDEE)**

| | |
|---|---|
| Resting metabolic rate (RMR) | 60 to 75% |
| Thermic effect of food (TEF) | 10% |
| Physical activity | 15 to 30% |

# Cardiovascular Endurance Exercise and Metabolism

Women usually choose to increase their TDEE by increasing their physical activity through traditional cardiovascular endurance exercise activities such as running, using a stair machine, or doing aerobics. Although doing cardio activities is a scientifically proven method for acute weight loss, it may not be the best method for long-term weight loss—keeping the weight off for months or years after starting an exercise program.

Once you start decreasing your FM with endurance exercise, you also decrease your LBM. Did you know that long, slow endurance exercise actually takes your hard-earned muscular tissue and uses it for energy? Since your LBM is directly associated with your RMR, when your LBM decreases, so does your RMR. This means that your body will use fewer calories at rest now that you weigh less than it did when you weighed more. Translated into gym lingo, this link means that to continue losing weight (or in some cases to keep off your lost weight) with the cardiovascular endurance exercise you do, you will either have to step on that stair climber longer or increase your intensity. As stated earlier, however, the physical activity component of your TDEE caps out at about 30 percent. Once you get to that high physical activity expenditure, your body starts to adapt and conserve. Therefore, a time will come when you hit a plateau and will not be able to lose one more pound without severe calorie restriction (probably our least favorite alternative).

Enter strength training. It is true that you expend more calories during a typical endurance-training session compared to a strength-training session. But it is also true that you use more calories throughout the day and even at rest if you have more muscle on your body. That's why it always seems as if guys can sit on the couch, eat anything they want, play a little football, and still maintain their weight, whereas you feel that you gain weight if you even *look* at a cupcake. Men typically have much more muscle mass than women and don't waste their time walking on the treadmill to nowhere. They play high-intensity sports or lift heavy weights and are simply born with more muscle, as we learned in the last chapter.

Gaining muscle mass increases a person's RMR, but merely by doing a strength-training workout you will elevate your metabolism throughout the day. A research study that compared a strenuous bout of weight training to a bout of steady-state stationary cycling showed that the strenuous weight training resulted in greater excess postexercise oxygen consumption compared to the steady-state endurance exercise of similar estimated energy cost. The increase in the RMR lasted for up to five hours after the weight training.

The old idea that if we do long, slow endurance exercise we will enter the fat-burning zone, and that high-intensity exercise doesn't burn fat, is somewhat misleading. The body works on a continuum—just as you can't do any number of leg lifts to spot reduce the fat on your thighs, neither can you burn only fat when exercising. The truth is, you burn *calories* when exercising, and to the body a calorie is just a calorie. The harder you exercise, the more calories you burn. If your goal for doing cardiovascular endurance exercise (or any exercise for that matter) is to lose weight, then the total number of calories you burn with that exercise (versus the calories you take in each day) is the only thing that matters, not where they came from.

## Adjusting Intensity

So why even bother with cardiovascular endurance exercise? If you enjoy it, that's one good reason to do it. Also, beneficial physiological adaptations happen in the body with this type of training that do not occur with weight training. Instead of just doing long, slow endurance cardio work, try to incorporate high-intensity cardiovascular endurance exercise into a strength training program to tap into the increased RMR that occurs after strenuous exercise. As a matter of fact, a research study of 33 college-age women who performed an aerobic circuit weight-training program backs up this approach. The results from the 45-minute circuit of 30 activities, including $5 \times 3$-minute aerobic exercises and $25 \times 30$-second weight training or calisthenic exercises, showed that the women improved their cardiovascular fitness, body composition, and muscular strength.

The most effective way to perform cardiovascular endurance exercise and get more benefits from it is to develop a plan that also incorporates elements of higher-intensity weight-training techniques. One way to do so is using a circuit like that described previously. Another way is to increase the intensity of your workout. Rather than running or stepping for 45 to 60 minutes at the same level in a steady state so that you can talk to your neighbor, cut the session down to 20 to 30 minutes and raise your level of intensity. You can't possibly do long, slow endurance exercise at your highest achievable intensity for an hour. If you think you can, then you aren't at the highest intensity you can attain.

## Using Interval Training

An even more effective cardio workout is to interval train. When you interval train, you divide your training period into *work* and *rest* sessions or intervals. During the work interval you train at a high intensity for a brief period of time. The rest session isn't exactly time to sit down, but time to slow the activity down a bit for recovery from the high-intensity interval. You can choose from many different work-to-rest ratios (WRR), but because the work intervals are supposed to be intense, they should only be performed for a short period of time.

Start your work intervals at 10 to 15 seconds and progress up to 30 to 90 seconds, but don't exceed 120 seconds. The shorter your rest intervals, the harder you will work, but never choose anything less than a 1:1 ratio of work to rest. For example, jog at a moderate speed for 1 minute (your rest interval) and then sprint for 10 to 15 seconds (your work interval). If you are on the treadmill, you may have to subtract the time it takes for the machine to speed up for your sprints. If you are swimming, you can just increase your speed in the water when it is time to sprint. When on a step machine, simply increase the level for your work time. On the bike, increase the level or tension.

# MEASURING INTERVAL INTENSITY

You can use two methods to measure how hard you are working based on effort during an interval training session—using a set scale or using your heart rate to determine your intensity.

By using a rating of perceived exertion (RPE) scale, you can rate your intensity and effort by the way it feels to you, assigning it a number. Some use a 15-point Borg scale with 6 representing no exertion and 20 representing maximal exertion (see table 3.2a). You can use a Category-Ratio scale, in which 0 is no effort at all and 12 is the absolute maximum (see table 3.2b; the "P" is perceived exertion, and "Max P" is the highest perception you have experienced).

## Table 3.2a  Borg RPE Scale

| | |
|---|---|
| 6 | No exertion at all |
| 7 | |
| 8 | Extremely light |
| 9 | Very light |
| 10 | |
| 11 | Light |
| 12 | |
| 13 | Somewhat hard |
| 14 | |
| 15 | Hard   (heavy) |
| 16 | |
| 17 | Very hard |
| 18 | |
| 19 | Extremely hard |
| 20 | Maximal exertion |

Borg RPE scale
© Gunnar Borg, 1970, 1985, 1994, 1998

G. Borg, 1998, *Borg's perceived exertion and pain scales* (Champaign, IL: Human Kinetics), 47.

## Table 3.2b  Borg CR10 Scale

| | | |
|---|---|---|
| 0 | Nothing at all | "No P" |
| 0.3 | | |
| 0.5 | Extremely weak | Just noticeable |
| 1 | Very weak | |
| 1.5 | | |
| 2 | Weak | Light |
| 2.5 | | |
| 3 | Moderate | |
| 4 | | |
| 5 | Strong | Heavy |
| 6 | | |
| 7 | Very strong | |
| 8 | | |
| 9 | | |
| 10 | Extremely strong | "Max P" |
| 11 | | |
| ● | Absolute maximum | Highest possible |

Borg CR10 scale
© Gunnar Borg, 1981, 1982, 1998

G. Borg, 1998, *Borg's perceived exertion and pain scales* (Champaign, IL: Human Kinetics), 50.

However, I think it's easier to simplify things and rate effort on a 0 to 10 scale, where 0 is no effort and 10 is maximal effort (see table 3.2c). Then you can correlate these numbers to percentages and say that a 5 is 50 percent effort and a 10 is 100 percent effort (the point at which you can't do any more). You should be at 5 at the end of your warm-up, at 3 at the end of your cool-down, and at 9 or 10 (for advanced interval trainers) during the work portion of the workout. For example, a beginner should warm up to 5, work at 6 to 7, recover at 5 to 6, and cool down at 5 to 3. Intermediates should warm up to 5, work at 7 to 8, recover at 6 to 7, and cool down at 5 to 4. Advanced trainers can warm up to 5, work at 8 to 10, recover at 7 to 8, and cool down at 5 to 4.

## Table 3.2c  10-Point Percentage Scale

| Rating | % of effort |
|---|---|
| 1 | 10 |
| 2 | 20 |
| 3 | 30 |
| 4 | 40 |
| 5 | 50 |
| 6 | 60 |
| 7 | 70 |
| 8 | 80 |
| 9 | 90 |
| 10 | 100 |

Using your heart rate maximum (HRmax) to determine intensity is a little difficult and sometimes inaccurate, because heart rate doesn't always correlate with effort, but wearing a heart rate monitor will simplify things. For safety for beginners, using the age-predicted maximum heart rate formulas and a heart rate monitor to assess your intensity is essential. To determine what heart rate to work at for your intense work sessions, calculate your age-predicted maximum heart rate (APHRmax) and multiply it by the appropriate intensity percentage. The American College of Sports Medicine (ACSM) recommends an intensity percentage between 60 and 90 percent for work sessions. For a beginner, work ratio intensities should be between 60 to 80 percent and then can progress up to 85 to 90 percent as you become more acclimated to interval training. Here's an example for a 30-year-old female beginner who wants a 70 percent intensity work bout:

$$\text{APHRmax} = 220 - \text{age } (220 - 30) = 190 \times .70 = 133$$

You can also arrange the heart rate percentage to reflect your selected recovery heart rate. Let's say that our 30-year-old beginner wanted to recover at 60 percent of her APHRmax:

$$\text{APHRmax} = 220 - \text{age } (220 - 30) = 190 \times .60 = 114$$

Then she wouldn't begin her next interval work repetition until her heart rate had recovered to 114 beats per minute.

---

The first time that you try interval training instead of your usual cardio program, you'll be pleasantly surprised at how difficult it is. If you are in the gym using cardio equipment that is computerized, record the METs (metabolic equivalents, based on a method of measuring energy expenditure in relation to the resting metabolic rate), miles, number of steps climbed, and so forth for your typical endurance session and compare it to your interval session. You will find that you are actually working harder for longer, but in a shorter overall period of time. Don't we want the biggest bang for our buck—the best workout in the shortest time period so that we can get on with our lives? Interval training can deliver that and more. The following are two interval workouts you can incorporate into your cardio program:

**Stadium intervals**—You can use stadium bleachers found on high school or college campuses, or you can use regular steps or stairs for this interval workout. Your work is walking or running up the steps, and your recovery is walking or running down the steps. Beginners should start by walking one step at a time with their arms at their sides, then move, when ready, to walking with arms overhead. Progress to running, then to taking two steps at a time, for a more intense work bout. Always begin with a five-minute warm-up and end with a five-minute cool-down. Gauge your work and recovery ratios by either the heart rate method or rating of perceived exertion (RPE) method (detailed in the following section).

**Bicycle or treadmill intervals**—You can also simply use an interval program or hill program on the standard computerized bicycles found in most gyms for an interval workout. The resistance you have to pedal against on the bicycle will increase during the work bout while you try to maintain a high RPM and will decrease during the recovery bout. Of course, you can also control the program manually if you prefer to control your work-to-rest ratio. Another way to intensify the work bout is to crank it up to the highest level of tension and then stand up and ride the bike (without your bottom touching the seat), while still trying to maintain the same RPM. Does this sound like one of those indoor cycling classes? Most of these classes do incorporate intervals. Some treadmills are also programmable, and some require a manual adjustment. You can choose a walk–jog, walk–run, walk–sprint, or jog–sprint, run–sprint WRR, depending on your level of fitness. Adjusting the incline on the treadmill is also a nice way to progress the intensity of the work session.

# Strength Training and Metabolism

What about giving up your cardiovascular endurance exercise altogether? Are you worried that you'll end up fat and out of shape or that you'll drop dead of a heart attack? It can't be true that the only exercise you can do for your heart and lungs is the aerobic exercise that we are familiar with. As you've already learned, there are many misconceptions about what aerobic training can do. Unfortunately, a lot of what you hear in the gym is based on old theories that may or may not have come from scientific research. Most importantly, you need to realize that physical fitness is a medical science and that science is always changing. What was correct and popular advice years ago may now be scientifically refuted. Realize that your heart is a muscle and you can do a lot of different things to train it. If you exercise at a high intensity, then your heart and lungs will be working.

A few years ago weight-machine circuits were all the rage. Weight machines were arranged in rows and you were instructed to go from one machine to the next, performing exercises on each machine for a prescribed amount of time, and continue until you ran out of machines. Basically you did a set with every body part that the machines were designed for, and you were then done with your workout for the day. Sometimes you got on a bicycle or treadmill in between the weight machines, to make rest periods more like periods of active rest and thereby increase energy expenditure. The popularity of these circuits died down for many reasons. One explanation is that they got pretty boring after a while, grinding out the same routine for every workout. Also, people weren't seeing huge changes in body composition from such workouts. In addition, athletes noticed the limitations of isolation exercises that used machines only and found that they weren't able to transfer strength gains into enhancing either their sport performances or their functional lives.

Sport scientists started looking for ways to devise weight-training programs that produced results that carried over to sports and functional performance. They painstakingly studied sports and documented each player's movements during a game, to determine their work and rest intervals. Playing most sports involves high-intensity, high-effort periods followed by periods of low-intensity or even total rest periods. Even during daily life the scientists saw periods of high- to moderate-intensity work followed by periods of relative rest. Those different periods of exercise intensity resulted in different metabolic rates (remember the physical activity component of the TDEE). So the scientists started using the phrase *metabolic training* to describe the correct way to train athletes, i.e., training athletes in the exact same intensities that they would use in a game or competition. The theory was that if you practice as you play, your metabolism will be efficient at the tasks it needs to perform during competition.

Most sports are multidimensional and use total-body movements. Metabolic training comes at a higher metabolic cost to the body than single muscle isolation movements. It burns a lot of calories, demolishes fat, decreases workout time, and builds muscle (which increases the metabolic rate even more). It is also a good general conditioning activity, because it involves more than one component of fitness. The common folk can't let a good idea go to waste, so now metabolic training has caught on in the mainstream training public. It is a catch phrase meaning a program that has high-intensity and low-intensity bouts—similar to the description of our cardiovascular interval programs, except that metabolic training uses strength-training exercises.

Metabolic weight circuits can bring your body new benefits, both physical and psychological. Using these programs, you can climb past plateaus and spice up your workouts. You can base your high-intensity weight-training intervals on either repetitions or time. For work based on repetitions, time how long it takes to perform 15 repetitions of an exercise and then rest for that same amount of time or more. For work based on time, work for a specific amount of time, such as 30 seconds, and then rest for 30 seconds or more. Get in as many reps as you can during that time. Your intensity during the weight or work session should range from 40 to 70 percent of your one-repetition maximum (1RM)—the amount of weight you can lift one

© Human Kinetics

In metabolic training, as in sport and daily life, periods of high-intensity activity are interspersed with periods of rest or low-intensity activity.

time. As your conditioning improves, maintain your intensity and decrease your rest ratios, or increase your intensity and maintain your rest ratios, for variety.

You should have a basic fitness level before embarking on a metabolic weight circuit since it is physiologically demanding. Be aware that doing this type of training for more than 30 minutes 3 days per week will likely lead to overtraining and injury. Stick with a 5-minute warm-up, a 5-minute cool-down, and 20 minutes of a metabolic weight circuit as an end goal. Because metabolic weight circuits are so challenging, it is wise to start with a 10-minute circuit (keeping the 5-minute warm-ups and cool-downs) and progress up to 20 minutes as your body adapts. Use a stopwatch to time your intervals so that you are consistent and not guessing. Although you want to maximize your effort and adhere to the interval times as closely as possible, you may have to vary and individualize the circuit to fit your conditioning level and experience. If you need more time to rest and recover before beginning the next exercise, you should take it. Likewise, some people have to begin the metabolic weight circuits with body weight alone. Don't think that's ineffective, though. Trying to push yourself to adhere to a program that isn't specifically designed for you could result in injury. Just remember to document the changes and strive to improve each time. The only person that you have to compete against is you.

In table 3.3, *a* through *d*, I provide an upper-body, lower-body, total-body, and outdoor metabolic circuit using the exercises that are described in part III of this book; it's also easy to design your own circuit. Because this type of exercise fatigues muscles quickly, alternate exercises to emphasize different areas. Some muscle groups are the primary workers during a certain exercise while others are resting so that they can be the primary workers in the next exercise; so for example, you could alternate pushing and pulling exercises in an upper-body circuit (see chapter 9). You can design a circuit with an exercise that hits every muscle group individually or as a whole. Thus, you can design a circuit with exercises for the shoulders, upper back, low back, biceps, triceps, and so forth; or you can have a circuit of total-body exercises like Olympic lifts. The possibilities are endless. Metabolic circuits are a lot of fun and can really benefit your health and fitness. To determine how to best fit a circuit or a cardiovascular interval-training session into your training program, see chapter 7 on designing your own program.

# METABOLIC STRENGTH CIRCUITS

Metabolic strength circuits can be easily performed in the gym, at home, or outdoors. Using body weight with some of the exercises, especially when first starting out, is totally appropriate. When adding weights, consider using dumbbells and medicine balls because of their compact design and ease of use. Perform 15 reps for each exercise or however many reps you can do in 15 seconds. If the exercise involves working a right or left extremity separately (as in lunges), count the right and left movement together as 1 rep. Rest for double the amount of time that it took you to exercise (a 1:2 work-to-rest-ratio) and move on to the next exercise immediately. Each strength circuit lasts approximately 5 minutes, so you will need to repeat it to add time to your workout. You can do an upper body circuit one day and a lower body circuit on another day, or you can combine both halves of the body with a total body circuit.

For the outdoor circuit, you'll need an area at least 50 feet in length. I've done outdoor metabolic strength circuits on driveways and porches and in parking lots, parks, and stadiums. Be creative with the area you have or travel around to find the perfect spot. This program consists of both weight exercises and burst exercises like skipping, jogging, or sprinting (that's why you need the 50 feet). You might have to travel back and forth over the 50 feet to achieve a work ratio of 15 seconds, or you can use a larger area.

### Table 3.3a  Upper-Body Metabolic Strength Circuit
Rest 30 seconds after each exercise.

| Exercise | Page # | Reps | Time (in seconds) |
|---|---|---|---|
| Push-up | 122 | 15 | 15 |
| Pull-up | 132 | 15 | 15 |
| Dumbbell bench press | 124 | 15 | 15 |
| Dumbbell row | 131 | 15 | 15 |
| Dumbbell overhead press | 130 | 15 | 15 |
| Lat pulldown | 134 | 15 | 15 |
| Dumbbell biceps curl | 139 | 15 | 15 |
| Dumbbell kickback | 144 | 15 | 15 |

### Table 3.3b  Lower-Body Metabolic Strength Circuit
Rest 30 seconds after each exercise.

| Exercise | Page # | Reps | Time (in seconds) |
|---|---|---|---|
| Squat | 159 | 15 | 15 |
| Butt lift | 165 | 15 | 15 |
| Sumo deadlift | 178 | 15 | 15 |
| Hip extension | 167 | 15 | 15 |
| Step-up | 165 | 15 | 15 |
| Lunge | 163 | 15 | 15 |
| One-leg squat | 160 | 15 | 15 |
| Stability ball leg curl | 168 | 15 | 15 |

### Table 3.3c  Total-Body Metabolic Strength Circuit

Rest 30 seconds after each exercise.

| Exercise | Page # | Reps | Time (in seconds) |
|---|---|---|---|
| Clean pull | 189 | 15 | 15 |
| Stability ball straight crunch | 101 | 15 | 15 |
| Jump squat | 161 | 15 | 15 |
| Stability ball diagonal crunch | 102 | 15 | 15 |
| Push press | 127 | 15 | 15 |
| Stability ball pull-in | 102 | 15 | 15 |
| Split jerk | 129 | 15 | 15 |
| Stability ball hyper-extension | 109 | 15 | 15 |

### Table 3.3d  Outdoor-Based Metabolic Strength Circuit

Rest 30 seconds after each exercise.

| Exercise | Page # | Reps | Time (in seconds) |
|---|---|---|---|
| Squat | 159 | 15 | 15 |
| Skip | — | — | 15 |
| Lunge | 164 | 15 | 15 |
| High-knee skip | — | — | 15 |
| Push-up | 122 | 15 | 15 |
| Sprint | — | — | 15 |
| Dumbbell overhead press | 130 | 15 | 15 |
| Sprint | — | — | 15 |

Here are a few final tips for maximizing the effectiveness of your metabolic strength circuits:

1. Complete the movements. With the weight exercises, don't sacrifice speed for form. Use full range-of-motion movements to get all of your muscles working.

2. Decrease the rest in between sets. As you advance, decrease your rest intervals. Aim for no rest at all for a superquick, highly charged session!

3. Increase the weight you use. When your body isn't fatigued and sore after training, up the weight. The heavier the weight, the more calories you'll burn.

4. Get fast and explosive. Put some spring in your step and increase your energy output.

5. Do another round—if you're up for the challenge, repeat the routine. Go through it as fast as you can.

# Part II

# Results-Oriented Training

# Training for Specific Results

Running a few miles or doing a few leg extensions is not enough anymore to say you're in shape. As the fitness industry has become more sophisticated through anecdotal reports and actual scientific research, certain trends have emerged. We now understand that physical fitness is a relative term that means different things to different people. For example, a marathon runner wouldn't consider herself physically fit if she was strong and muscular, but lacked the endurance to run 26 miles. She might look good, and society might judge her to be in shape, but without the endurance she wouldn't be able to compete in her sport. Likewise, a powerlifter who can run for long distances but can't perform a one-rep maximum bench press would have terrible fitness for her sport. Her cardiovascular endurance may be excellent, but that won't win her any medals in powerlifting. These athletes need to train for the specific demands of their sports.

What about the stay-at-home mom whose physical need is to be able to chase her kids around all day without becoming fatigued? She would love to have a fantastic body, but perhaps it's more important to her to be fit enough to keep up with her children. She needs to train specifically for the physical demands of her day. Specific training leads to specific results, whereas haphazard training leads to haphazard results. You might think you are physically fit if you can run a few miles and do some leg extensions, but it depends on how you define what physical fitness is for you. What are your physical fitness needs? Defining your needs is as specific to each person as choosing the exercises to meet those needs.

When we get in a car, we usually have in mind both a destination and a route to get there. We don't drive willy-nilly all around town hoping that we'll wind up at work, the dry cleaner's, and the grocery store. It should be the same with your exercise program. Think of your physical fitness program as a journey to reach a specific goal. What is your goal for exercise? Do you want to enter a strength competition? If so, you will have to incorporate very different training techniques than if you want to lose a dress size. Your specific goals determine the type and amount of training you must do. Familiarize yourself with the following components of fitness to help you determine your goals. In chapter 7, I'll tell you how to design the perfect program to meet those goals.

# Components of Fitness

Five basic components make up the total physical fitness picture. If you wanted to say that you are a complete physical fitness specimen, then technically you would have to excel in all five: agility, balance, flexibility, endurance, and strength. But is excelling in all five really possible? Actually, it's not. What trainers and coaches have discovered through years of trial and error in training athletes is that the body gets good at the things it does the most and it tends to do the most of the things it is good at. This may seem like circular logic—but try looking at it in a different way.

Suppose you are in college and are striving to become the most knowledgeable person you can be, so you take classes in a wide variety of disciplines. You enjoy learning a little about ancient history, composition, philosophy, and economics. Soon it becomes apparent that you have a certain aptitude for remembering dates and places, and you receive A's on all of your ancient history tests. You are not doing poorly in your other classes, since you are an extremely smart woman and are maintaining B's. However, the A's are encouraging and you find history fascinating, so you decide to take another history class the next semester. Before you know it, you are majoring in history and the economics classes are a thing of the past. This example is similar to what happens to the body when you present it with training for the five components of fitness. You can likely succeed in all five components, but more often than not, one or two of the components suffer (relatively) for the gains made in others. Usually you concentrate on the component that you are the most successful at, which is probably something that fits your body type. That is why at the elite level it is as rare to see a short, stocky, muscular marathon runner as it is to see a tall, thin powerlifter. Your body gravitates to what it is good at—what it is built to do. Let's look at the components of fitness to gain a better understanding of what being in good shape means to you.

## Agility

If you can change direction quickly, start and stop on a dime, and look coordinated doing it, then you have good agility. Many sports like soccer, volleyball, basketball, and tennis require athletes who are agile. You can train for agility by running obstacle courses or by practicing techniques or drills that are specific to the movements you encounter in your sport, such as faking left but running right. Being agile is beneficial for nonathletes too. Certainly navigating an obstacle course made up of your kids' toys on the ground without twisting your ankle is a valuable skill. Being able to avoid a car that's suddenly pulling out of a parking spot is also important. Agility training is imperative as we grow older; research has shown that the decrease in agility and balance that often occurs as we age can lead to falls and fractures.

Agility movements aren't typically found in a strength-training program but are easy to add. The metabolic strength circuits I provide in chapter 3 incorporate some aspects of agility work. Some of the exercises I describe in part III, when done on one leg or with a stability ball, can improve your agility. But to be truly agile, you have to devote more time to this component than a typical strength-training program will allow.

## Balance

Balance is the ability to maintain a stable position for a certain period of time. We usually think of balance as a lower-body activity, but it is a coordinated effort of the body and mind. Our overall sense of balance comes from communication among the eyes, ears, and brain. The ears and eyes communicate changes of head position to the brain. Sports require balance because when you are participating in most sports, you are rarely standing still on two legs. Balance is equally integral to daily activities (with the exception of the time you spend sitting at your office desk, in your car, or on your couch).

Having balance in the muscles that surround your joints protects the joints and prevents injury. Strength training is an excellent way to improve your balance because your muscles have to provide balanced support for both your body and the weights you are using. Using free weights forces the muscles on either side of a joint to co-contract, providing balance for the musculature as well as the apparatus you are holding. You can incorporate even more balance work into your strength training by doing single-leg exercises, narrowing your base of support, or using devices like stability balls that challenge your balance. Closing your eyes during an exercise is also an excellent way to train your balance because the eyes give the body spatial clues.

## Flexibility

Flexibility is the range of motion of a joint. Our muscles are actually long enough to allow for a full range of motion in our joints. It is the tension in our muscles that makes us less flexible. That tension can come from actual psychological tension that spills over into the muscles (think of that tension headache you get in your head, neck, and shoulders when your kids are running around like banshees or your boss is giving you yet another project to complete on a tight deadline) or from repeated and prolonged positions (like sitting at your computer all day long). Genetics, age, gender, exercise, and body and external temperature also influence your flexibility. Although few research studies have been able to prove that safely improving flexibility decreases one's risk for injuries, many authorities believe that it does. Moreover, some experts think that being inflexible can actually predispose you to an injury.

Being flexible does have its advantages in sports and daily life. Flexibility may allow your arm to stretch a little farther to hit a backhand or to reach a plate on the top shelf of a cabinet. In addition, your body feels much better when you are flexible—don't underestimate the value of simply feeling good. You can improve flexibility through static and dynamic stretching techniques. You most commonly see people stretching statically. Static stretching focuses on one group of muscles, putting them in a stretched position and holding that stretch continuously for a period ranging from 30 seconds to 1 to 2 minutes. It can be effective in elongating tissue, but it is most effective if done after strength training sessions and on a daily basis. Research has found that aggressive static stretching done before a strength-training session actually decreases muscular power and strength. Dynamic stretching, on the other hand, has a positive effect on strength-training sessions and athletic events, because it stretches muscles through movement patterns found in exercise and sports. Dynamic stretching involves multiple joints in active motions. You'll find a dynamic stretching warm-up program in chapter 7.

## Endurance

How long can you do an activity and still maintain quality? The better endurance you have, the less quickly you become fatigued. When you are fatigued, your performance either falters or just stops. Fatigue is a complex issue with both mental and physical aspects. You can become mentally fatigued from boredom, from having an intense emotional experience, or from having a low pain tolerance or motivation for a particular activity. Physically, your body can become fatigued from weak muscles, low muscular energy stores, and low muscular oxygen capacity.

The two types of endurance are muscular endurance and cardiovascular endurance. You use muscular endurance in activities that require a muscle or group of muscles to work at a high intensity for many repetitions or for a prolonged period. Think of performing 15 or more repetitions of an exercise as using muscular endurance. Likewise, holding on to a very heavy object for a long period of time shows muscular endurance. Muscular endurance activities typically cannot last longer than two minutes, because the muscles cannot generate or store that much energy. You'll find more details about muscular endurance in chapter 5.

Cardiovascular endurance is the type of endurance that marathon runners have. You can think of it as whole-body endurance, as opposed to stamina in only one muscle or muscle group. In order to sustain the entire body for a prolonged bout of exercise, muscles need the oxygen that is delivered to them by the cardiovascular and respiratory systems.

## Strength

We talk about everyday strengths like strength of character, strength of convictions, and strength of the family unit. Basically we are talking about a force, something that is powerful and intense. This is exactly the classic definition of strength—the ability to exert force. Even though it seems like a cut-and-dried definition, in chapter 5 you'll find out that there is a lot more to it. There is absolute strength and relative strength and, to confound the issue, there is also speed-strength and strength-endurance.

Obviously you picked up this book because you are interested in doing strength training, or at least in finding out what it is. If you do decide to devote your fitness program to training for strength, it doesn't necessarily mean that you can't incorporate all of the five components of fitness. It does mean that you will sacrifice excelling in some for excelling in others, because as much as we want to, we just can't have it all.

# Specificity of Exercise

Personal trainers and strength coaches have been talking about the benefits of *functional training* for quite some time now. Functional training simply means that the exercises you choose are specific to what you are training for. For example, a functional exercise for a woman whose primary job is taking care of a house and her kids is very different from a functional exercise for a female professional soccer player. Whereas the domestic goddess needs strong and powerful legs to squat down to pick up her kids, the soccer player needs strong, powerful, and fast legs to run around the field and kick a ball accurately. In this way, functional training is very goal oriented.

Before developing a functional training workout that is right for you, you need to determine what your functional goals are and select your exercises with them in mind. What exactly does the mother of two want in a training program? Maybe she simply wants to be strong enough to pick up her kids and not hurt her back. Perhaps she wants to practice soccer with her kids in the backyard and teach them a few new moves. In each case the exercises will be different, yet functional for her goal. The five components of fitness are very closely tied to the specificity of exercise. A "soccer mom" will probably do some agility training and maybe incorporate a little cardiovascular endurance training. But a postmenopausal woman who is concerned about osteoporosis will focus on strength and balance training.

Because human activities, whether playing sports or merely walking around, are multidimensional, the basis of functional strength training is too. It uses total-body movements in multiple planes as opposed to traditional bodybuilding, which uses isolated muscular movements in one plane. We rarely have a specific daily activity that requires us to sit in a chair and extend both legs out in front of us and then bend them back, as we do when we are seated in a leg extension machine. Exercises in machines are not considered functional because we don't play sports in machines and we don't live in machines (unless you count your car). You can work the quadriceps just as well (or better) by doing a squat, which is functional because you do it every day when you squat down to sit or to pick something up. The free-weight squat also requires balance, as does squatting in everyday activities, whereas sitting inside a machine requires no balance whatsoever.

Bone and muscle both need multidimensional activities to grow to their maximum potential. We saw in chapter 2 that the more diverse stresses you can put on bone from different angles, the more you increase bone density. The same is true for muscles that have to function in all different directions. If you exercise them only one specific way, they will only get strong in that way. Working in machines or using two-dimensional exercises is definitely not functional training for an athlete. Sports are dynamic, and athletes need exercises that mimic dynamic motion and the actions of their particular sport.

Why is something called *core training* often lumped in with functional strength training? The philosophy behind core training is that the trunk or core is the stabilizer and the power for the entire body. The core muscles are considered the abdominals, back, hips, and butt. Chapter 8 is entirely devoted to core exercises. Movement in life occurs (and often occurs without injury) because we have been able to stabilize our core and have used it to generate power. We can reach for the glass on the top shelf without injuring our shoulders because our trunk is maintaining a base of support that our arm can work off of.

If you have watched children develop from infancy, you've seen core training in action. Babies' muscles are nothing more than wet noodles. Without a solid base, they can't go anywhere. Their first muscular mission is to get a strong neck so that they can hold their heads up and see the world. As the spinal muscles strengthen, they gain more mobility and can roll from side to side. If they are supported in a bouncy seat or lying on their backs they can reach for objects, but not if they are left unsupported—their core muscles aren't strong enough yet. Soon they are crawling and are able to move around using their extremities. As they develop greater balance and strength, they learn to stand and walk. Core training, then, is really functional strength training in its most basic definition.

You can realize different goals with different kinds of training methods, and that's what this whole book is about. You can stay safe with tried-and-true routines that you have done to death, or you can take a leap and challenge your body with a new stimulus. You'll find that if you want to develop maximal strength, a bodybuilding workout will never let you achieve that goal. If you want to be fast and explosive, lifting the total amount of weight you can lift in one repetition isn't going to cut the cake. On the other hand, weight training works on a continuum, and training routines for hypertrophy, strength, power, body composition, and general health do overlap and have mutually beneficial side effects.

## Training to Improve Body Composition

Millions of women across the country are trying to improve their physiques by altering their body composition. Specifically, they want to reduce their body fat. The cardiovascular endurance exercise session is the traditional favorite exercise of choice to achieve this goal. Many women hop on the treadmill or step machine for 45 minutes to expend calories and decrease fat stores. Although research has proven that this approach might be a sure solution to short-term weight loss (for about the first three months), it may not be the best strategy for long-term weight loss and maintenance.

Let's take a look at a hypothetical example to see why. Our subject is a 200-pound woman who eats 2,000 calories a day and doesn't exercise. For her New Year's resolution, she decides to start a diet and exercise program in an effort to lose 60 pounds. She cuts her calories down to 1,700 a day and adds cardiovascular endurance exercise to burn an additional 300 calories a day. She successfully loses 15 pounds in the first three months, so now she is down to 185. Believe it or not, when she was 200 pounds it cost her body more calories simply to move around. Now that she has lost weight, her body has to burn less energy to move her lighter weight, so it doesn't cost as many calories just to live. She is starting to hit a plateau.

To continue losing weight, the woman needs to decrease her caloric intake again, increase the time or intensity of her cardiovascular endurance exercise, or try another approach. Going below

By building muscle, strength training helps you burn more energy and achieve a more sculpted look.

1,500 calories might leave her hungry, depressed, and lacking some nutrients. If she stays with that strategy, is she going to have to keep decreasing calories until she hits her target weight of 140? That's still 45 pounds away. She can increase the length of time that she stays on the cardio equipment to burn more calories, but she is already doing 45 minutes every day of the week. She might be able to increase the intensity of the exercise (raise the level or difficulty), but she won't be able to sustain the exercise session for as long. At some point she needs to do something that will cost her body calories without having to starve herself or risk joint injury from over-training. Enter strength training, which will affect her body composition in two ways. First, she is adding another training modality that will cost energy (calories). Second, and most importantly, she is adding lean body weight in the form of muscle. Muscle is metabolically active—it burns energy. You can see how these effects could be a double whammy for her body fat. In addition, lean muscular tissue gives the sculpted look that people who train for body composition desire.

Body composition training and strength training are not enemies, especially not in the long term. But even in the short term, strength training makes sense; otherwise, the body reaches a plateau all too soon. Why wait until the muscles have decreased in size because of the cardiovascular endurance training and until the metabolic cost of living has gone down because of the weight loss? If you pair strength training with the traditional cardiovascular endurance exercise in a planned program, you can create an effective symbiotic relationship.

## Training for Health Versus Competition

A classic saying among competitive athletes states, "Health ends where competition begins." The general public thinks that highly competitive amateur and professional athletes not only possess the skill and talent to take them to the top of their sports, but also possess superior health because of their rigorous training schedules and devotion to becoming the best. After all, we see their fantastic bodies and rejoice with their successes; we know that they must be extremely healthy to have achieved such lofty goals. That competitive athletes are perfect physical specimens is a misconception in the lay community. This notion couldn't be farther from the truth for some athletes. The reality of competitive athletics is that all bets are off and the rules are few. Many competitive athletes are continually overtrained, resulting in lowered immune systems, lack of sleep, and constant muscle soreness. Many competitive athletes will do anything it takes to be competitive and win—even experimenting with drugs, untested supplements, unscientific diets, and unproven training methods. Depending on the sport, many competitive athletes are basically beaten up. Don't try to push yourself into competition or strive to be an elite athlete if your goal is to train for general health and fitness.

Consider professional basketball, for example. Although these men and women kick butt on the court and look terrific doing it, they may not be able to get out of bed the next morning because of the stress they endured during the game. What about the constant overuse injuries that plague tennis players? They play so many games a year on the tennis circuit that their bodies get worn out and their general health suffers. Bodybuilders look the picture of health as they flex their massive muscles on the stage, but they practically starve themselves before a competition and purposely dehydrate themselves to the point of risking death. Does that strike you as healthy?

Being healthy is a balancing act. You need to eat a balanced diet, get the appropriate amount of sleep, exercise reasonably, work moderately, and enjoy time with friends and family. Health care professionals use many physiological markers to determine a person's health, and only one of them has to do with appearance. Don't be misled that the only way to be healthy is to compete against others. There is more than a fine line between competitive athletics and general health and fitness—it can actually be a wide chasm. The only competition you need to wage is against yourself.

## Training for Hypertrophy

Three to four sets of 10 repetitions with short rests in between—is this a training method déjà vu for you? If you are like most women who have been following the classic resistance-training program, then you are very familiar with such a regimen. This type of moderate-intensity (8 to 12 repetitions), high-volume (3 or more exercises per muscle group, 2 or more muscle groups, 3 to 4 sets) routine with short rests (10 to 60 seconds between sets and exercises) is common among bodybuilders because of the muscle fiber hypertrophy it produces. The hypertrophy result probably has also led to its popularity as the official exercise program adopted by the general gym-going public.

With bodybuilding programs, you primarily train individual muscles and groups of muscles for the sole purpose of looking muscular and symmetrical. You don't train specific movements or movement patterns for sports or daily activities. For example, a bodybuilding program might call for you to train your arm muscles on one day and your shoulder and chest muscles on another day. You'll do a lot of isolation exercises like biceps curls and triceps pushdowns. You won't find a total-body exercise (like the clean and jerk) or an exercise used to simulate a tennis stroke (like a diagonal plane rotational movement) in a bodybuilding routine. Bodybuilding also requires pushing yourself to muscular failure during your repetitions. In other words, pick a weight that is light enough that you can do 8 to 12 repetitions, but heavy enough that your muscles fail to lift the weight again at some point in that repetition range. The short rest periods and inadequate recovery of muscular energy sources help this process along. If you have been following a bodybuilding-type program for some time now, I suggest that you change it up and try something different, like one of the strength-training programs found in chapter 7. If you are new to weight training altogether or are just coming back from an injury, a bodybuilding rep-and-set scheme can work well for you. It will give you a base of muscular hypertrophy. The exercises are easy to follow, and you can progress to a strength-training program after you have completed a six- to eight-week cycle.

## Training for Strength

It would be so nice if we could say that there is a perfect number of reps and sets that will magically make everyone strong. Researchers believe that when training specifically for strength, the load (intensity) should be high, the repetitions (volume) should be few, and the rest periods should be long enough for a full recovery of muscular energy (ATP). A pure strength movement is actually your one-repetition maximum (1RM)—how much weight you can lift, push, or pull just one time. The accepted protocol is to lift 85 percent of your 1RM for 6 or fewer reps, doing 2 to 3 sets per exercise. Training for strength causes muscle to hypertrophy, because as each successive motor unit is called on to produce force, it increases in size. When the body requires more force to lift heavier weights, it activates more motor units. Simply gaining more muscle makes you stronger, but the building process involves a complex interaction of the muscular and nervous systems. Anyone can follow a strength-training program, from beginners to advanced trainers, or from those working for body composition changes to those interested in staving off osteoporosis. It is safe for beginners because they will be lifting 85 percent of their 1RM, and their 1RM will probably be a light weight. More advanced trainers need to vary their programs so that if they haven't yet tried a particular strength protocol, they will experience gains from doing it.

## Training for Power

Frequently called explosive training, power training combines elements of strength and speed. Power is seen in an entire movement as in Olympic lifts such as the clean or snatch or sports movements such as a baseball swing or a volleyball spike. Most power movements are very technical and require help from the nervous system for proper timing and excellent coordination. To ensure that the proper technique is mastered and the lifter doesn't falter because of fatigue, the volume and reps are kept low. Keeping the load moderate (75 to 85 percent of 1RM) helps to ensure proper technique. Maximal force can't be generated with a power movement anyway. The extremely short period in which the power movement takes place isn't enough time for maximal muscular force to accumulate. You can train for power using weights, elastic tubing, and medicine balls, or by doing plyometrics (jumping exercises).

## Training for Muscular Endurance

I can think of no term used in training language that is more misleading than the word *toning*. People say things like, "I just want to tone—I don't want to get big," or "If you do a lot of reps you will just tone instead of build." In truth, there is no scientific explanation for toning. Your muscles either hypertrophy or they do not. The amount and quality of hypertrophy vary among people and depend on the training method they use. Technically, *muscle tone* is used in a neurological setting to describe the resting tension of a muscle and to denote how that muscle responds to either passive stretching or stretching by a therapist. Most people have normal tone in their muscles. Abnormal tone is the result of a central nervous system (brain and spinal cord) problem. It has nothing to do with how long or hard you are working out or how good you look.

Maybe people who talk about toning are referring to the muscular endurance exercises that they typically see in the gym. It has been (incorrect) dogma for quite some time that women should lift light weights for many repetitions to sculpt their bodies, whereas men should go heavy with fewer repetitions to define their muscles. Lifting light weights for many repetitions only succeeds in giving you the muscular endurance to do that particular movement over and over again. It does not produce muscular hypertrophy, it does not have a high caloric cost (because it's not difficult), and it does not increase your RMR or help you burn fat. If you want to achieve the lean, athletic look that many associate with so-called toning, incorporating strength-training exercises is the key.

# Setting Your Training Goals

I've given you a lot of food for thought as you consider your training program. By now you should have a pretty good idea of what results you want to achieve in your body. Let's take those desired results and develop goals to help you achieve them. The specific outcome you want coupled with the goals you set determines what kind of training program you need to follow.

Be realistic and specific about your goals and plan some short-term goals that you can reach on your way to the final goal. Meeting smaller goals and milestones helps ensure motivation and success over the long run. For example, your ultimate goal might be to lose body fat. This goal is not specific, however, and can't be attained in a week. How about specifying that your long-term goal is to decrease your body fat to 20 percent in 16 weeks, and your short-term goal is to decrease your body fat by 5 percent each month?

Another long-term goal might be to fit into a certain clothing size. You could make your long-term goal to fit comfortably into a size 6 by the summer, and then set short-term goals that reflect decreasing sizes. If your long-term goal is to get stronger, specify how you are going to do it by quantifying your objective. A better long-term goal would be to squat and bench 135 pounds by the end of 8 weeks. Then you could adjust your training and short-term goals to reflect that intention. How about making it a long-term goal to win a powerlifting competition? You have to be realistic and consider your exercise experience and history. If you are a beginner in strength training, then you need to concentrate on the basics for a while and set many short-term goals to attain before you even plan to train for a competition. If you have already been strength training seriously, then you can plan your training cycle so that you will hit your peak on the day of the competition (check out chapter 13).

If you are training for general health and fitness then you won't really have a specific goal—you'll just keep exercising to stay healthy. However, you can monitor some general health markers like heart rate, blood pressure, and cholesterol levels on a monthly basis to make sure that you are still on the right track. Your training program will reflect your goal of general health and fitness, and you can incorporate a lot of variety into such a program.

Results-oriented training means that you are training for a specific purpose and that all of your exercises are devoted to that purpose. You don't want to go to the gym and merely get a workout done. You need to have a final destination in mind, and then design a road map to get you there. Having a goal doesn't mean that once the destination is reached, your job is done. On the contrary—there will always be new goals to strive for and new territory to explore.

# Gaining Superwoman Strength

Surely this is the age of the Superwoman. We want to do it all. We want to be Superwoman moms, girlfriends, and wives and have Superwoman careers. There is no reason why we can't have Superwoman strength as well. Just because 20 years ago women were jumping around in aerobics classes and wearing leg warmers as a fashion statement (and to help their shin splints) doesn't mean that we have to now. Ideas about fitness and health have evolved throughout the years, as has every other aspect of life.

In the 1800s people generally believed that any kind of exercise a woman did was harmful to her body. Now we know that strength training is one of the best things a woman can do for herself. Embrace the Superwoman of Strength inside yourself. Every woman can make strength gains and be stronger than she currently is; she just needs a little guidance in devising the best program for doing so, given her busy schedule.

The classic definition of strength is simply the ability to exert force. If that definition told the whole story, however, then we could all consider ourselves strong—every day we exert force just to get out of bed and walk to the shower. And if you compare the strength of those of us who can exert enough force to get out of bed to that of a 90-year-old woman who can't, we really are strong. What about the woman who can squat 300 pounds and deadlift a truck? Certainly she is stronger than someone who just manages to get out of bed and make it through her day. Strength is definitely a relative term and we need to have some agreement on how to measure it.

You can measure strength absolutely or relatively. Absolute strength is the total amount of strength that a person can exert, regardless of her body weight. Relative strength, on the other hand, takes body weight into account. For example, in absolute terms a 100-pound woman who can bench press 200 pounds is just as strong as a 200-pound woman who can bench press the same weight. Relatively speaking, though, the 100-pound woman is much stronger because she can bench press twice her body weight, whereas the 200-pound woman can bench press only her total body weight.

Coaches and scientists have developed normative values throughout the years that give us an indication of what *strong* means for certain movements like the bench press and squat. Also, research data indicate what it means for certain body heights, body weights, genders, and ages. So we have to qualify all of the variables when it comes to claiming that someone is strong; that is, we need to define what type of strength we mean.

5

# Speed-Strength Versus Strength-Endurance

Another way to define muscular strength is by the speed of contraction, or *speed-strength*. You can contract your muscles slowly, as you do when you complete a typical barbell bench press. Or you can contract them quickly and explosively, as you do for a vertical jump or Olympic power clean (see page 190). The barbell bench press is an example of low-speed muscular strength whereas the explosive vertical jump or Olympic power clean shows high-speed muscular strength. Low-speed muscular strength involves lifting the heaviest weight possible for one repetition, as in powerlifting or lifting a child from the ground into your arms. High-speed muscular strength involves a factor called *power*, which means exerting force very quickly (as you learned in chapter 4).

We see high-speed muscular strength in virtually all sports, and we also experience it in certain aspects of our lives. Examples from daily living include jumping up from a chair to answer the doorbell or rushing up a set of stairs when you are late. You can incorporate speed-strength into a pure strength-training program without doing Olympic lifts, simply by decreasing the weight you lift and increasing the speed at which you lift it. Choose one exercise in your routine for the day and concentrate on how fast you can move the weight (while still maintaining proper form) rather than how much weight you can move. Vary the exercises you choose throughout the weeks so that you can experience speed-strength with different movements.

If strength is the ability to exert force and endurance is the ability to maintain an activity, then *strength-endurance* is really the ultimate combination that everyone seeks to achieve. It would be awesome if we could maintain maximal muscular activation and contraction for extended periods, but is the combination even possible? Aren't the two abilities, by their very definitions, at odds with each other? Is strength-endurance even a relevant concept for the average person to consider?

Muscular strength and muscular endurance do seem to be the opposite of one another. They tend to differ in which muscle fibers they incorporate (see chapter 2), in the way those muscles work, and in the way that they use energy from the body. Their goals are also totally different. Demonstrating strength requires you to complete a short, intense event, whereas showing endurance requires you to finish a long, moderate- to low-intensity event. Logically it might seem that your body couldn't do both. But what happens when the two abilities have to combine for a special occasion? Are they able to work in unison or does one win out over the other?

Strength and endurance come in closest contact with each other during sports movements. Some sporting events require both great strength and exceptional endurance at the same time. Think about the decathlon, mountain climbing, rowing, and adventure racing. What they all have in common is the need to recruit large numbers of muscle fibers to move the body powerfully for long distances. We know that typical gains in muscular strength occur with lower numbers of repetitions, and gains in muscular endurance occur with higher numbers of repetitions. Higher repetition ranges also take longer to complete than the lower ranges. Strength-endurance training uses the principle known as "going to failure" on exercises. Going to failure means you lift as heavy a weight as you can for as many repetitions as you can, until you can't lift it anymore (usually somewhere in the range of 75 to 85 percent of 1RM for 8 to 12 repetitions). For strength-endurance exercises you take your time with sets, going slowly so that the whole set takes up to 1 minute to complete. The reasoning is that what we call time under tension produces both strength and endurance gains in muscles.

The physical demands of athletic events don't often closely simulate the demands of our daily lives, even if we are construction workers or engage in physically demanding professions. Our usual routine consists of periods of rest (some shorter than others) interspersed with low, medium, and high levels of activity. Although each day paints a different picture, in general we lead pretty routine lives. With the exception of weekends, special occasions, and vacations, we are creatures of habit. Even if we do have a physically demanding job, we don't go all out every minute of the day; we take intermittent breaks for a bathroom visit, lunch, or chat.

We need strength-endurance in our daily lives when we perform tasks such as carrying in groceries on a big shopping day. Let's say that one bag weighs 25 pounds. No matter who you are or how strong you are, that bag is still going to weigh 25 pounds. If your 1RM in the deadlift is 100 pounds, then that 25-pound bag represents 25 percent of your 1RM. Since it weighs only 25 percent of the total amount of weight you could lift one time, the bag would be light for you and you wouldn't have to exert much effort. The greater your strength and the higher your 1RM, the lighter the 25-pound bag is going to be for you. If it seems like a light weight to you, you will be able to lift it many more times before becoming fatigued—carrying in 12 bags of groceries won't be a major undertaking in your day.

You can argue that strength-endurance is exactly what we use in our daily activities. Nevertheless, your strength—how much weight you can lift one time—is actually the basic issue. In the preceding example, carrying in the groceries came on the heels of walking around the grocery store, standing in the checkout line, and sitting in the car on the way home—activities that don't require exceptional strength or endurance. Taking the groceries into the house probably doesn't take long, but if the groceries seem light to you, you can do it even faster. You can also unpack and store everything more quickly and easily so that you have time for a short break before starting to make dinner. The point is that our bodies are used to our daily routines and therefore do not typically need additional endurance for us to last longer doing these things; we can usually push ourselves to do whatever needs to be done. However, we do need additional

Increasing the total amount you can lift at one time through strength training allows you to accomplish your daily lifting tasks more quickly and easily.

strength to make everything that we do in a day feel easier. Increasing our strength, then, is the best way not to feel worn out at the end of the day. Because the activities in our lives largely involve whole-body movements, we should include multijoint exercises that use many muscles so that our strength-training sessions closely simulate how we use our bodies every day.

# Strength-Training Methods

Given all of the ways in which we can define strength, there must be many ways that we can train to increase these types of strength. The method you use depends on what your goals are and what your level of training is. Virtually anything that involves exerting a force affords strength gains in a previously untrained woman, but women who have consistently been lifting weights require something extra. We saw how important the specificity of training is in chapter 4. Women who are participating in sports must have a strength-training routine that incorporates methods that are specific to that sport. Often they use many different training methods in their training program. Let's take a look at the different ways that we can strength train.

## Isometric Training

Remember when you were in middle school and you chanted the rhyme "We must, we must, we must increase our bust!" while pushing your hands together in a prayer position as hard as possible? You were doing an isometric exercise, pushing against an immovable object in the hope that doing so would increase your muscular size. In an isometric exercise your muscles are contracting, but there is no joint movement. Because the joint isn't moving, your muscles will not strengthen through a full range of motion. They will get strong in the position at which they are held, but not at other positions (unless you train at those positions too).

You would want to incorporate isometric exercises if you were training for strongwoman and powerlifting competitions. Many strongwoman events, like the truck push, include isometric components. Isometrics also help powerlifters get through the sticking points in their dynamic exercises—points at which they have trouble pushing through or completing a movement for a full lockout. Of course, isometrics can benefit anyone's sticking point by strengthening the muscles at a particular range of motion (see the section on isometrics in chapter 13).

## Isotonic Training

Isotonic muscular contractions have a concentric phase, in which you lift the weight and the muscle shortens, and an eccentric phase, in which you slowly lower the weight and the muscle lengthens under tension. Isotonics involve a constant external resistance, like gravity, barbells, or dumbbells. Although the resistance is always the same, the force to move that resistance varies with the joint angle as the weight is lifted and lowered. Depending on the exercise, an isotonic movement can require more force to lift the weight at the end of the movement (squat), the beginning of the movement (deadlift), or the middle of the movement (biceps curl). The lifter also controls the speed of the movement. These components of isotonic exercise mimic our movements in life and sports, so doing isotonic exercises can be very functional. The majority of exercises in this book are isotonic for several reasons: they simulate life and sports activities, they are easy to do, and they don't require special equipment or a gym membership.

The exercises in this book focus on free weights because of all of the advantages they have over machines. With free weights, the possibilities are endless. You can use gravity, barbells, dumbbells, medicine balls, and even trucks. Stretch cords and tubing have value as training adjuncts for travel (because of their portability) and in rehab, but they are not very useful for strength training. Tubing can't put the same amount of loading on the muscle and bone as free weights. This book describes some exercises that use a stability ball as an accessory, as part of a good strength-training program. As an alternative to performing the strength-training exercises on stationary benches, using stability balls is a fun way to incorporate balance and function.

## Variable-Resistance Training

I was a gal who trained with variable resistance from the beginning. My first gym experience was at the University of Florida, with Nautilus equipment. Arthur Jones, the inventor of Nautilus equipment, thought he had invented a way for the entire muscle to be trained equally throughout the exercise range of motion with his revolutionary Nautilus cam system. Jones designed the weight-stack machines with a cam shaped like a nautilus shell to equally distribute the weight lifted throughout an entire range of motion. He wanted to eliminate the biomechanical disadvantages that are inherent in free-weight training, such as unequal force curves.

Unfortunately, Jones's system didn't really train muscles equally throughout their ranges of motion, and neither does any pulley, lever, or cam machine invented since. Machines can be a nice adjunct to a strength-training program, but isotonics should be the core. Most machines can't stimulate the same amount of muscular hypertrophy, bone mass, and strength as isotonic exercises, particularly exercises that employ free weights. Very few exercises in this book use machines because using free weights has many more advantages.

# ADVANTAGES OF FREE WEIGHTS

Why do so many trainers (including me) emphasize free weights over machines? Here are a few advantages that free weights have over machines:

1. Balance—Using free weights allows your body to develop and improve balance. You have to hold dumbbells and barbells in a balanced position, or you risk injury and embarrassment from plates falling off the bar. To provide balance the body has to work overtime, and that's a good thing. You use accessory muscles (muscles that help in the exercise but are not necessarily the ones you are training) and burn more calories. For instance, if you are performing a standing biceps curl, your core and lower-body muscles have to hold your body tightly in place or you will fall over. Also, your upper-back muscles have to contract isometrically to provide a base of support so that your arms can actually curl the weight and not just drop it on the floor.

2. Functional application—Life does not take place in one dimension, so the exercises you do to enhance life shouldn't either. You bend, twist, and lift in all dimensions during the day to get the job done. If you simulate the activities that your body needs to do every day when you use weights, then your daily tasks will become easier. Why sit in a machine to strengthen your legs when you really need them to be strong while you are standing? Holding dumbbells and medicine balls is just like holding your children or weighty packages in your arms.

3. Cost and convenience—If you like to work out at your house and want to invest financially as little as possible, then free weights are the way to go. You can get a workout for your entire body from just a couple of sets of dumbbell exercises. You need minimal instruction and you don't need a lot of room. Add a stability ball, and you've got the perfect beginner's gym. In a few months, after you are hooked on strength training, you can add Olympic bars and benches. You can find some of the best deals on such items at used sports equipment stores.

4. Posture—Get a double whammy and exercise your core muscles while you are exercising another muscle group. Free weights challenge your core, whereas machines allow you to relax and rest. The problem is that the majority of the public has poor posture from the kind of world we live in. We slouch at the computer and sprawl out on the couch. We don't pay too much attention to our posture until our muscles ache from fatigue. But if you work your postural muscles, you can decrease that fatigue and improve your appearance. Try squeezing your shoulder blades together while bench pressing. You'll see your bench press go up with ease and your posture remain perfect.

5. Psychological benefit—Lifting with free weights can really psych you up. Loading up the bar and holding on to the big dumbbells (as opposed to lifting light weights and doing endless repetitions) simply makes you feel strong. There is nothing girly about it. You gain a definite psychological advantage when you use free weights.

6. Perfect fit—Have you noticed that some machines don't seem to fit you? It could be because most machines are made for the specifications of an average man (5 feet 11 inches, 180 pounds). Free weights are a better fit for women simply because they don't have to worry about the fit. No matter what your size, free weights can accommodate you. You'll also eliminate the possibility of injuring yourself from working out on a piece of equipment designed for someone else.

7. Fat-busting properties—Training with free weights burns a ton of calories. First, it burns calories when you grab a pair of dumbbells, hold them, walk to the nearest bench, and set up your lift—likewise when you work with barbells. How many calories do you expend by sitting in a machine and leaning over to move a pin? Second, if your lift is a total-body lift like a squat or a deadlift, almost every muscle in your body is working and demanding energy in the form of calories. If you are doing a single muscle group exercise like a biceps curl, you'll still burn more calories lifting with free weights than with machines; the other muscles in your body are working hard to provide stabilization.

## Isokinetic Training

As a physical therapist assistant and a certified athletic trainer, I am very familiar with isokinetic equipment. Used extensively in physical therapy clinics and sports-training centers, isokinetic equipment tries to solve the problems of both isotonics and variable resistance by using accommodating resistance at a set velocity. You perform the exercise at a specific velocity, and no matter how much force your muscle produces, the isokinetic machine matches that force. This force matching makes it an excellent rehab device, because it makes the exercise quite safe. If you are rehabilitating an injury and can't produce much force, the machine will only give you what you can take. You can practice different velocities (speeds) to closely mimic the speeds of normal or sports activities. Unfortunately, isokinetic machines are very expensive and require someone who is trained to operate them. They are great for rehab and certain sport-specific training, but you probably won't use them regularly.

## Eccentric Training

We use eccentric, or lengthening, contractions often in daily life simply by fighting gravity in all of our movements. Walking down the stairs without falling and rolling down them requires eccentric muscular action. Slowly lowering a child you're holding in your arms to the floor without dropping him also requires eccentric muscular action.

Because an eccentric contraction recruits many more muscle fibers than a concentric contraction, eccentric training is extremely effective for strength improvements. Unfortunately eccentric contractions also generate the most damage and soreness in muscles, so you should use them in moderation and only if you have a weight-training background. Frequently eccentric exercises are recommended as part of a rehabilitation protocol under the supervision of a rehab professional.

Whereas eccentric contractions have to follow concentric contractions in isotonic exercise programs, eccentric training focuses on performing only the eccentric portion of the exercise. How do you do it? Some exercises require spotters or special equipment, but some are easy to do on your own. For instance, you can lift a weight with both arms or legs and lower it with just one arm or leg. That way you are getting an overloaded resistance on one limb in the eccentric phase. Eccentric training can rectify strength discrepancies between limbs and also improve overall strength. Because of the complexity of this kind of training program and the potential for injury, I do not include eccentric programs in this book.

## Plyometric Training

If you have ever watched kids while they are engaged in active outdoor play, you are familiar with plyometrics. Without conscious effort on their part, children store elastic energy in their muscles to run, jump, and bounce all over a playground. This stored elastic energy results in more powerful movements.

Usually people describe plyometrics as jumping exercises, but any exercise that allows the muscle to quickly prestretch before performing the actual movement is plyometric. A prestretch is a countermovement or a movement that is the opposite of the intended movement. Let's look at a simple standing long jump. Stand in place, and without bending your knees, jump for as long a distance as you can. Then bend your knees and explode forward as you jump. You go a lot farther, right? Most sports incorporate plyometric movements, so many athletes incorporate plyometric exercises into their routines. These exercises can speed up reaction time, improve force production, and increase velocity. Plyometric exercises involve Type II muscle fibers, just as strength training does. You may find, after adding some of these exercises into your routine, that you can improve your power and lift your weights faster—which may even lead to more calorie burning.

You'll find a few plyometric exercises in part III, like the jump squat, push press, and overhead throw-down exercises. Proper technique and moderation in adding plyometrics to your training program are essential to avoid injury. Plyometric programs vary greatly depending on the person and her goal. They are not a significant part of strength-training programs, but are certainly a nice supplement to them.

# Fueling Your Strength

6

Dieting is a multibillion-dollar industry in the United States. Every diet claims to be the answer to your fat-loss prayers. Why is it, then, that in the United States obesity trends have been rising dramatically since 1985? If any particular diet were successful, then we would expect to see segments of the population who were resistant to weight gain. Instead, we find that the entire country has gotten fatter. The fattening of America, and other developed countries for that matter, is multifactorial. In addition to silly fad diets, a big reason is a significant reduction in physical activity patterns. As our country has become more technologically advanced, our activity levels have dropped substantially. Findings from the National Weight Control Registry indicate that a combination of diet and exercise yields the best results for people trying to lose weight and keep it off.

Believe it or not, 95 to 98 percent of all diets fail. This figure means that all but 2 to 5 of every 100 people dieting will eventually regain the weight they lose. You may already have experienced such a reversion, or you may in the future. In almost every case, though, simple mistakes cause diets to fail. We all know someone who picked up a book, followed the diet, and lost weight. We also know other people who failed miserably while trying the same diet. It may seem logical that if a diet worked for your friend, it should work for you—it's on the bestseller list and everyone is doing it, so it's got to be right. But copying your friend's diet doesn't take into account your individual needs. Maybe you have a sedentary job, whereas she is on her feet all day. What if she has high cholesterol and you have high blood sugar? To avoid wasting time and to maximize the amount of progress you make, the rules are simple: Get a medical checkup, take objective measurements, monitor yourself, and follow up and adjust when necessary. You can maximize the positive effects of a strength-training program with a smart and individualized nutrition plan.

## Start With a Physical

If you haven't had a routine physical exam in the past year, consider getting one (especially if you're just starting an exercise program). It makes far more sense to get a checkup and have a medical doctor tell you that everything is fine than to find out the hard way that it isn't. A complete physical exam should include the following: height and weight measurements, body fat percentage and blood work to check for complete blood count (CBC) with differential, blood lipids, complete metabolic panel (CMP), homocysteine, high-sensitivity C-reactive protein (hsCRP), lipoprotein (a) (LP(a)), and a maximal stress test with EKG on a treadmill. Each of these tests is necessary because they are health markers for immune function, kidney function, and cardiovascular disease risk.

Discuss these suggested tests with your doctor and see whether there are any additional markers that may be more appropriate. For example, some doctors order glycosylated hemoglobin ($Hgb_{A1c}$) levels for diabetics to monitor their long-term glucose control. Your doctor may want to check certain additional markers, depending on your family history.

If your doctor will not prescribe these tests for your preventative health, then you might want to consider a more progressive doctor who will respond to your needs. If your insurance company will not pay for preventative medicine (and many will not), then consider paying for it on your own. You can also volunteer with the exercise physiology and cardiac rehab departments at universities and medical schools to be a research subject so that you can possibly get the testing done for free, depending on the research going on.

Most people evaluate the success of a program by how they feel or by how they look in the mirror. Consider, however, that most people do not succeed in this sense. This dilemma indicates that maybe our notions about how we feel and how we look are too vague—they don't give us the detailed information we need to evaluate and improve our health and fitness levels. These details aren't hard to get, and before you begin a new program, you must know your actual starting point. How do you know whether you've gotten someplace if you don't know where you started? Some measurements are easy to do on your own, whereas other measurements should be done by a competent healthcare professional. If your medical doctor determines you are healthy and can begin a diet and exercise program, then purchase a body-weight scale, a tension-controlled tape measure, a food scale, and an oral thermometer. If you have diabetes or cardiovascular disease, or if you need to lose more than 30 pounds, also purchase a blood glucose monitor, blood pressure monitor with heart rate, and a blood cholesterol tester.

# Measure and Monitor

Monitor yourself regularly to determine whether you are meeting your goals. Select one day each week for four weeks to monitor and record your progress, using table 6.1. Do your measurements first thing in the morning. After you wake up and go to the bathroom, take a nude weight using your scale. Make sure the scale lies flat on a hard surface in a place where it won't get moved a lot. Then, using the tension-controlled tape measure, take your circumference measurements. If you started off with a health condition, it is a good idea to monitor your heart rate and blood pressure each week as well. If you need to, check your glucose and cholesterol levels according to the follow-up protocol outlined by your doctor.

Monitoring your results and writing them down will help you see your objective data and then judge whether they indicate the need for improvements. In addition to tracking this health information, you'll also want to keep a record of what exercises you do each week, what weights you lift, and how many repetitions you do (see chapter 7). Your health and nutrition plan should follow the same principle. Measure and monitor so that you can objectively determine whether a program is helping you meet your goals or whether something needs to be changed.

Another way to monitor yourself, if you are strength training as part of a weight control effort, is to weigh your food with a food scale and measure liquid volumes in a measuring

## Table 6.1   Weekly Weight-Control Checklist

| Measure | Week 1 | Week 2 | Week 3 | Week 4 |
|---|---|---|---|---|
| Weight | | | | |
| Body fat % | | | | |
| Heart rate | | | | |
| Systolic blood pressure | | | | |
| Diastolic blood pressure | | | | |
| Blood glucose | | | | |
| Blood cholesterol | | | | |
| Neck | | | | |
| Shoulders | | | | |
| Chest[a] | | | | |
| Middle of R upper arm | | | | |
| Middle of L upper arm | | | | |
| Top of R forearm | | | | |
| Top of L forearm | | | | |
| Upper waist[b] | | | | |
| Lower waist (just above hips) | | | | |
| Widest part of hips | | | | |
| Top of R thigh[c] | | | | |
| Top of L thigh | | | | |
| Middle of R calf | | | | |
| Middle of L calf | | | | |

[a] Run the tape measure around the chest so that it is slightly below your armpits but above your breasts.
[b] Just below your ribs—usually the smallest part of your waist.
[c] Where your rear end and leg meet.
Table courtesy of Thomas Incledon.
From *Strength Training for Women* by Lori Incledon, 2005, Champaign, IL: Human Kinetics.

cup. You won't always have to, but developing an awareness of your portion size and control is essential in the beginning. Research indicates that people consistently underestimate how much food they consume and how large their portions are. Researchers note that the more body fat people have, the more they underestimate their portion sizes. Prevent a possible pitfall by measuring all your foods until you feel comfortable with your own portion control.

Monitoring your temperature with a thermometer is an indirect way of assessing your thyroid hormone status—often a problem for women. If your morning temperature is consistently below 98.6 degrees Fahrenheit, your thyroid hormone may be low. If it is higher than 98.6 degrees Fahrenheit and you are not sick, it may indicate excessive thyroid hormone. In either of these situations, it is important to seek qualified medical follow-up.

# Make Adjustments

Starting anything new is difficult, and changing your nutrition and exercise program is no exception. You have to decide that your nutrition plan and your strength-training program are not fads that you will get tired of after a few days, but a new way of life. Dedicate yourself to the program and you will see the positive changes.

Brightly colored, nutrient-dense fruits and vegetables should be key components of your long-term nutrition plan.

Keep in mind that many people drop the most weight in the first three weeks of a program, but it is not necessarily fat weight. During this time most of the weight lost is water and lean body mass. After about three weeks, the body starts to adapt by conserving water and lean body mass. After this time is when you begin to see the most fat loss, especially in people lifting weights. If you don't monitor yourself weekly and instead only follow up every few weeks, you might think that you have reached your goals prematurely. This is one reason quick weight-loss plans ultimately fail. Keep in mind that you may not reach your goals if your caloric intake or energy expenditure is out of balance. It is best to follow up and evaluate your diet and exercise programs frequently, to avoid mistakes that can add up over the long run.

# Individualize Your Nutrition Plan

Your goal is to determine how much energy you require each day. This is an important step that should not be overlooked. Simply guessing at this number can sabotage all of your efforts. The Estimated Energy Requirement (EER) is a relatively new term that means the dietary energy intake predicted to maintain an energy balance consistent with good health in healthy, normal-weight individuals of a specific age, gender, weight, height, and level of physical activity. In basic terms, your EER tells you how much food you should eat each day to maintain your current weight.

To get started you'll need to know some basic health variables about yourself. Complete worksheet 6.1 to calculate your Body Mass Index (BMI) and body fat percentage. Now take a look at the BMI range and body fat range in table 6.2. If you are in the normal range, then use worksheet 6.2a (page 60) to estimate your energy needs. If you are in the overweight or obese range, then use worksheet 6.2b (page 61) to estimate your energy needs. To calculate your energy needs, select the correct physical activity level coefficient (PA coefficient) from table 6.3.

## Worksheet 6.1  Calculation of Body Mass Index (BMI) and Body Fat Percentage

1. Enter your weight in lb ____; multiply by .454 to get weight in kg.        ____

2. Enter your height in in. ____; multiply by .0254 to get your height in m.    ____

3. Multiply your height in m by itself to get height in m².                    ____

4. Divide your weight in kg by your height in m² to get your BMI.              ____

5. Measure your hip girth at the largest width.                               ____

6. Measure your upper waist girth at the smallest width.                      ____

7. Add lines 5 and 6.                                                         ____

8. Measure your neck circumference.                                           ____

9. Subtract line 8 from line 7.                                              ____

10. Check appendix A to get body fat %.                                       ____


Example: woman, 145 lb, 5 ft 6 in.

1. Enter your weight in lb 145; multiply by .454 to get weight in kg.          66

2. Enter your height in in. 66 ; multiply by .0254 to get your height in m.   1.68

3. Multiply your height in m by itself to get height in m².                   2.82

4. Divide your weight in kg by your height in m² to get your BMI.             23.4

5. Measure your hip girth at the largest width.                                38

6. Measure your upper waist girth at the smallest width.                       30

7. Add lines 5 and 6.                                                         68

8. Measure your neck circumference.                                         12.25

9. Subtract line 8 from line 7.                                             55.75

10. Check appendix A to get body fat %.                                       28%

Worksheet courtesy of Thomas Incledon
From *Strength Training for Women* by Lori Incledon, 2005, Champaign, IL: Human Kinetics.

## Table 6.2  Body Weight Classification by BMI and Body Fat Content

| BMI range (kg/m²) | Classification | Body fat % | |
|---|---|---|---|
| | | Men | Women |
| 18.5 to 25 | Normal | 13 to 21 | 23 to 31 |
| 25 to 30 | Overweight | 21 to 25 | 31 to 37 |
| 30 to 35 | Obese | 25 to 31 | 37 to 42 |
| Above 35 | Clinically obese | Above 31 | Above 42 |

Reprinted with permission from *Dieteary reference intakes from energy, carbohydrate, fiber, fat, fatty acids, cholesterol, protein and amino acids (macronutrients)* © 2002 by the National Academy of Science, courtesy of the National Academies Press, Washington, DC.

## Table 6.3   Physical Activity Coefficients

| Category | Activity level[a] (walking in miles per day) | PA coefficient |
|---|---|---|
| Sedentary | None | 1.00 |
| Low active | 1.5 to 2.9 | 1.12 |
| Active | 3.0 to 9.9 | 1.27 |
| Very active | 7.5 to 31.0 | 1.45 |

[a] Note that the walking estimates are in addition to your activities of daily living.

Reprinted with permission from *Dietary reference intakes from energy, carbohydrate, fiber, fat, fatty acids, cholesterol, protein, and amino acids (macronutrients)* © 2002 by the National Academy of Science, courtesy of the National Academies Press, Washington, DC.

## Worksheet 6.2a   Estimation of Energy Needs for Normal BMI and Body Fat %

1. Multiply your weight in kg (from line 1 in worksheet 6.1) by 9.36 to get value A.   \_\_\_\_   A
2. Multiply your height in m (from line 2 in worksheet 6.1) by 726 to get value B.   \_\_\_\_   B
3. Add values A and B together to get value C.   \_\_\_\_   C
4. Multiply value C by your PA coefficient (from table 6.3) to get value D.   \_\_\_\_   D
5. Add 354 to value D above to get value E.   \_\_\_\_   E
6. Multiply your age (in years) by 6.91 to get value F.   \_\_\_\_   F
7. Subtract value F from value E to get the number of Calories you need per day.   \_\_\_\_

Example: active 30-year-old woman, 145 lb, 5 ft 6 in.

1. Multiply 66 kg by 9.36 to get value A = 617.76.   618   A
2. Multiply 1.68 m by 726 to get value B = 1219.68.   1220   B
3. Add values A and B to get value C: 618 + 1220 = 1838.   1838   C
4. Multiply value C by 1.27 to get value D: 1838 × 1.27 = 2334.26.   2335   D
5. Add 354 to 2335 to get value E = 2689.   2689   E
6. Multiply your age (in years) by 6.91 to get value F: 30 × 6.91 = 207.3.   208   F
7. Subtract value F from value E to get the number of Calories you need per day:
2689 – 208 = 2481

Worksheet courtesy of Thomas Incledon.
From *Strength Training for Women* by Lori Incledon, 2005, Champaign, IL: Human Kinetics.

## Worksheet 6.2b   Estimation of Energy Needs For Obese or Overweight BMI and Body Fat %

1. Multiply your weight in kg (from line1 in worksheet 6.1) by 11.4 to get value A.  ____ A
2. Multiply your height in m (from line 2 in worksheet 6.1) by 619 to get value B.  ____ B
3. Add values A and B together to get value C.  ____ C
4. Multiply value C by your PA coefficient (from table 6.3) to get value D.  ____ D
5. Add 448 to value D above to get value E.  ____ E
6. Multiply your age (in years) by 7.95 to get value F.  ____ F
7. Subtract value F from value E to get the number of Calories you need per day.  ____

Example: low-active 30-year-old woman, 165 lb (75 kg), 5 ft 6 in.

| | | |
|---|---|---|
| Multiply 75 kg by 11.4 to get value A = 855. | 855 | A |
| Multiply 1.68 m by 619 to get value B = 1039.92. | 1040 | B |
| Add values A and B to get value C: 855 + 1040 = 1895 | 1895 | C |
| Multiply value C by 1.12 to get value D: 1895 x 1.12 = 2122.4 | 2123 | D |
| Add 448 to 2123 to get value E = 2571 | 2571 | E |
| Multiply your age by (in years) by 6.91 to get value F: 30 x 6.91 = 207.3 | 208 | F |

Subtract value F from value E to get the number of Calories you need per day:
2571 – 208 = 2363

Worksheet courtesy of Thomas Incledon.
From *Strength Training for Women* by Lori Incledon, 2005, Champaign, IL: Human Kinetics.

Once you calculate your energy needs, you can follow a strategy to maintain weight, lose weight, or gain weight. I devote a section to each strategy that will guide you through the steps necessary to develop your individualized nutrition plan. After you identify your strategy, keep in mind the following simple nutritional guidelines:

- Try to eat six small meals spread evenly throughout the day. The body can more easily burn a small caloric load than a large one. With larger calorie meals, the excess calories have the potential of going to fat storage. Small, frequent meals help maintain blood glucose levels, keeping you on an even keel all day long. Frequent eating can raise your RMR (remember the thermic effect of food?) and decrease your food cravings.
- Emphasize vegetables and fruits in the diet. Research consistently shows that eating vegetables and fruits lowers the risks for many diseases and that those who eat them on a consistent basis are much healthier than those who don't.
- Eat as many different colors of foods in the diet as possible. Colors are associated with different phytonutrients that work to keep you healthy by providing antioxidants to reduce inflammation in the body.
- Eat meats that are as lean as possible, except fish. The saturated fat in meats raises your LDL cholesterol (the "bad" cholesterol). Fatty fish have polyunsaturated fat, which lowers your LDL cholesterol.
- Eat healthy fats in foods like nuts, olive oil, canola oil, fish oil, and flaxseed oil. Those who eat healthy fats lower their risk for cardiovascular disease, depression, and diabetes.

## Maintaining Your Weight

If you are already at an appropriate weight and body composition, congratulations! You just need to ensure that you consume enough calories and the appropriate macronutrients to maintain your weight and health. After estimating your caloric needs, determine your macronutrient needs—how much protein, fat, and carbohydrate you need each day. The estimates for each macronutrient are the following:

- Grams of protein per day = .82 × body weight in pounds.
- Convert grams of protein into Calories: 1 gram of protein = 4 Calories
- Grams of fat each day = 30 percent of your estimated caloric needs.
- Convert grams of fat into Calories: 1 gram of fat = 9 Calories
- Grams of carbohydrate each day = remaining calories.
- Convert grams of carbohydrate into Calories: 1 gram of carbohydrate = 4 Calories

For example, a 132-pound woman who requires 2,383 Calories each day to maintain her weight would consume approximately 109 (.82 × 132) grams of protein each day. This amount of protein is equal to 436 Calories (109 × 4). She would also consume about 715 (.30 × 2,382) Calories from fat. To convert these fat calories into fat grams, we divide 715 by 9 (715 / 9) to equal approximately 80 grams of fat each day. To estimate carbohydrate needs, subtract the 436 protein Calories and the 715 fat Calories from the estimated daily energy intake (2,383 – 436 – 715 = 1,232) to find that this woman needs 1,232 Calories from carbohydrate daily. To convert this number of carbohydrate calories into grams, divide it by four to equal 308 grams of carbohydrate each day (1,232 / 4 = 308). To review, the 132-pound active female would eat

109 grams of protein × 4 (Calories per gram) = 436 Calories.

80 grams of fat × 9 (Calories per gram) = 720 Calories.

308 grams of carbohydrate × 4 (Calories per gram) = 1,232 Calories.

A meal plan for this woman might look something like the sample provided in table 6.4.

## Losing Weight

If you need to lose weight, subtract 15 percent or 500 Calories, whichever is smaller, from your daily energy needs as calculated previously. As you lose weight, you need to reevaluate your daily energy needs and goals using the tables. Let's use an example of a 165-pound woman who is not very active, who needs 2,363 Calories per day. She could reduce her intake by 500 Calories each day and eat 1,863 Calories, but research indicates that large caloric reductions reduce important thyroid hormone levels significantly and also may result in reduced compliance to her diet.

A better strategy would be for the woman to reduce her caloric intake by 15 percent and add extra activity like strength training or even walking. Using this strategy, she would ingest 2,009 Calories per day and add exercise to expend more energy. For example, walking burns about 50 to 70 Calories per mile. By walking an extra 4 miles per day she could burn 200 to 280 additional Calories. She could walk 2 miles in the morning and 2 miles in the evening. Imagine how many more calories she could burn by lifting weights and increasing her muscle mass and metabolic rate. She would eat 135 (.82 × 165) grams of protein each day. This amount of protein is equal to 540 (135 × 4) Calories. She would also consume 603 (.30 × 2,009) Calories from fat, which means 67 (603 / 9) grams of fat each day. To estimate carbohydrate needs, subtract the 540 Calories from protein and the 603 Calories from fat from the estimated daily energy intake (2,009 Calories), which comes to 866 Calories from carbohydrate (2,009 – 540 – 603 = 866).

## Table 6.4 Sample Meal Plan for Maintaining Weight

| Meal | Food item | Amount | kcal | Pro (g) | Fat (g) | CHO (g) |
|------|-----------|--------|------|---------|---------|---------|
| 1 | Whole eggs | 2 large | 128 | 12 | 8 | 2 |
|   | Stir-fried peppers | 3 oz | 12 | 0 | 0 | 3 |
|   | Skim milk | 1 cup | 88 | 9 | 0 | 13 |
|   | Whole-grain bread | 1 slice | 93 | 3 | 1 | 18 |
|   | Meal totals | | 321 | 24 | 9 | 36 |
| 2 | Whey protein | 1/2 scoop | 57 | 10 | 1 | 2 |
|   | Blueberries | 7 oz | 100 | 1 | 0 | 24 |
|   | Flaxseed oil | 1 tbsp | 126 | 0 | 14 | 0 |
|   | Orange juice | 1 cup | 108 | 1 | 0 | 26 |
|   | Meal totals | | 391 | 12 | 15 | 52 |
| 3 | Chicken breast | 3 oz | 110 | 21 | 2 | 2 |
|   | Tossed salad | 9.7 oz | 52 | 1 | 0 | 12 |
|   | Whole-grain bread | 2 slices | 186 | 6 | 2 | 36 |
|   | Olive oil dressing | 2 tbsp | 126 | 0 | 14 | 0 |
|   | Meal totals | | 474 | 28 | 18 | 50 |
| 4 | Whey protein | 1/2 scoop | 57 | 10 | 1 | 2 |
|   | Strawberries | 7 oz | 100 | 1 | 0 | 24 |
|   | Flaxseed oil | 1 tbsp | 126 | 0 | 14 | 0 |
|   | Orange juice | 1 cup | 108 | 1 | 0 | 26 |
|   | Meal totals | | 391 | 12 | 15 | 52 |
| 5 | Lean beef | 3 oz | 110 | 21 | 2 | 2 |
|   | Broccoli | 4 oz | 32 | 3 | 0 | 5 |
|   | Sweet potato | large | 202 | 2 | 2 | 44 |
|   | Meal totals | | 344 | 26 | 4 | 51 |
| 6 | Skim milk | 1 cup | 80 | 8 | 0 | 12 |
|   | Apple | 2 med - 5 oz ea | 177 | 0 | 1 | 42 |
|   | Peanut butter | 2 tbsp | 200 | 8 | 16 | 6 |
|   | Meal totals | | 457 | 16 | 17 | 60 |
|   | Daily totals | | 2378 | 118 | 78 | 301 |
|   | % of kcal | | 100 | 19.8 | 29.5 | 50.6 |

Meal plan courtesy of Thomas Incledon.

To convert these calories into grams, divide by 4, which means 217 grams of carbohydrate each day (866 / 4 = 217). Here is a summary of what the 165-pound inactive female would eat:

135 grams of protein × 4 (Calories per gram) = 540 Calories.

67 grams of fat × 9 (Calories per gram) = 603 Calories.

217 grams of carbohydrate × 4 (Calories per gram) = 868 Calories.

A one-day meal plan for this woman might look something like that presented in table 6.5.

Table 6.5    **Sample Meal Plan for Losing Weight**

| Meal | Food item | Amount | kcal | Pro (g) | Fat (g) | CHO (g) |
|---|---|---|---|---|---|---|
| 1 | Whole eggs | 2 large | 128 | 12 | 8 | 2 |
| | Stir-fried peppers | 3 oz | 12 | 0 | 0 | 3 |
| | Skim milk | 1 cup | 88 | 9 | 0 | 13 |
| | Whole-grain bread | 1 slice | 93 | 3 | 1 | 18 |
| | Fruit | 1/2 cup | 56 | 1 | 0 | 13 |
| | Meal totals | | 377 | 25 | 9 | 49 |
| 2 | Whey protein | 1/2 scoop | 57 | 10 | 1 | 2 |
| | Psyllium | 1 tsp | 0 | 0 | 0 | 0 |
| | Flaxseed oil | 2 tsp | 90 | 0 | 10 | 0 |
| | Meal totals | | 147 | 10 | 11 | 2 |
| 3 | Chicken breast | 3 oz | 102 | 21 | 2 | 0 |
| | Tossed salad | 12 oz | 68 | 2 | 0 | 15 |
| | Olive oil dressing | 2 tsp | 90 | 0 | 10 | 0 |
| | Pear | 6 oz | 113 | 1 | 1 | 25 |
| | Meal totals | | 373 | 24 | 13 | 40 |
| 4 | Whey protein | 1/2 scoop | 57 | 10 | 1 | 2 |
| | Psyllium | 1 tsp | 0 | 0 | 0 | 0 |
| | Flaxseed oil | 2 tsp | 90 | 0 | 10 | 0 |
| | Olive oil | 1 tsp | 45 | 0 | 5 | 0 |
| | Meal totals | | 192 | 10 | 16 | 2 |
| 5 | Salmon | 4 oz | 188 | 29 | 8 | 0 |
| | Broccoli | 4 oz | 32 | 3 | 0 | 5 |
| | Rice | 4 oz | 97 | 4 | 1 | 18 |
| | Meal totals | | 317 | 36 | 9 | 23 |
| 6 | Nonfat yogurt | 2 cups | 249 | 26 | 1 | 34 |
| | Raisins | 3 oz | 260 | 1 | 0 | 64 |
| | Almonds | .5 oz | 89.5 | 3 | 7.5 | 2.5 |
| | Meal totals | | 598.5 | 30 | 8.5 | 100.5 |
| | Daily totals | | 2004.5 | 135 | 66.5 | 216.5 |
| | % of kcal | | 100 | 26.9 | 29.9 | 43.2 |

Meal plan courtesy of Thomas Incledon.

# Gaining Weight

If you need to gain weight, add 15 percent or 500 Calories, whichever is smaller, to your daily energy needs. As you gain weight, you need to reevaluate your daily energy needs and goals using the tables. Let's use the example of a 135-pound woman who is very active and requires 2,481 Calories per day. She needs to gain 13 pounds to get stronger and be more competitive in a heavier weight class for powerlifting. She could increase her intake by 500 Calories each day and ingest 2,981 Calories, but research indicates that most of these extra calories could wind up as extra body fat.

To increase her strength, the woman must maximize the ratio of muscle that she adds to her body relative to the fat that she adds to her body. A better approach would be to increase calories by only 15 percent. Using this tactic, she would increase her caloric intake by an extra 372 Calories to 2,853 Calories per day. It is essential for her to maintain some regular activity like strength training and interval cardiovascular exercise so that she gains primarily muscle and so that she maintains her fitness and health levels. Thus, a 135-pound active female would eat the following:

135 grams of protein × 4 (Calories per gram) = 540 Calories.

80 grams of fat × 9 (Calories per gram) = 720 Calories.

365 grams of carbohydrate × 4 (Calories per gram) = 1,460 Calories.

A sample one-day meal plan for weight gain for her might look like table 6.6 on page 66.

# Eat Right for Training

Eating right makes sense for more reasons than just your health. Eating right also helps with recovery from training and may even allow for greater muscular growth—a big bonus for women who are strength training. If you work out in the morning, eat meal 1 about an hour before training and then eat meal 2 (a shake) immediately after training. If your schedule does not allow that much time before training, then drink your shake (meal 2), have your workout, and eat meal 1 immediately after the workout. The main point of surrounding your training session with meals is to ensure nutrients are available to your body when your body needs them the most. If you train later in the day, plan your training and meals so that you have a solid meal about 1.5 to 2 hours before training or a liquid meal .5 to 1 hour before training. After training, eat a planned meal (solid or liquid) as soon as possible.

## Staying Hydrated

After oxygen, water is the most vital nutrient for our bodies. Despite its importance to our health, few people drink sufficient quantities each day. A healthy water intake enhances both the removal of metabolic waste products from the blood and their excretion by the kidneys. A rough rule of thumb has been to drink 6 to 8 glasses of water per day. Critics of this guideline indicate that a one-size-fits-all approach is not optimal for everyone. It wouldn't make sense for a female athlete to drink the same amount of water as a female nonathlete. For women who want to estimate their fluid intake on their own, a general guideline is .5 to 1 ounce of fluid for each pound of body weight, every day. If you are exercising, weigh yourself before training, drink water or other fluids during training, and weigh yourself again after training. Your weight should be the same as before. If you have lost weight, continue drinking fluids until you reach your preworkout weight. This workout fluid intake is in addition to the general daily intake recommended.

## Table 6.6　Sample Meal Plan for Gaining Weight

| Meal | Food item | Amount | kcal | Pro (g) | Fat (g) | CHO (g) |
|------|-----------|--------|------|---------|---------|---------|
| 1 | Whole eggs | 2 large | 128 | 12 | 8 | 2 |
| | Stir-fried peppers | 3 oz | 12 | 0 | 0 | 3 |
| | Skim milk | 1 cup | 88 | 9 | 0 | 13 |
| | Whole-grain bread | 2 slices | 186 | 6 | 2 | 36 |
| | Orange juice | 1 cup | 112 | 2 | 0 | 26 |
| | Meal totals | | 526 | 29 | 10 | 80 |
| 2 | Whey protein | 1/2 scoop | 57 | 10 | 1 | 2 |
| | Blueberries | 7 oz | 100 | 1 | 0 | 24 |
| | Flaxseed oil | 1 tbsp | 126 | 0 | 14 | 0 |
| | Olive oil | 1 tsp | 45 | 0 | 5 | 0 |
| | Orange juice | 1 cup | 112 | 2 | 0 | 26 |
| | Meal totals | | 440 | 13 | 20 | 52 |
| 3 | Chicken breast | 4 oz | 138 | 28 | 2 | 2 |
| | Tossed salad | 9.7 oz | 52 | 1 | 0 | 12 |
| | Whole-grain bread | 2 slices | 186 | 6 | 2 | 36 |
| | Olive oil dressing | 2 tbsp | 126 | 0 | 14 | 0 |
| | Meal totals | | 502 | 35 | 18 | 50 |
| 4 | Whey protein | 1/2 scoop | 57 | 10 | 1 | 2 |
| | Strawberries | 7 oz | 100 | 1 | 0 | 24 |
| | Flaxseed oil | 1 tbsp | 126 | 0 | 14 | 0 |
| | Olive oil | 1 tsp | 45 | 0 | 5 | 0 |
| | Orange juice | 1 cup | 112 | 2 | 0 | 26 |
| | Meal totals | | 440 | 13 | 20 | 52 |
| 5 | Salmon | 4 oz | 188 | 29 | 8 | 0 |
| | Broccoli | 4 oz | 32 | 3 | 0 | 5 |
| | Sweet potato | large, 6.4 oz | 188 | 3 | 0 | 44 |
| | Orange juice | 1 cup | 112 | 2 | 0 | 26 |
| | Margarine (no TFAs) | 1 tsp | 45 | 0 | 5 | 0 |
| | Meal totals | | 565 | 37 | 13 | 75 |
| 6 | Nonfat yogurt | 1 cup | 120 | 13 | 0 | 17 |
| | Raisins | 1 oz | 88 | 1 | 0 | 21 |
| | Almonds | 1 oz | 179 | 6 | 15 | 5 |
| | Meal totals | | 387 | 20 | 15 | 43 |
| | Daily totals | | 2860 | 147 | 96 | 352 |
| | % of kcal | | 100 | 20.6 | 30.2 | 49.2 |

Meal plan courtesy of Thomas Incledon.

# Knowing Your Supplements

Every day new studies point to the relationship between inadequate amounts of nutrients and disease (or impaired health). Therefore it makes sense for most people to take a daily multiple vitamin–mineral supplement. There is no guarantee that taking a supplement will prevent a disease, but it does reduce one's risk. Table 6.7 (page 68) lists the recommended daily intakes for most nutrients, which can help you decide whether a product meets your needs. A common concern about supplements is whether the product actually contains what the label says. Feel free to contact the company and ask for a Certificate of Analysis (COA). If they balk or stall at providing this certificate, then you should be concerned. Companies that routinely test and check their products for contents have these documents on hand for each and every lot. If they don't test, how can they know what they are selling you? Better to buy a product from a different company that you can trust. You can also read www.consumerlab.com to see which products passed their analysis.

Certain logos, like the CL (consumer lab) Seal or the NSF Mark (The Public Health and Safety Company, a nonprofit, nongovernmental organization—see www.nsf.org/consumer/about_NSF/mark.asp), indicate that a product has passed independent testing and is more likely to contain what it claims on the label. This does not always mean the product is free from contaminants and certainly does not indicate whether the product will work. Supplement companies that have specific research on their products usually post it on their Web sites. But be careful when reading research, because one common trick is the use of borrowed science. This practice occurs when one company does a study, and another company uses that study as support that its own product works. You need to see the exact name of the product that was used in the study being cited to know that it is the same product.

All kinds of supplements are on the market, so how do you determine which is best for you? Working with a competent dietitian who has a background in exercise physiology is ideal. The dietitian can review your diet, suggest possible areas for improvement, and recommend blood tests to verify any nutritional concerns. Be wary of using a nutritionist, however. The term *nutritionist* is very vague, and many people offering nutritional advice do not have the appropriate training to help you. The gold standard is a college degree in nutrition, not a weekend certification. Find out the credentials of the person helping you, and don't be afraid to ask for proof of education and a list of client references.

The numerous products on the market may or may not help you achieve your goals. There is nothing ethically wrong with trying a supplement to see whether it will help you improve, unless that supplement is banned by a sport that you compete in. If you plan on competing, find out the rules of your sport so that you don't take something banned by mistake. If you do take a supplement (or medication), you should be monitored under the care of a competent health care professional. For medications either an MD or a DO (doctor of osteopathy) is the preferred credential, and for supplements an RD (registered dietitian) is preferred. Health care professionals usually recommend blood tests for your liver and kidney function, white blood cells, red blood cells, and blood lipids. They also check your heart rate, blood pressure, and respiration. These tests allow both you and them to know whether any side effects develop from taking the products.

## Table 6.7   Vitamin and Mineral Dietary Reference Intakes (DRIs) for Women

| | Units | Age (years) | | | | | |
| --- | --- | --- | --- | --- | --- | --- | --- |
| | | 9-13 | 14-18 | 19-30 | 31-50 | 51-70 | > 70 |
| **Vitamins** | | | | | | | |
| Biotin | µg/d | 20 | 25 | 30 | 30 | 30 | 30 |
| Choline | mg/d | 375 | 400 | 425 | 425 | 425 | 425 |
| Folate | µg/d | 300 | 400 | 400 | 400 | 400 | 400 |
| Niacin | mg/d | 12 | 14 | 14 | 14 | 14 | 14 |
| Pantothenic acid | mg/d | 4 | 5 | 5 | 5 | 5 | 5 |
| Riboflavin | mg/d | 0.9 | 1.0 | 1.1 | 1.1 | 1.1 | 1.1 |
| Thiamin | mg/d | 0.9 | 1.0 | 1.1 | 1.1 | 1.1 | 1.1 |
| Vitamin A | µg/d | 600 | 700 | 700 | 700 | 700 | 700 |
| Vitamin $B_{12}$ | µg/d | 1.8 | 2.4 | 2.4 | 2.4 | 2.4 | 2.4 |
| Vitamin $B_6$ | mg/d | 1.0 | 1.2 | 1.3 | 1.3 | 1.5 | 1.5 |
| Vitamin C | mg/d | 45 | 65 | 75 | 75 | 75 | 75 |
| Vitamin D | µg/d | 5 | 5 | 5 | 5 | 10 | 15 |
| Vitamin E | mg/d | 11 | 15 | 15 | 15 | 15 | 15 |
| Vitamin K | µg/d | 60 | 75 | 90 | 90 | 90 | 90 |
| **Minerals** | | | | | | | |
| Calcium | mg/d | 1300 | 1300 | 1000 | 1000 | 1200 | 1200 |
| Chromium | µg/d | 21 | 24 | 25 | 25 | 20 | 20 |
| Copper | µg/d | 700 | 890 | 900 | 900 | 900 | 900 |
| Fluoride | mg/d | 2 | 3 | 3 | 3 | 3 | 3 |
| Iodine | µg/d | 120 | 150 | 150 | 150 | 150 | 150 |
| Iron | mg/d | 8 | 15 | 18 | 18 | 8 | 8 |
| Magnesium | mg/d | 240 | 360 | 310 | 320 | 320 | 320 |
| Manganese | µg/d | 1.6 | 1.6 | 1.8 | 1.8 | 1.8 | 1.8 |
| Molybdenum | mg/d | 34 | 43 | 45 | 45 | 45 | 45 |
| Phosphorus | mg/d | 1250 | 1250 | 700 | 700 | 700 | 700 |
| Selenium | µg/d | 40 | 55 | 55 | 55 | 55 | 55 |
| Zinc | mg/d | 8 | 9 | 8 | 8 | 8 | 8 |

Reprinted with permission from *Dietary reference intakes from energy, carbohydrate, fiber, fat, fatty acids, cholesterol, protein, and amino acids (macronutrients)* © 2002 by the National Academies Press, Washington, DC.

# 7

# Designing Your Program

Sure, it's great to pick up a new book with strength-training programs already written for you. It's even better to have a personal trainer design the perfect program for you and help you implement it. Well, we aren't all lucky enough to have a personal trainer, and what do you do when you complete all of the book's programs? You have to learn how to design your own training program. Even if you never actually have to use it, it's nice to learn how the process works so that you'll know whether the programs that you're following are meeting your goals.

Now that you have a good understanding of the whys of strength training, it is time to figure out the hows. Several common principles apply to any specially planned and designed training program.

## Determine Your Goals and Needs

You have read all about how specific training yields specific results and about how to set your personal goals in chapter 4. Hopefully by now you have established some long- and short-term goals for your strength training. If not, now is the time to do it. Start with your long-term goals and make them objective. Put some numbers in so that you can quantify your success. The numbers can run the gamut from goals for body weight, to pant size, to the amount of weight lifted, to cholesterol level.

Also, make sure to add an end date to your goal. If it is open-ended, you can never reach it. The longer away your end date is, the more short-term goals you need to reach it. Planning a short-term goal that lasts four weeks provides an excellent reevaluation point. Four weeks is not so far away that if you find you are headed in the wrong direction, you can't correct things without much harm being done. And it's not too short a time period to see changes in your body. Be realistic when coordinating your end date and your goals. If your long-term goal is to win a powerlifting competition and you are a newcomer to strength training, then your end date may be years from now. You will need a lot of short-term goals to keep you on track and motivated.

Once you've set your goals, you have to determine how you will achieve them. Are you going to follow a program to increase strength, increase power, or lose fat (or do you want it all)? Scrutinize your goals and use the knowledge you've gained from the previous chapters to match your goals up with training methods. For example, if your long-term goals include gaining strength and losing fat, then consider a strength-training program mixed in with metabolic weight-training circuits (see chapter 3). If your long-term goal is to improve your bone density score, then you'll design a bone-building program (provided at the end of this chapter).

# Decide on Frequency and Intensity

As important as exercise should be in your life, you also need to consider real-world demands. Although you might need to exercise five days a week to achieve all of your goals, perhaps you have a stressful job that only gives you time for a workout three days a week, possibly four if you push it. In this case it isn't reasonable or realistic for you to design a training program for four days, and certainly not for five days. Give a lot of thought to how many days a week you can definitely work out, and don't lie to yourself. Design your program for the bare minimum of time you reasonably expect you'll have for training. If you aim low, you can exceed your expectations. You can always add in an extra day of an exercise or yoga class, a walk around the block with a friend, or a bike ride with your kids if you're feeling energetic and have the time. If you find that you're consistently adding in an extra day, then design a program to include that day.

Related to how frequently you decide to exercise is an important variable called recovery, or rest. Recovery is how much rest you'll need between exercises, sets, and training sessions. In general, you should rest a muscle or muscle group for 24 to 48 hours before training it again. The rest periods that you plan between exercises and sets are closely related to your exercise intensity (see table 7.1).

Intensity, also referred to as load, is estimated as a percentage of the one-repetition maximum (1RM) or of any RM for a particular exercise. A 1RM is how much weight you can lift for only one repetition—that's 100 percent intensity. A 6RM for any exercise is how much weight you can lift for 6 repetitions to failure. It means you can perform 6 reps with perfect form and maximum effort and absolutely cannot complete another rep or even come close to trying. Another way to quantify intensity is to measure it as a percentage of your 1RM. So if your 1RM in the squat is 135 pounds (100 percent intensity), at 70 percent intensity you'll lift 94.5 pounds. But of course, you can lift that weight for more than 1 repetition. How do you decide, then, how much weight to lift and for how many repetitions and sets?

Many scientific studies have examined the RM formulas to determine the best way to assign training loads. However, the overall conclusion is that it's best to use formulas as a guideline—an estimate only—and not as an absolute truth. Some of the many drawbacks in the formulas are that they are geared toward men, they are based on three free weight exercises only (bench

## Table 7.1  Adjusting the Intensity of Strength-Training Workouts

|  | Light | Moderate | Heavy |
|---|---|---|---|
| Rep range | 12-15RM | 8-10RM | 3-5RM |
| Set range | 3-4 | 3-4 | 4-5 |
| Rest between sets | 1 min | 2 min | 3-4 min |

press, back squat, and power clean), they aren't based on multiple sets, and exercises that involve smaller muscle areas will yield less repetitions. Machine exercises will also yield more repetitions. So what's a girl to do? Use the following tables to determine approximate weights for your training program, keep a training record diligently, and be flexible. There are some hard rules that you can adhere to, though. Use heavy resistance (85 to 100 percent of your 1RM) for building strength and power, moderate resistance (75 to 85 percent of your 1RM) for developing muscular hypertrophy (increasing muscular size), and light resistance (65 to 75 percent of your 1RM) to gain muscular endurance.

Heavy resistance sets are usually in the 3- to 5RM range, requiring 4 or 5 sets with 3 to 4 minutes between sets. Moderate resistance sets are usually what you can lift at 8- to 10RM, requiring 3 to 4 sets with a 2-minute rest between sets. Light resistance is a weight that you can lift at 12- to 15RM, in 3 to 4 sets, with a 1-minute rest between sets. As you can see in table 7.1, the heavier the weight is, the fewer repetitions you can perform, and the more time you'll need to rest in between sets. Lifting heavy weights also feels more intense than lifting lighter weights. Don't confuse working hard with working long, though. As a matter of fact, the opposite is often true. If you are working with an appropriate amount of intensity on a heavy workout day, your actual working time will be shorter than on a light or moderate day. However, your rest periods will be longer so the total session time will probably be about the same.

Your current conditioning, training background, and exercise history are important factors to consider when determining the intensity of your program. Because of its high intensity, perform exercises involving weights in the heavy range no more than three times a week.

To meet your strength-training goals you'll likely want to mix heavy and moderate intensities, either throughout a particular session or during the week. You can split a workout that is focusing on a body part into heavy and moderate exercises; for example, a chest and arm workout might include heavy bench presses, moderate push-ups, and heavy incline dumbbell presses. You can divide a workout week into heavy day, rest day, moderate day, active recovery day (a sports activity unrelated to lifting weights), heavy day, and rest day. You can also divide an entire four-week program into a heavy or moderate program. Just remember to alternate body areas in the programs and to vary exercises between heavy and moderate intensities, to avoid injury and boredom.

You can use table 7.2 to determine your RM percentages and training loads. Here is an example of how to find a training load when you know any of your RMs. To squat in the heavy resistance range, you must squat the maximum weight you can 3 to 5 times (3RM to 5RM). First look at the training load number that you know. Let's say you know you can squat 105 pounds for 10 reps. Look at the max reps on the top of the table and cross reference the RM you know to the load numbers beneath, to find the specific number of the weight you can lift at that RM (in this case, 105). Now look to the left on the row 105 is in and cross reference 3, 4, and 5 reps to get your training load for a heavy resistance workout. The loads you should have gotten are 3 reps at 130 pounds, 4 reps at 126 pounds, and 5 reps at 122 pounds. Here's another example. Maybe you are deadlifting one day in training and decide to throw on some weight and see where it takes you. You are on fire and deadlift 225 pounds twice. This is your new 2RM, but the next time you deadlift you need to go at a moderate intensity of 8 to 10RM. What will be your new training weights? Go to the 2RM column and follow your finger down to 225. But wait—it's not there. We have to fudge a little here and pick either 219 or 228. Since this was your first time at that weight, you should err on the conservative side and opt for the lower weight. If you thought that it was really easy, go for the bigger one. Now trail your finger to the right in this column to match the number up to 8, 9, and 10RM for your new training weights.

## Table 7.2　Estimating 1RM and Training Loads

| Max reps (RM) | 1 | 2 | 3 | 4 | 5 | 6 | 7 | 8 | 9 | 10 | 12 | 15 |
|---|---|---|---|---|---|---|---|---|---|---|---|---|
| %1RM | 100 | 95 | 93 | 90 | 87 | 85 | 83 | 80 | 77 | 75 | 67 | 65 |
| Load (lb or kg) | 10 | 10 | 9 | 9 | 9 | 9 | 8 | 8 | 8 | 8 | 7 | 7 |
| | 20 | 19 | 19 | 18 | 17 | 17 | 17 | 16 | 15 | 15 | 13 | 13 |
| | 30 | 29 | 28 | 27 | 26 | 26 | 25 | 24 | 23 | 23 | 20 | 20 |
| | 40 | 38 | 37 | 36 | 35 | 34 | 33 | 32 | 31 | 30 | 27 | 26 |
| | 50 | 48 | 47 | 45 | 44 | 43 | 42 | 40 | 39 | 38 | 34 | 33 |
| | 60 | 57 | 56 | 54 | 52 | 51 | 50 | 48 | 46 | 45 | 40 | 39 |
| | 70 | 67 | 65 | 63 | 61 | 30 | 58 | 56 | 54 | 53 | 47 | 46 |
| | 80 | 76 | 74 | 72 | 70 | 68 | 66 | 64 | 62 | 60 | 54 | 52 |
| | 90 | 86 | 84 | 81 | 78 | 77 | 75 | 72 | 69 | 68 | 60 | 59 |
| | 100 | 95 | 93 | 90 | 87 | 85 | 83 | 80 | 77 | 75 | 67 | 65 |
| | 110 | 105 | 102 | 99 | 96 | 94 | 91 | 88 | 85 | 83 | 74 | 72 |
| | 120 | 114 | 112 | 108 | 104 | 102 | 100 | 96 | 92 | 90 | 80 | 78 |
| | 130 | 124 | 121 | 117 | 113 | 111 | 108 | 104 | 100 | 98 | 87 | 85 |
| | 140 | 133 | 130 | 126 | 122 | 119 | 116 | 112 | 108 | 105 | 94 | 91 |
| | 150 | 143 | 140 | 135 | 131 | 128 | 125 | 120 | 116 | 113 | 101 | 98 |
| | 160 | 152 | 149 | 144 | 139 | 136 | 133 | 128 | 123 | 120 | 107 | 104 |
| | 170 | 162 | 158 | 153 | 148 | 145 | 141 | 136 | 131 | 128 | 114 | 111 |
| | 180 | 171 | 167 | 162 | 157 | 153 | 149 | 144 | 139 | 135 | 121 | 117 |
| | 190 | 181 | 177 | 171 | 165 | 162 | 158 | 152 | 146 | 143 | 127 | 124 |
| | 200 | 190 | 186 | 180 | 174 | 170 | 166 | 160 | 154 | 150 | 134 | 130 |
| | 210 | 200 | 195 | 189 | 183 | 179 | 174 | 168 | 162 | 158 | 141 | 137 |
| | 220 | 209 | 205 | 198 | 191 | 187 | 183 | 176 | 169 | 165 | 147 | 143 |
| | 230 | 219 | 214 | 207 | 200 | 196 | 191 | 184 | 177 | 173 | 154 | 150 |
| | 240 | 228 | 223 | 216 | 209 | 204 | 199 | 192 | 185 | 180 | 161 | 156 |
| | 250 | 238 | 233 | 225 | 218 | 213 | 208 | 200 | 193 | 188 | 168 | 163 |
| | 260 | 247 | 242 | 234 | 226 | 221 | 206 | 208 | 200 | 195 | 174 | 169 |
| | 270 | 257 | 251 | 243 | 235 | 230 | 224 | 216 | 208 | 203 | 181 | 176 |
| | 280 | 266 | 260 | 252 | 244 | 238 | 232 | 224 | 216 | 210 | 188 | 182 |
| | 290 | 276 | 270 | 261 | 252 | 247 | 241 | 232 | 223 | 218 | 194 | 189 |
| | 300 | 285 | 279 | 270 | 261 | 255 | 249 | 240 | 231 | 225 | 201 | 195 |
| | 310 | 295 | 288 | 279 | 270 | 264 | 257 | 248 | 239 | 233 | 208 | 202 |
| | 320 | 304 | 298 | 288 | 278 | 272 | 266 | 256 | 246 | 240 | 204 | 208 |
| | 330 | 314 | 307 | 297 | 287 | 281 | 274 | 264 | 254 | 248 | 221 | 215 |
| | 340 | 323 | 316 | 306 | 296 | 289 | 282 | 272 | 262 | 255 | 228 | 221 |
| | 350 | 333 | 326 | 315 | 305 | 298 | 291 | 280 | 270 | 263 | 235 | 228 |
| | 360 | 342 | 335 | 324 | 313 | 306 | 299 | 288 | 277 | 270 | 241 | 234 |
| | 370 | 352 | 344 | 333 | 322 | 315 | 307 | 296 | 285 | 278 | 245 | 241 |
| | 380 | 361 | 353 | 342 | 331 | 323 | 315 | 304 | 293 | 285 | 255 | 247 |
| | 390 | 371 | 363 | 351 | 339 | 332 | 324 | 312 | 300 | 293 | 261 | 254 |

| Max reps (RM) | 1 | 2 | 3 | 4 | 5 | 6 | 7 | 8 | 9 | 10 | 12 | 15 |
|---|---|---|---|---|---|---|---|---|---|---|---|---|
| %1RM | 100 | 95 | 93 | 90 | 87 | 85 | 83 | 80 | 77 | 75 | 67 | 65 |
| Load (lb or kg) | 400 | 380 | 372 | 360 | 348 | 340 | 332 | 320 | 308 | 300 | 268 | 260 |
| | 410 | 390 | 381 | 369 | 357 | 349 | 340 | 328 | 316 | 308 | 274 | 267 |
| | 420 | 399 | 391 | 378 | 365 | 357 | 349 | 336 | 323 | 315 | 281 | 273 |
| | 430 | 409 | 400 | 387 | 374 | 366 | 357 | 344 | 331 | 323 | 288 | 280 |
| | 440 | 418 | 409 | 396 | 383 | 374 | 365 | 352 | 339 | 330 | 295 | 286 |
| | 450 | 428 | 419 | 405 | 392 | 383 | 374 | 360 | 347 | 338 | 302 | 293 |
| | 460 | 437 | 428 | 414 | 400 | 391 | 382 | 368 | 354 | 345 | 308 | 299 |
| | 470 | 447 | 437 | 423 | 409 | 400 | 390 | 376 | 362 | 353 | 315 | 306 |
| | 480 | 456 | 446 | 432 | 418 | 408 | 398 | 384 | 370 | 360 | 322 | 312 |
| | 490 | 466 | 456 | 441 | 426 | 417 | 407 | 392 | 377 | 365 | 328 | 319 |
| | 500 | 475 | 465 | 450 | 435 | 425 | 415 | 400 | 385 | 375 | 335 | 325 |
| | 510 | 485 | 474 | 459 | 444 | 434 | 423 | 408 | 393 | 383 | 342 | 332 |
| | 520 | 494 | 484 | 468 | 452 | 442 | 432 | 416 | 400 | 390 | 348 | 338 |
| | 530 | 504 | 493 | 477 | 461 | 451 | 440 | 424 | 408 | 398 | 355 | 345 |
| | 540 | 513 | 502 | 486 | 470 | 459 | 448 | 432 | 416 | 405 | 362 | 351 |
| | 550 | 523 | 512 | 495 | 479 | 468 | 457 | 440 | 424 | 413 | 369 | 358 |
| | 560 | 532 | 521 | 504 | 487 | 476 | 465 | 448 | 431 | 420 | 375 | 364 |
| | 570 | 542 | 530 | 513 | 496 | 485 | 473 | 456 | 439 | 428 | 382 | 371 |
| | 580 | 551 | 539 | 522 | 505 | 493 | 481 | 464 | 447 | 435 | 389 | 377 |
| | 590 | 561 | 549 | 531 | 513 | 502 | 490 | 472 | 454 | 443 | 395 | 384 |
| | 600 | 570 | 558 | 540 | 522 | 510 | 498 | 480 | 462 | 450 | 402 | 390 |

Reprinted, by permission, from T.R. Baechle, R.W. Earle, D. Wathen, 2000, Resistance training. In *Essentials of strength training and conditioning,* 2nd ed., edited by T.R. Baechle and R.W. Earle (Champaign, IL: Human Kinetics), 410, 411.

# Select Your Exercises

Selecting your exercises depends greatly on how many days a week you are training and how long your sessions will take. In general, aim to complete the entire workout in 1 hour, from warm-up to training to cool-down. One hour is a manageable block of time to take out of your day, and you can get a lot accomplished in an hour if you are motivated and efficient. How many exercises you can attempt in that hour (which will probably be just 45 minutes after a 10-minute warm-up and a 5-minute cool-down) depends on your intensity and goals and varies by individual. You might find the best approach to be trial and error—seeing what is too little or what is too much. First decide how you are going to arrange your exercise program within the number of days that you can train. In other words, how are you going to train your entire body? Will you train upper body one day, lower body the next day, and do a metabolic circuit on the third? Table 7.3 on page 74 offers a few examples of how you can structure your workout weeks.

Guidelines to arranging the individual exercises during the training session are summarized as follows:

**Work from power to strength**—Start with power movements like the snatch and clean and then do strength movements like the bench press and squat.

**Work from multijoint exercises to single-joint**—Start with multijoint movements like the squat and deadlift and progress to single-joint movements like the leg extension and leg curl.

**Work from large muscle groups to smaller muscle groups**—Start with large muscle groups like the leg muscles and progress to small muscle groups like the arm muscles.

**Alternate pushing and pulling movements**—Alternate pushing moves like the bench press with pulling moves like the barbell row.

**Alternate upper- and lower-body work**—Bench press, then squat, then overhead press, then step-up.

Table 7.3    **Ideas for Structuring Your Workout Week**

|  | A | B | C | D |
|---|---|---|---|---|
| Day 1 | Upper body | Total body | Total body | Chest and back |
| Day 2 | Lower body | Total body | Metabolic circuit | Legs |
| Day 3 | Core and metabolic circuit | Total body | Upper body | Shoulders, lats, and arms |
| Day 4 |  |  | Lower body and core | Deadlift and core |

# Include Rest

Wait a minute; this is a book on training, right? We can't rest—we've got too much muscle to build and too little time! Well, that's precisely why we need to rest. You must plan recovery time into every training session and weekly routine. Rest includes plenty of passive recovery like sleeping and eating and some active recovery like playing a sport just for fun, not competitively. Passive recovery allows the muscles time to grow and heal from the damage created during grueling training sessions, and active recovery can prevent or decrease physiological and psychological burnout. Include rest days in your weekly training schedule. Get plenty of rest, and you'll have the energy to incorporate these new training suggestions and take your training to the next level.

# Maintain a Training Log and Add Variety

The easiest way to guarantee success in your training is to maintain a training log. I've designed each strength-training and competition workout program provided in this book in a format that allows for logging information. Just as you would never go on a long car trip without a map, so you must use a training log as your map to your workout goals. It shows you where you started, how you are getting there, and when you will reach your final goal. Bring your training log with you to the gym so that you can mark down your exercises completed, weight amounts lifted, reps, sets, and rest periods. Look at your log often to see how much weight you've lifted in the past so that you can exceed it. Keeping a log can also help you know what exercises you have been doing and can tell you when you need to change things up a bit to add more variety.

Whether you have recently started strength training or are an experienced veteran, surely you are enjoying the positive changes you see in your body composition, general health, and mental attitude. Of course you have to begin with the basic movements and routines, but eventually you need to look for some other ideas. Learning and incorporating new techniques into your training program is essential to stimulating muscle growth and preventing boredom. The following list offers some suggestions for kicking your training up a notch:

**Unilateral movements**—Performing exercises on one side of the body improves balance, decreases strength discrepancies, and strengthens the core muscles. Try doing one-leg squats (page 160) or any movement that you normally do on two legs.

**Metabolic circuit training**—Tired of losing that hard-earned muscle while you're trying to lose body fat? Get down from the stair machine and start circuit training with weights. You get a big bang for your buck with this extremely metabolic type of training. Check out chapter 3 to see examples of some metabolic circuits. These short, simple circuits can help you lose body fat while helping you keep your muscle.

**Short rest periods**—Stop checking out the people in the gym between sets and start checking your watch. Most weightlifters and powerlifters know that to make maximal gains in strength, you need to rest muscles well before the next set begins. But to increase muscular size, short rest periods of 30 to 60 seconds are the way to go. Short rest periods stimulate the release of more growth hormone than longer rest periods, maximizing muscular growth and fat loss. Use the 30- to 60-second technique or try a work-rest ratio of 1:1, in which you rest between sets for the same amount of time it took you to perform the set you just completed.

**Supersets of agonist-antagonist muscle groups**—Want to decrease your workout time, yet still increase your volume? Then do what are called supersets with movements that oppose each other. A superset involves two different exercises that you perform together as one set, without rest in between the exercises, taking the rest after completing the full set of two exercises. You commonly do supersets with agonist and antagonist muscles—muscles that oppose each other on either side of a joint. The agonist muscle is the prime mover and the antagonist is on the opposite side of the joint, slowing that motion down. Some examples of supersets are performing a bench press with a barbell row, a leg extension with a leg curl, and a biceps curl with a triceps pushdown. Another name for this technique is push-pull sets. Exercise supersets that use the exact opposite muscles give the first group of muscles time to rest while the second group is working. Training muscles that surround a joint creates stability around that joint and prevents injuries.

**Training while balancing**—Do you sometimes feel off balance or lose your footing? Not only does balance training improve your body awareness, but it also allows you to lift heavier weights, which can translate into bigger muscles. Try doing one-leg squats without holding on to anything. Vary the position of your free leg for each set so that it is in front of you, beside you, and in back of you. To make it even more challenging, try holding dumbbells in each hand. How about doing squats on a rocker board or foam rolls—items your gym may have that are specifically geared toward enhancing your balance during exercises? Any uneven surface will do. Challenge your upper body by putting your hands on a stability ball and doing push-ups (see page 123). Don't have a stability ball? Well, that's what old tire tubes are for. Forget about floating down Grandma's stream. Instead, stand on the tube while performing weight-training exercises for a down-home balance experience.

**Plyometrics.** Do you miss hopping, jumping, skipping, and playing with balls as you did when you were a kid? Then incorporate plyometrics into your workout program. Plyometrics are simply movements preceded by a prestretch because of a sudden change from the eccentric to the concentric phase of a movement. Any exercise can be made into a plyometric one just by performing the eccentric portion as rapidly as possible, and then quickly reversing direction and performing the concentric phase of the movement as quickly as possible. Most people think of jumping movements as plyometric exercises. However, virtually any quick movement can qualify as a plyometric. Try jump squats (page 161) or overhead throw-downs (page 108) for plyometric fun.

**Tempo changes or pauses**—Forget the old-school recommendation of lifting the weight (concentric action) on a two count and lowering it (eccentric action) on a four count. Perform the same exercises, but change the tempo. Do all of the reps very quickly, or very slowly, or one quick and one slow. Use pauses on the eccentric movement and vary both the number of pauses and the hold times. For example, during the lowering or the eccentric portion of a pull-up (see page 132), try to pause three times and hold for 5 seconds at each pause. Or after the eccentric portion of the bench press, pause the bar on your chest for 3 to 5 seconds and explode off your chest for the concentric movement. Have your training partner vary the pause times and cue you when to lift.

**Increasing the overload**—Traditionally, lifters handled supramaximal weights only during negative-type movements like lowering a heavy weight very slowly or during partial movements like lifting a heavy weight over a shorter range of motion. But it's time to come out of hibernation and see what's outside the cave. Thanks to Louie Simmons and the Westside Barbell Club training methods, here's a useful strategy for tapping into the benefits of overloading. Try hanging chains off of your bar while squatting. As you descend, the weight gets lighter (more chain is in contact with the ground). As you ascend, the weight gets heavier (less chain is in contact with the ground). You can add this type of overload with many exercises like bench presses, rows, or deadlifts. Use chains with one-half inch link sizes or greater, with hooks or clamps to attach to the barbell. Such chains can be found at most home improvement stores. Another option is to use heavy elastic surgical or rehab tubing, or bungee cords. Attach one end to the bar and anchor the other end to the floor.

**Wave work sets**—Are you trying to push past a weight plateau? If you are having trouble lifting a particular weight, or if you want to progress to a heavier weight but can't seem to get there, this technique is for you. Let's say that you've been squatting about 135 pounds for reps, but you just can't seem to get to 145 yet. Do your warm-up sets first, and then perform a wave in this manner: 95 pounds × 5, 115 pounds × 5, and 135 pounds × 5, with a 3- to 5-minute rest period between sets. Rest for 3 to 5 more minutes and perform the next wave: 105 pounds × 5, 125 pounds × 5, and 145 pounds × 5. Do the wave on any exercise and wave bye-bye to your old personal records as you welcome in all-time personal bests.

**Explosive power movements**—Learn what the Olympians know: To increase power, strength, and speed, perform explosive power movements like power snatches and power cleans. Read chapter 13 and get a good coach who can teach you the proper technique behind these useful exercises. Pick one exercise and do it early in the workout session when you are fresh. Keep reps to 5 or less and perform 3 to 5 sets. Initially your goal is to learn proper technique, not to see how much weight you can lift. Let your technique or coach be the guide for increasing the weight on the bar. It takes some time to learn these exercises, but the return is well worth the investment.

**Double stimulation weight sets**—For some real variety and cutting-edge training, choose the double stim method. A double stimulation workout places a high demand on the neuromuscular system, which leads to great gains in strength, speed, and power. Perform 2 warm-up sets of a movement. Next perform a segment of 1 set for 5 reps, rest for 3 to 5 minutes, and then perform a set with a heavier weight for 1 rep. Repeat this segment twice more. Focus on lifting the weights as quickly as possible. If you know how much you can lift one time (1RM), use the following percentages and reps (with all rest times at 3 to 5 minutes):

- Warm-up: 60% × 5 reps, rest, 70% × 5, rest (optional third warm-up set of 75% × 3, rest)
- 80% × 5, rest, 90% × 1, rest
- 80% × 5, rest, 90% × 1, rest
- 80% × 5, rest, 90% × 1

## STAYING MOTIVATED

We are always shopping for the best outfit to wear to the gym or the latest belts, wraps, and straps to help our workouts. But we seldom realize that the best equipment for our workouts is something that we already have and rarely take advantage of—our mind. The mind is a powerful muscle that can make or break a single workout and even all your fitness goals. Your training philosophy is as important as your training program, so take some time to train your brain.

Here are some tips to help psych up your workout:

1. Prepare yourself—A primary key to having an effective training session is preparing your mind for the hard work to come. Having a written training plan is essential to being prepared. You can relieve the anxiety of not knowing what exercise to do next and eliminate wandering aimlessly around the gym, wasting time and effort.

2. Use imagery—Let your mind's eye see that perfect training session or that ultimate lift. Mentally practice your lifting technique, your entire workout routine, and even how you will look and feel after a grueling workout.

3. Motivate yourself—Even if you have a training partner who is great at shouting encouragement, you have to be able to motivate yourself. Find out what makes training important for you, and then use that as motivation. Are you trying to get healthier? Go to a doctor and get information on your baseline health parameters like cholesterol, blood sugar, body composition, and blood pressure and shoot for improving those numbers. If you are training to lose weight, reward yourself with new clothes after each drop in size.

4. Believe in yourself—You have to be confident that your effort in the gym will translate into your goals outside of the gym. If you have the conviction that you can successfully curl the weight you have on the bar, your intensity and persistence will pay off with a top performance.

# Sample Programs

The basic strength programs I have provided here are all for five days per week and are not sport-specific. It is not necessary to go to a gym or health club, since you can do most of these exercises at home. But because they rely mostly on body weight and free-weights, they do require some equipment. If you choose to exercise at home, you need adequate space and you must purchase some supplies. Where you like to train is a very personal matter. Some women are uncomfortable going to gyms and working out in front of other people, whereas some don't care or see it as a challenge or a way to make friends. Whichever you choose, try to enlist a partner to train with for moral support, advice, and injury prevention. Even someone who is a beginner can help—it's a great way to learn. Don't be worried if you are both beginners, either—two heads are better than one. It is essential to do the exercises correctly, however, to prevent injury—never sacrifice perfect form for increased weight.

The programs that follow emphasize muscular hypertrophy and strength, so you'll see different rest periods and repetitions depending on the focus that day. If you have never strength trained before, have trained mostly on machines, or have never even exercised before, the beginner's program is for you. Follow the program for 4 to 6 weeks, and then you can graduate to the intermediate program. If you are currently training with free weights and strength movements, you can start with the intermediate program for 4 to 6 weeks. If you are already a Superwoman and want a cutting-edge program to take you to the max, then the 12-week advanced program is for you. When you have completed that program, you might want to try some of the competition programs in chapter 13 or incorporate some of the competition exercises into your program. You'll find detailed descriptions and photographs of all the exercises in part III, in case you are not familiar with a certain exercise.

## Warm-Up and Cool-Down

Before starting each day of your training program, perform a warm-up routine that consists of a general warm-up, dynamic stretching, and a specific warm-up. Use a 5- to 10-minute general warm-up to increase your entire body's circulation, warm up your muscles and joints, and get your body and mind ready to exercise. You can walk, jog, climb stairs, or use a stair-climbing machine. After your general warm-up, choose three to four dynamic stretches from the following list. Dynamic stretches are preferable to static stretches for warming up the body because dynamic stretches involve multiple joints in active motions, which is what you want when you are lifting.

The cool-down is the time you can devote to gaining flexibility, through the use of static stretching techniques. These are the long, slow-duration stretches that you commonly see and probably do yourself. If you want to gain flexibility, you need to perform static stretching on a daily basis. Statically stretching individual muscle groups after exercise can help cool down your body by helping your blood pressure slowly return to normal. You can also finish a strength-training session with light walking or biking. Not much of a cool-down is needed with strength-training programs because although your heart rate and blood pressure rise, they quickly return to preexercise levels during your rest sessions (unlike cardiovascular endurance programs, in which there is no rest).

### KNEE HUG

1. Stand on the left leg and bring the right leg with bent knee to the chest.
2. Rise up onto the right toes, and hug the right leg to the chest while pulling it upward.
3. Repeat with the other leg and perform 10 reps with each leg.

### LEG CRADLE

1. Stand on the left leg and bring the right leg to the chest in a figure-four position. Use one hand to hold the leg at the ankle and one at the knee.
2. Rise up onto the left toes, and pull the right leg upward.
3. Repeat with the other leg and perform 10 reps with each leg.

## WALKING BACKWARD LUNGE WITH TWIST

1. With the feet together, step backward with the right leg into a lunge.
2. Arch and lean back slightly, twist the torso over the right leg, and reach both hands to the sky.
3. Push back out of that position into the next lunge on the left leg.
4. Repeat 10 times on each leg.

## FORWARD ARM SWING

1. Stand up tall with the scapulas retracted and the feet shoulder-width apart.
2. Keep the elbows straight and swing the arms forward and backward. Start with a small range of movement (ROM) and progress to full ROM.

## SIDE ARM SWING

1. Bend at the hip and make a 90-degree angle between the upper and lower body. Let the arms hang straight down.
2. Keep the elbows straight and swing the arms to each side. Start with a small range of movement (ROM) and progress to full ROM.

## HEEL TO BUTT

1. Stand on the left leg and bend the right leg toward the rear end. Use the right hand to hold the leg at the ankle and raise the other arm in the air.
2. Rise up onto the left toes and pull the right leg upward.
3. Repeat with the other leg and perform 10 reps with each leg.

## PLANK WALKOUT

1. Start in downward-facing dog position (from yoga). Place the feet and hands flat on the ground.
2. Keeping the legs straight and the abdominal muscles tight, walk the hands out as far as possible.
3. Still keeping the legs straight, walk the feet back up to the hands.
4. Perform 10 reps.

## WALKING FORWARD LUNGE

1. Lunge forward on the left leg. Place the hands on either side of the left foot to support the body's weight.
2. Stretch into the lunge while keeping the back knee off the ground.
3. Push the hips back, straighten the legs, and pull the left toe up off the ground.
4. Take a step forward and repeat with the right leg. Perform 10 reps on each leg.

a                                        b

## CHEST LEAN FORWARD

1. Using a weight cage or a doorway, position the arms straight out to the sides in a T formation such that the arms are touching the cage or doorway. Keep the feet close together.
2. Lean the body forward and backward in an oscillating fashion to gently stretch the upper body.
3. Start with a small range of motion (ROM) and progress to full ROM.
4. Move hand placement up the cage or doorway to end with a Y formation.

## SCAPULAR LEAN BACKWARD

1. Align the left side of the body to the left side of an open doorway or a weight upright. Pronate the left hand (palm down) and grasp the edge of the doorway or upright. Keep the feet together.
2. Lean the body backward and forward in an oscillating fashion. Let the scapula protract from a small range of motion (ROM) to full ROM.
3. Repeat on the right side.

*a*

*b*

Once you have completed these dynamic stretches, you are ready to hit the weights. In the specific warm-up within the sample programs, you'll perform the actual exercise in your program with a light weight, progressively increasing the weight for each set until you reach your top weight—the weight you will be working with for the prescribed number of sets. If you are lifting heavy weights, you'll definitely need 3 specific warm-up lifting sets. If you are lifting lighter weights, you may just need 1 set. Here is an example of a specific warm-up for a lift:

Set 1: Olympic bar or 50 percent of your top weight for the day for 5 reps

Set 2: 75 percent of your top weight for the day for 3 reps

Set 3: 90 percent of your top weight for the day for 2 reps

## Beginner Program

Attempt 8 repetitions per set for the exercises in this program (see table 7.4). Choose a weight that is heavy enough that the last 2 reps are tough. If the reps seem easy, increase the weight by 2 1/2 to 5 pounds. In beginners' programs, a 5-pound weight increase can feel like a lot of weight. It is also difficult to find weights that jump in 2 1/2-pound increments. If you have just made an increase in weight, allow yourself a little leeway on the repetitions. Getting 6 repetitions with perfect form is better than doing 8 with lousy form.

## Intermediate Program

Attempt 5 repetitions for each set in the exercises in table 7.5 on page 84. Choose a weight that is heavy enough so that reps 4 and 5 are tough. If the reps seem easy, increase the weight by 2 1/2 to 5 pounds. If you have just made an increase in weight, allow yourself a little leeway on the repetitions. Again, getting 4 repetitions with perfect form is better than doing 5 with lousy form.

## Advanced Program

The program outlined in table 7.6 (page 86) follows an undulating periodization model in which the repetition count varies with every workout, from 3 to 6 to 9. If you use this program for 6 weeks, each body part will experience the same rep count for two workouts. Start week 1 using weights with which you are confident you can complete the prescribed rep count. Aim for quality of movement and make a realistic determination of what you can handle. That way you minimize soreness and injury and prepare a road map of weight increases that you can follow as you progress. You can stay on the program for up to 12 weeks, as long as you are making progress. The change in the rep count is a great way to stimulate new gains and decrease boredom within a training program.

## Table 7.4  Weekly Beginner Strength-Training Program

Date:

| Day: focus | Exercise | Page | Load | Set 1 | Set 2 | Set 3 |
|---|---|---|---|---|---|---|
| 1: Legs | Barbell back squat | 159 | Weight | | | |
| | | | Reps | | | |
| | Step-up | 164 | Weight | | | |
| | | | Reps | | | |
| | Lunge | 163 | Weight | | | |
| | | | Reps | | | |
| | Stability ball leg curl | 167 | Weight | | | |
| | | | Reps | | | |
| 2: Chest and upper back | Push-ups | 122 | Weight | | | |
| | | | Reps | | | |
| | Ys, Ts, and Is | 119 | Weight | | | |
| | | | Reps | | | |
| | Dumbbell bench press | 124 | Weight | | | |
| | | | Reps | | | |
| | Dumbbell row | 131 | Weight | | | |
| | | | Reps | | | |
| 3: Rest | | | | | | |
| 4: Deadlift and core | Conventional deadlift | 175 | Weight | | | |
| | | | Reps | | | |
| | Ball walkout | 111 | Weight | | | |
| | | | Reps | | | |
| | Stability ball straight crunch | 101 | Weight | | | |
| | | | Reps | | | |
| | Stability ball hyperextension | 109 | Weight | | | |
| | | | Reps | | | |
| | Stability ball diagonal crunch | 102 | Weight | | | |
| | | | Reps | | | |
| 5: Shoulders, lats, and arms | Dumbbell overhead press | 130 | Weight | | | |
| | | | Reps | | | |
| | Lat pulldown | 134 | Weight | | | |
| | | | Reps | | | |
| | Scaption | 118 | Weight | | | |
| | | | Reps | | | |
| | Dumbbell biceps curl | 139 | Weight | | | |
| | | | Reps | | | |
| | Overhead dumbbell extension | 145 | Weight | | | |
| | | | Reps | | | |
| 6: Metabolic intervals | | | | | | |
| 7: Rest | | | | | | |

From *Strength Training for Women* by Lori Incledon, 2005, Champaign, IL: Human Kinetics.

## Table 7.5  **Weekly Intermediate Strength-Training Program**

Date:

| Day: focus | Exercise | Page | Load | | Set 1 | Set 2 | Set 3 |
|---|---|---|---|---|---|---|---|
| 1: Legs | Barbell back quat | 159 | Weight | | | | |
| | | | Reps | | | | |
| | Step-up | 164 | Weight | | | | |
| | | | Reps | | | | |
| | Lunge | 163 | Weight | | | | |
| | | | Reps | | | | |
| | Leg curl | 169 | Weight | | | | |
| | | | Reps | | | | |
| | Romanian deadlift | 180 | Weight | | | | |
| | | | Reps | | | | |
| 2: Chest and upper back | Barbell bench press | 124 | Weight | | | | |
| | | | Reps | | | | |
| | Barbell row | 131 | Weight | | | | |
| | | | Reps | | | | |
| | Barbell bench press (incline) | 124 | Weight | | | | |
| | | | Reps | | | | |
| | Dumbbell row | 131 | Weight | | | | |
| | | | Reps | | | | |
| | Hands on stability ball push-up | 123 | Weight | | | | |
| | | | Reps | | | | |
| | Cable row | 133 | Weight | | | | |
| | | | Reps | | | | |
| 3: Rest | | | | | | | |
| 4: Deadlift and core | Conventional deadlift | 175 | Weight | | | | |
| | | | Reps | | | | |
| | Hanging leg raise | 105 | Weight | | | | |
| | | | Reps | | | | |
| | Good morning | 112 | Weight | | | | |
| | | | Reps | | | | |
| | Wood chop | 106 | Weight | | | | |
| | | | Reps | | | | |
| | Trunk side raise | 107 | Weight | | | | |
| | | | Reps | | | | |

| Day: focus | Exercise | Page | Load | Set 1 | Set 2 | Set 3 |
|---|---|---|---|---|---|---|
| 5: Shoulders, lats, and arms | Barbell overhead front press | 126 | Weight | | | |
| | | | Reps | | | |
| | Pull-up | 132 | Weight | | | |
| | | | Reps | | | |
| | Dumbbell overhead press | 130 | Weight | | | |
| | | | Reps | | | |
| | Straight-arm lat pull-down | 120 | Weight | | | |
| | | | Reps | | | |
| | Standing barbell biceps curl | 138 | Weight | | | |
| | | | Reps | | | |
| | Close grip bench press | 148 | Weight | | | |
| | | | Reps | | | |
| 6: Metabolic intervals | | | | | | |
| 7: Rest | | | | | | |

From *Strength Training for Women* by Lori Incledon, 2005, Champaign, IL: Human Kinetics.

## Table 7.6 Multiweek Advanced Strength-Training Program

| Weeks | Day | Exercise | Page | Load | Set 1 | Set 2 | Set 3 |
|---|---|---|---|---|---|---|---|
| 1, 4, 7, 10 | Day 1 | One-leg squat | 160 | Weight | | | |
| | | | | Reps | 3 | 3 | 3 |
| | | Step-up | 164 | Weight | | | |
| | | | | Reps | 3 | 3 | 3 |
| | | Deadlift—barbell | 176 | Weight | | | |
| | | | | Reps | 3 | 3 | 3 |
| | | Abdominal rotation | 107 | Weight | | | |
| | | | | Reps | 3 | 3 | 3 |
| | Day 2 | Barbell bench press—flat | 124 | Weight | | | |
| | | | | Reps | 6 | 6 | 6 |
| | | Barbell row | 131 | Weight | | | |
| | | | | Reps | 6 | 6 | 6 |
| | | Barbell bench press—incline | 124 | Weight | | | |
| | | | | Reps | 6 | 6 | 6 |
| | | Cable row | 133 | Weight | | | |
| | | | | Reps | 6 | 6 | 6 |
| | | Standing barbell biceps curl | 138 | Weight | | | |
| | | | | Reps | 6 | 6 | 6 |
| | | Close grip bench press | 148 | Weight | | | |
| | | | | Reps | 6 | 6 | 6 |
| | Day 3 | Rest | | | | | |
| | Day 4 | Romanian deadlift | 180 | Weight | | | |
| | | | | Reps | 9 | 9 | 9 |
| | | Barbell back squat | 159 | Weight | | | |
| | | | | Reps | 9 | 9 | 9 |
| | | Walking forward lunge | 80 | Weight | | | |
| | | | | Reps | 9 | 9 | 9 |
| | | Hanging leg raise | 105 | Weight | | | |
| | | | | Reps | 9 | 9 | 9 |
| | Day 5 | Pull-up | 132 | Weight | | | |
| | | | | Reps | 3 | 3 | 3 |
| | | Barbell overhead front press | 126 | Weight | | | |
| | | | | Reps | 3 | 3 | 3 |
| | | Lat pulldown | 134 | Weight | | | |
| | | | | Reps | 3 | 3 | 3 |
| | | Dummbell overhead press with top hold | 130 | Weight | | | |
| | | | | Reps | 3 | 3 | 3 |
| | | Preacher curl | 141 | Weight | | | |
| | | | | Reps | 3 | 3 | 3 |
| | | Cable pushdown | 146 | Weight | | | |
| | | | | Reps | 3 | 3 | 3 |
| | Day 6 | Metabolic intervals | | | | | |
| | Day 7 | Rest | | | | | |

| Weeks | Day | Exercise | Page | Load | Set 1 | Set 2 | Set 3 |
|---|---|---|---|---|---|---|---|
| 2, 5, 8, 11 | Day 1 | One-leg squat | 160 | Weight | | | |
| | | | | Reps | 6 | 6 | 6 |
| | | Step-up | 164 | Weight | | | |
| | | | | Reps | 6 | 6 | 6 |
| | | Deadlift—barbell | 176 | Weight | | | |
| | | | | Reps | 6 | 6 | 6 |
| | | Abdominal rotation | 107 | Weight | | | |
| | | | | Reps | 6 | 6 | 6 |
| | Day 2 | Barbell bench press—flat | 124 | Weight | | | |
| | | | | Reps | 9 | 9 | 9 |
| | | Barbell row | 131 | Weight | | | |
| | | | | Reps | 9 | 9 | 9 |
| | | Barbell bench press—incline | 124 | Weight | | | |
| | | | | Reps | 9 | 9 | 9 |
| | | Cable row | 133 | Weight | | | |
| | | | | Reps | 9 | 9 | 9 |
| | | Standing barbell biceps curl | 138 | Weight | | | |
| | | | | Reps | 9 | 9 | 9 |
| | | Close grip bench press | 148 | Weight | | | |
| | | | | Reps | 9 | 9 | 9 |
| | Day 3 | Rest | | | | | |
| | Day 4 | Romanian deadlift | 180 | Weight | | | |
| | | | | Reps | 3 | 3 | 3 |
| | | Barbell back squat | 159 | Weight | | | |
| | | | | Reps | 3 | 3 | 3 |
| | | Walking forward lunge | 80 | Weight | | | |
| | | | | Reps | 3 | 3 | 3 |
| | | Hanging leg raise | 105 | Weight | | | |
| | | | | Reps | 3 | 3 | 3 |
| | Day 5 | Pull-up | 132 | Weight | | | |
| | | | | Reps | 6 | 6 | 6 |
| | | Barbell overhead front press | 126 | Weight | | | |
| | | | | Reps | 6 | 6 | 6 |
| | | Lat pulldown | 134 | Weight | | | |
| | | | | Reps | 6 | 6 | 6 |
| | | Dumbbell overhead press with top hold | 130 | Weight | | | |
| | | | | Reps | 6 | 6 | 6 |
| | | Preacher curl | 141 | Weight | | | |
| | | | | Reps | 6 | 6 | 6 |
| | | Cable pushdown | 146 | Weight | | | |
| | | | | Reps | 6 | 6 | 6 |
| | Day 6 | Metabolic intervals | | | | | |
| | Day 7 | Rest | | | | | |

*(continued)*

Table 7.6  **Multiweek Advanced Strength-Training Program** (continued)

| Weeks | Day | Exercise | Page | Load | Set 1 | Set 2 | Set 3 |
|---|---|---|---|---|---|---|---|
| 3, 6, 9, 12 | Day 1 | One-leg squat | 160 | Weight | | | |
| | | | | Reps | 9 | 9 | 9 |
| | | Step-up | 164 | Weight | | | |
| | | | | Reps | 9 | 9 | 9 |
| | | Deadlift—barbell | 176 | Weight | | | |
| | | | | Reps | 9 | 9 | 9 |
| | | Abdominal rotation | 107 | Weight | | | |
| | | | | Reps | 9 | 9 | 9 |
| | Day 2 | Barbell bench press—flat | 124 | Weight | | | |
| | | | | Reps | 3 | 3 | 3 |
| | | Barbell row | 131 | Weight | | | |
| | | | | Reps | 3 | 3 | 3 |
| | | Barbell bench press—incline | 124 | Weight | | | |
| | | | | Reps | 3 | 3 | 3 |
| | | Cable row | 133 | Weight | | | |
| | | | | Reps | 3 | 3 | 3 |
| | | Standing barbell biceps curl | 138 | Weight | | | |
| | | | | Reps | 3 | 3 | 3 |
| | | Close grip bench press | 148 | Weight | | | |
| | | | | Reps | 3 | 3 | 3 |
| | Day 3 | Rest | | | | | |
| | Day 4 | Romanian deadlift | 180 | Weight | | | |
| | | | | Reps | 6 | 6 | 6 |
| | | Barbell back squat | 159 | Weight | | | |
| | | | | Reps | 6 | 6 | 6 |
| | | Walking forward lunge | 80 | Weight | | | |
| | | | | Reps | 6 | 6 | 6 |
| | | Hanging leg raise | 105 | Weight | | | |
| | | | | Reps | 6 | 6 | 6 |
| | Day 5 | Pull-up | 132 | Weight | | | |
| | | | | Reps | 9 | 9 | 9 |
| | | Barbell overhead front press | 126 | Weight | | | |
| | | | | Reps | 9 | 9 | 9 |
| | | Lat pulldown | 134 | Weight | | | |
| | | | | Reps | 9 | 9 | 9 |
| | | Dumbbell overhead press with top hold | 130 | Weight | | | |
| | | | | Reps | 9 | 9 | 9 |
| | | Preacher curl | 141 | Weight | | | |
| | | | | Reps | 9 | 9 | 9 |
| | | Cable pushdown | 146 | Weight | | | |
| | | | | Reps | 9 | 9 | 9 |
| | Day 6 | Metabolic intervals | | | | | |
| | Day 7 | Rest | | | | | |

# Bone-Building Program

Successful programs for building bone are relatively intense, and you perform them with little rest during the exercise session. Research proves that 3 days of high-impact cardiovascular endurance activity such as jogging, stair climbing, or aerobics done for 20 minutes, alternated with 3 days of total-body weight training, increase the bone mineral density in the hip and spine.

- Focus on the basic free-weight exercises such as squats (page 159), deadlifts (page 177), cleans (page 190), rows (page 131), presses page 124), and curls (page 139).
- Use exercises in which you have to move your own body weight, such as crunches (page 101) and push-ups (page 122).
- Choose exercises that force you to support your weight from different angles and directions—try one-leg movements, lunging sequences to different directions, and balance-challenge exercises. You must choose exercises that have you moving upward, downward, and to the side to emphasize bone growth.
- Hike or run on inclines or uneven surfaces.
- Play sports that involve some running, cutting, and jumping like tennis, basketball, and volleyball.
- Participate in step aerobics classes, climb stadium steps, or use a step machine.

Table 7.7 on page 90 provides an example of a bone-building program that incorporates the basics. Perform each exercise for 3 sets of 8 repetitions, with a 1-minute rest between sets and between exercises.

## Table 7.7   **Bone-Building Program**

| Day | Exercise | Page | Load | Set 1 | Set 2 | Set 3 |
|---|---|---|---|---|---|---|
| Monday | Barbell back squat | 159 | Weight | | | |
| | | | Reps | | | |
| | Lunge to a diagonal holding dumb-bells. Perform a dumbbell biceps curl between reps. | 163 | Weight | | | |
| | | | Reps | | | |
| | Push-up | 122 | Weight | | | |
| | | | Reps | | | |
| | Pull-up or chin-up | 132 | Weight | | | |
| | | | Reps | | | |
| | Push press | 127 | Weight | | | |
| | | | Reps | | | |
| Tuesday | Step machine or step class | | | | | |
| Wednesday | Conventional deadlift | 177 | Weight | | | |
| | | | Reps | | | |
| | Step-up | 165 | Weight | | | |
| | | | Reps | | | |
| | Dumbbell bench press incline | 124 | Weight | | | |
| | | | Reps | | | |
| | Dumbbell overhead press | 130 | Weight | | | |
| | | | Reps | | | |
| | Dumbbell row | 131 | Weight | | | |
| | | | Reps | | | |
| | Dumbbell biceps curl | 139 | Weight | | | |
| | | | Reps | | | |
| | Dumbbell kickback | 144 | Weight | | | |
| | | | Reps | | | |
| Thursday | Walk, run, or hike on an incline or uneven surface. | | | | | |
| Friday | Barbell front squat | 159 | Weight | | | |
| | | | Reps | | | |
| | Romanian deadlift one-leg | 182 | Weight | | | |
| | | | Reps | | | |
| | Barbell bench press | 124 | Weight | | | |
| | | | Reps | | | |
| | Barbell overhead front press | 126 | Weight | | | |
| | | | Reps | | | |
| | Barbell row | 131 | Weight | | | |
| | | | Reps | | | |
| | Standing barbell biceps curl | 138 | Weight | | | |
| | | | Reps | | | |
| | Lying French press | 145 | Weight | | | |
| | | | Reps | | | |
| Saturday | Play a game like tennis, volleyball, or basketball. | | | | | |
| Sunday | Rest | | | | | |

From *Strength Training for Women* by Lori Incledon, 2005, Champaign, IL: Human Kinetics.

# Part III

# Movements and Muscles

# 8

# Strengthening Your Core

We crave them, we obsess about them, and we're constantly holding them in. They are the sexiest things to look at and the hardest things to get. Some claim that getting them takes only five minutes a day, but others toil for a half hour. Many use machines and devices, but most prefer to work au naturel. I'm talking about abdominal muscles, of course. But do you realize that it would be impossible to have fantastic abs without the big role that your low back muscles play?

You've probably heard the term *core training*. The basic theory is that if you train your core or trunk muscles (your abdominals and low back) you will improve the strength, stability, and possibly power of many movements. That's because the power that generates a lethal tennis serve or a killer volleyball spike comes from the center of the body (the core) and transfers out to the arms. Think about this: Many injuries that result from accidents and overuse can trace their origins back to poor trunk control and strength. If your core is not strong and you perform high-level activities like deadlifting a toddler or playing tennis, you may be putting stress on muscles that are too small, too weak, and too mechanically disadvantaged to perform those movements.

Think about the developmental processes that occur from the time you are a helpless newborn to the time you can walk. If you've had a baby, this development will be easier for you to follow since you've seen it, or will see it, firsthand. Even if you haven't, the process makes sense and is easy to grasp. Our bodies are constantly undergoing change, no matter how old we are. But as babies, the growth and development that take place are remarkable and fast. The nervous system (brain, spinal cord, and peripheral nerves) doesn't fully develop until we are well into our twenties. So a newborn has only some primitive survival skills and appears to make random movements, basically responding to the environment. And those responses are immature and largely ineffective. Newborns can't withstand the challenges of gravity, much less move against it. They can't hold their heavy heads up, not only because their muscles aren't strong enough yet, but also because their nervous systems aren't completely formed. As the newborn and her nervous system mature, she is able to control movement and eventually master it. The development starts proximally (trunk) and proceeds distally (extremities), starts with gross motor movements and proceeds to fine motor control, and starts with head control and proceeds to postural control.

A baby must reach certain developmental milestones as she grows in order to proceed to the next stage (see table 8.1). For example, an infant doesn't walk before she can crawl and doesn't use a fork before she can hold a bottle. As a matter of fact, infant motor development is divided into four stages: mobility (0 to 3 months), stability (4 to 6 months), controlled mobility (7 to 9 months), and skill (10 to 12 months). Within these phases are specific motor developmental milestones that a baby goes through, some faster and some slower than the average.

### Table 8.1   Milestones in Motor Development

| Age (in months) | Motor developmental milestone |
| --- | --- |
| 1 | Has prone head control |
| 3 | Pushes up on elbows while prone |
| 4 | Reaches for and holds objects; rolls back to belly |
| 6 | Rolls belly to back; sits with minimal support |
| 7 | Pushes up to quadruped posture (on hands and knees); shifts weight and rocks in quadruped position |
| 8-9 | Crawls; holds bottle |
| 9-11 | Side sits, squats, kneels, and half kneels; can play with two objects simultaneously |
| 12 | Stands; walks with support and progresses to true walking; finger feeds |

So what does all of this baby talk have to do with strength training? Motor learning doesn't only take place from birth to the age of 12 months; it takes an entire lifetime. We can't play tennis if we have never held a racket in our hands, and we can't hold a baby in our arms if we're not skilled enough to hold a bag of flour. We are in a constant state of learning, developing, and refining that development. If we teach our body to sit on the couch, then it will adapt to sitting on the couch. If we teach it to lift weights, then it will adapt to that too. If we lift heavier weights, our body will accommodate us. But don't ask it to lift heavy weights when it's been sitting on the couch—that's when we get injured. Our bodies can learn many wonderful and complicated skills, but they need a base on which to build. That base is your core.

## Understanding Trunk Anatomy

To begin a discussion on the bones of the trunk, we have to start with the spinal column, which is the basis or core for our entire body. The bones that form the spinal column are the cervical vertebrae (neck), the thoracic vertebrae (upper back to midback), and the lumbar vertebrae (low back). Sandwiched between vertebrae are the intervertebral discs that provide shock absorption and stability to the spinal column. These discs can become injured and cause significant pain and disability. The top of the spinal column is attached to the skull, and the lower end of the column attaches to the sacrum and coccyx. The sacrum is encircled by the pelvis, which has a receptacle on each side for the head of the femur (thigh bone). The ribs attach to the thoracic vertebrae in the back and the sternum in the front. However, some ribs are called false or floating ribs, because they do not attach directly to the sternum but attach by cartilage to the other ribs to help form the entire rib cage.

The trunk muscles on the back of the body are built in layers upon layers (see figure 8.1*a*). The muscular layers are necessary and practical, because as a group they help stabilize the trunk in all planes of movement and provide additional protection to the spinal cord. Their primary job is to hold the body upright against gravity, but they also extend and rotate the neck and trunk. The numerous muscles throughout the back are named for their action, like the erector spinae (spinal extension) and rotators (spinal rotation); or for their origin and insertion point, like the semispinalis thoracis (which originates on the transverse process of the thoracic vertebrae and inserts on the spinous process of the thoracic vertebrae). The quadratus lumborum covers the area where your kidneys are and is involved in side bending and hip hiking.

The trunk musculature on the front of the body is collectively known as the abs, but actually there are a few different abdominal muscles that work together (see figure 8.1*b* on page 96). The muscle that is known as the six-pack is the rectus abdominis (RA). It flexes the trunk so that the rib cage moves toward the pelvis. It covers the so-called corset of your trunk, the transverse abdominis, which is responsible for keeping your internal organs internal. The external oblique muscle fibers stretch diagonally over each side of the trunk, assisting the rectus abdominis in trunk flexion when working together, or flexing the trunk laterally and rotating it to the other side when working unilaterally. The external oblique muscle fibers run in the opposite direction from the internal oblique muscle fibers. In addition to assisting the rectus abdominis with trunk flexion, they are lateral flexors and rotate the trunk to the same side. Table 8.2 lists the various trunk muscles and their functions.

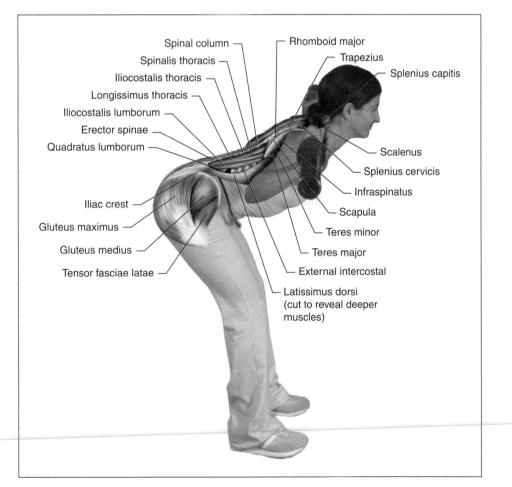

**Figure 8.1a**   Anatomy of the back.

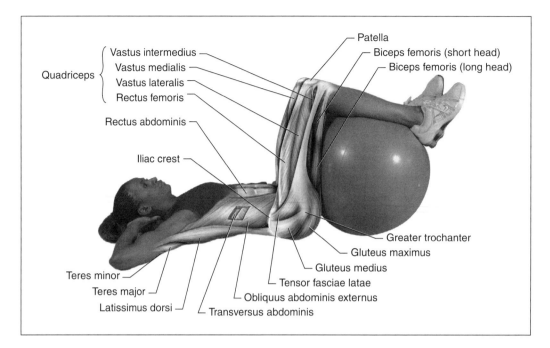

**Figure 8.1***b*　Anatomy of the abdomen.

The trunk musculature is closely associated the with hip and butt musculature. Whereas the trunk muscles attach to the top of the pelvis, the hip and butt muscles attach to the sides and bottom of the pelvis. They all need to be strong for stabilization, and they have to work in unison. Sometimes core exercises include hip and butt components for this reason.

## Table 8.2　**Trunk Muscles and Their Functions**

| Muscle | Function |
|---|---|
| Quadratus lumborum | Lateral flexion of trunk, elevation of pelvis |
| Splenius capitis, cervicis | Extension of neck, rotation of head to same side |
| Erector spinae | Extension and lateral flexion of spine |
| Semispinalis and multifidus | Extension of spine, rotation to opposite side |
| Rotatores | Extension of spine, rotation to opposite side |
| Interspinales | Extension of spine |
| Intertransversarii | Lateral flexion of spine |
| Rectus abdominis | Flexion of trunk |
| External oblique | Flexion of trunk, lateral flexion, rotation to opposite side |
| Transverse abdominis | Compression of abdominal contents |

# Creating a Functional Core

Your core strength is important for functional activities as well as sports activities. Stabilization and power come from the trunk of the body. If you had a weak, hunched-over trunk, your arms and legs wouldn't be particularly strong either. Although most sports and daily life activities require you to bend and twist your trunk in a standing position, most people don't train their abdominal muscles that way. People typically do abdominal training lying on their backs on the floor with their knees bent. Are there any sports or daily activities that require you to be in that position and use your abdominal muscles? Functional training says to choose exercises that mimic sports or activities and to train for movements, not for muscles. So if you want to improve your golf swing, you can reproduce that movement with resistive tubing or weighted cables, doing a moderate number of sets and reps to increase strength, or doing a low number with faster speed to increase power. If you want to make it easier to bend down to pick up and hold your child or to pull weeds, train your abdominal muscles in that movement pattern. Because this type of training also tends to be metabolic, you may shed some unwanted body fat, leading to quite functional-looking abs.

## Protecting the Back

At some time in their lives, virtually everyone is going to sustain a back injury. It can range from an everyday muscle strain to a larger problem like a herniated disc. Why are low back problems such a common malady? Just as there are many reasons for the injuries, there are also many ways to prevent them.

Something that many people don't consider is that from an evolutionary standpoint, we are not too far evolved from walking on all fours and using our arms to help with locomotion. As we mature as a species, the genetic traits that help us survive will outlast those that don't. Throughout evolution our vertebrae and pelvises have gotten wider and thicker to support upright posture, and our muscles have adapted. But we're not perfect yet—it stands to reason that we will encounter some challenges along the way.

Also consider that whereas our lives used to be highly active and physical, now we are quite sedentary. In the early years of human development, we had to hunt and gather our food and roam the countryside looking for food and shelter. Now we sit in the car and drive to the grocery store for a microwavable meal that we eat while sitting on our comfy couch watching television. We have gone from a life in which existing was the only exercise we needed (or had time for) to a culture in which we actually hire people to whip us into shape in our spare time.

If we haven't used them, our muscles become deconditioned; sometimes they even have a hard time fighting gravity. Our abdominal and low back muscles are sometimes called postural muscles, because their primary job is to fight gravity and keep us upright. But we have to consciously perform isometric contractions of these muscles to make our posture perfect. If we don't, we slouch. This improper posture leads to overly lengthened back muscles, shortened abdominal muscles, muscular fatigue, and injury (especially if you are calling on these muscles to do hard work like picking something heavy off the floor or playing 18 holes of golf). What if you don't keep these muscles tight throughout your strength-training sessions, even if you are not working specifically on them? If they are not strong enough to provide support during unloaded situations, then loaded situations become a recipe for disaster.

Body mechanics is how you use your body in all situations, from sitting at the computer, to playing with your children, to lifting weights. Injuries rarely occur when you use excellent technique and optimize your body mechanics. With good technique, it is impossible to lift more weight than your body is capable of lifting or to perform so-called cheating movements that could result in injury. Using your back as a lever when you are reaching down to pick something up, as opposed to bending at the knees and letting your strong thigh muscles take the burden, puts enormous pressure on the intervertebral discs and the long, thin spinal erector muscles that are not designed to withstand such forces. Repeatedly bending over from the back, day after day, is usually the cause of herniated discs. That bent-over position puts so much pressure on the low back discs that eventually they fracture and spill out into the spinal column, where they impinge on other tissues and nerves.

Finally, you must be aware of your body weight and how that weight is distributed. Is it any wonder that pregnant women complain of low back pain? They are carrying extra weight directly centered over their abdominal region. In order for their bodies to maintain a normal upright posture, they have to shift their center of gravity. This adjustment forces the low back into constant hyperextension, shortens the muscles, and impinges the vertebrae and intervertebral discs. The same holds true for any extra weight that we hold on the belly, so take care to keep your midsection trim.

The bottom line in preventing low back injury is this: Stay active; stay strong, especially in the core; stay aware of your body and the way you use it at all times (i.e., use your legs to lift); and stay lean.

## Developing the Abs

The abdominal muscles are the most talked about muscles by far. Everyone wants the perfect washboard abdomen; theories abound about how you can get it. The only problem is that there are so many myths, misunderstandings, and mysteries about abs that few people actually attain the elusive six-pack.

Common gym folklore would have you train your abs every day, doing at least 100 crunches. Some have said that abdominals and low back muscles are endurance muscles, so they can withstand that treatment and even benefit from it. However, the abdominal muscles are made up of the same muscle tissue as any other muscle; like any other muscle they should only be weight trained concentrically and eccentrically once every 48 hours at the maximum. You wouldn't dream of lifting with your legs every day, would you? Your abs need some rest to grow too. The abdominal muscles do have some endurance qualities, since they have to isometrically contract all day long to help you maintain your posture and prevent low back injury, but that work doesn't mechanically stress the muscle fibers as strength training does. When you strength train your abdominals, they hypertrophy and get stronger. When that happens, you just may start to see the six-pack.

The real reason that you don't see ripped abs on everybody, however, isn't related to the number of sit-ups they do or even the amount of weight they lift. It is all about fat. Well-defined abs are not so much a product of exercise as they are of diet. You must peel away all of the layers of body fat for the abdominal muscles to peek through. They can increase in size (hypertrophy) with exercise, but you must decrease your body fat for all of that exercise to show itself as defined abs.

What about the latest rage of doing ab work using stability balls? This is another old practice that has turned into a new training method. Physical therapists have used stability balls in therapy for years to help people with injuries or disabilities to exercise, but now such balls are popular in the gym scene. These accessories add more to your workout than variety. Performing crunch exercises on a ball increases abdominal muscular activity and places a higher demand on the motor control system than doing crunches on a stable surface. Ball use also appears to specifically strengthen the external oblique muscles significantly, even when you perform straight crunches, because of all the muscles needed to stabilize the body during the movement. Crunches on balls change both the level of muscular activity and the way that the muscles coactivate to stabilize the spine and the entire body. Definitely not a rip-off, inexpensive stability balls can help you through a low back rehabilitation program and advance you to a challenging exercise routine.

Can you really concentrate your abdominal training on just upper abs, lower abs, or obliques? There is no validity to the argument that you can train only your upper abs by doing a certain movement and only your lower abs by doing a different movement. The rectus abdominis muscle is one continuous muscle that spans the length of the abdominal area, and when it is called on to perform its job of forward trunk flexion, all of the fibers work as a unit. Indeed, even the obliques assist with trunk flexion. Certain exercises, however, emphasize more of the upper abdomen, like the partial crunch or ab-roller crunch. These exercises work on the upper abdomen because you only complete the movement partially and don't work a full range of motion. The typical exercises people do to target their lower abs, like hanging leg raises and reverse crunches, actually do not totally isolate that area. Reverse crunches may emphasize the lower part of the rectus abdominis as opposed to the upper because that is where the movement is starting, but the hip flexors play a significant role too. During hanging leg raises the abdominals work only as stabilizers, isometrically contracting to allow the hip flexors to curl the lower body. It certainly feels challenging, because it is difficult to stabilize the spine while the body is hanging without support. Rotating movements emphasize the obliques, but the rectus abdominis works during these movements also.

Pilates is a popular discipline that is based on trunk control. Instructors teach you to curl the trunk up and down, vertebra by vertebra, during abdominal exercises, while you do straight-leg sit-ups. By contrast, someone probably taught you to bend your knees to protect your low back during sit-ups, and maybe even to anchor your feet under a table or bench. However, when the feet or legs are restrained during abdominal exercises, the iliopsoas muscle group (hip flexors) is primarily working, not the abdominals. Essentially, you are bending at the hips to raise your trunk. In addition, anchoring the feet leads to an arched back and possible shearing stress on the lumbar spine; some studies have found that performing sit-ups with bent knees doesn't significantly reduce lumbar spine compression. Your feet are never glued to the ground when your trunk moves during everyday life or during sports. To prevent injury and increase performance, your trunk needs to know how to coordinate movements in real-life situations, not just in the gym.

If you are healthy and free from back problems, you need to get off the floor and experiment with some new ab exercises like those discussed in this chapter. If you are lying flat on the floor and only doing crunches, you are missing out on some important ranges of motion for strengthening and function. Maximal muscular tension is developed with a prestretch on the muscle, so try initiating the ab crunch from beyond neutral, or from about 15 degrees of hyperextension. Try using resistive tubing, weighted cables, stability balls, or a curved Roman chair. Also experiment with different functional patterns like diagonals. Such moves will not only increase the use of all of your abdominal musculature, but will also train your ab strength for use in daily activities and sports.

What is the best ab exercise you can do if you have a low back problem or are just a beginner? There is no single best exercise that recruits all of the abdominal muscles simultaneously. Your conditioning level, medical history, and progression are important to keep in mind. With that said, the straight-leg sit-up and bent-leg sit-up create the greatest muscle challenge—but they also involve the greatest lumbar compression. In other words, they may work your abdominals well but could possibly harm your spine. Perform these exercises only if you have previous training experience and don't have a low back problem. The partial crunch produces less spinal compression, but also creates less of a muscle challenge. It is a good exercise for beginners or for those with a previous back injury. One exercise that really challenges the obliques without lumbar compressive loading is one you hardly ever see people doing. The trunk side raise is performed by lying on your side and raising the torso up off a decline sit-up bench or a hyperextension bench. This exercise also strengthens the quadratus lumborum muscle of the low back, a spinal stabilizer.

## DON'T BUCKLE UP

You see them in the gym in all shapes, sizes, colors, and patterns. Every month there seems to be a new version. Women love to match them to their outfits, and men are leaving the old worn leather ones for the style and comfort of the latest model. Many think that weightlifting belts are a necessity for preventing injury in the gym, but some people use them indiscriminately and too often. The abuse of weightlifting belts may be increasing the risk of injuries instead of preventing them.

Weightlifting belts are not new. Olympic weightlifters first used them to prevent trunk hyperextension during overhead lifts. Marketers then promoted the devices to workers who lifted heavy loads daily in an industrial setting. Bodybuilders took the idea and ran with it. Once used for a specific purpose, the weightlifting belt has been turned into a fad by the bodybuilding community.

The real purpose of a belt is to provide support for the back by increasing the intra-abdominal pressure (IAP) and the intrathoracic pressure (ITP). The IAP and ITP compress or prevent the protrusion of the abdominal compartment, which in turn reduces the force the low back muscles must exert to support a heavy load. Some researchers report that reducing how hard the low back muscles have to work may prevent disc compression injuries. But if the purpose is to increase IAP and ITP by compressing the abdominal contents, not supporting the back, then why is the widest part of the belt centered on the back instead of on the abdomen? The design of the traditional weightlifting belt is all wrong.

Many studies have shown that the low back muscles are not taxed while the weightlifting belt is worn. While this effect may seem beneficial, it actually has a detrimental effect in the long run on your functional and sports activities. It may be fine to use the weightlifting belt in the gym, but what happens when you need to move a couch in your family room or pull weeds in the yard? Your abdominals and low back muscles must be strong. The constant use of a weightlifting belt during strength training can give you a false sense of security. You could then expose your spine to greater loads, increasing the potential for injury outside the gym setting in sports or other activities.

Even the National Institute for Occupational Safety and Health (NIOSH) doesn't recommend that healthy people use back belts. Studies have proven that weightlifting belts don't decrease muscular fatigue or prevent injuries. One study has even shown that holding one's breath properly during lifting increased the IAP more significantly than wearing a weightlifting belt.

Although some of the best weightlifters in the world do not use weightlifting belts, there are certain competitive weightlifting and powerlifting situations in which weightlifting belts are appropriate and beneficial. When performing a lift like the clean and jerk or the squat, weightlifting belts are effective in increasing IAP for lifts at 90 percent of the 1RM (one repetition maximum). This effect may translate into lifting heavier weights. If the lifter wears a belt in the gym with heavy loads, then she should wear it in competition (and vice versa).

# Abdominal Exercises

Each of the abdominal exercises that follow provides variations for those who are beginners, intermediate, and advanced. Only after you've mastered one form can you progress to the next. Concentrate on keeping your abdominals as tight as possible throughout the entire movement. Curl and uncurl your body slowly, vertebra by vertebra.

# STABILITY BALL STRAIGHT CRUNCH

Stability ball exercises work your entire abdominal region. The inherent instability of the ball not only forces the abdominals to work, but also the low back, glutes, and entire leg.

1. Lie back on a stability ball with the low back and midback supported by the ball. Bend the knees and keep the feet flat on the floor.

2. Place the hands in the appropriate position, depending on the level of difficulty:

   • Beginner—Position the shoulder blades just off the ball and cross the hands over the chest.

   • Intermediate—Place the hands behind the head.

   • Advanced—Place the arms straight overhead.

   • Advanced plus—Place the arms straight overhead holding a weight plate.

3. Crunch up straight to the appropriate level of strength (small range of motion for beginner level and full range of motion for intermediate and advanced) and slowly lower back down to the starting position, trying to place one vertebra at a time down on the ball.

*a*

*b*

## STABILITY BALL DIAGONAL CRUNCH

The oblique muscles get the emphasis in this exercise, but don't think that other muscles are ignored. All of the trunk and lower-body muscles get a workout to keep you balancing steadily on the ball.

1. Lie back on a stability ball with the low back and midback supported. Bend the knees and keep the feet flat on the floor.

2. Place the hands in the appropriate position depending on level of difficulty:

   • Beginner—Position the shoulder blades just off the ball and cross the hands over the chest.

   • Intermediate—Place the hands behind the head.

   • Advanced—Place the arms straight overhead.

   • Advanced plus—Place the arms straight overhead holding a weight plate.

3. Crunch up diagonally to the appropriate level of strength (small range of motion for beginner level and full range of motion for intermediate and advanced). Aim the left elbow toward the right knee.

4. Slowly lower, trying to place one vertebra at a time on the ball.

5. Crunch up diagonally, aiming the right elbow toward the left knee.

6. Slowly lower to starting position.

*a*

*b*

## STABILITY BALL PULL-IN

This exercise is a dynamic way to strengthen the abs in conjunction with the lower body. Beginners will bring the ball in only halfway to their chests, whereas intermediates can concentrate on a full range of motion (ROM). Advanced exercisers should have one leg on the ball, pulling it in toward the chest, and one leg extended straight out.

1. Get on the knees on the floor with a stability ball touching the thighs.

2. Extend the body over the ball until the hands reach the floor.

3. Slowly walk the hands out until the shins rest on the ball.

4. Tighten all muscles and hold the body like a plank.

5. Keeping the back straight, pull the toes up to hold on to the ball and pull the knees in toward the chest, allowing the ball to roll forward and underneath the body.

6. Hold for a moment and contract the abs.

7. Straighten the legs and roll the ball back to the starting position.

*a*

*b*

## STABILITY BALL REVERSE CRUNCH

This crunch is similar to the previous exercise, because you initiate the movement from the lower body instead of the upper body.

1. Lie on the back and rest the lower legs on top of a stability ball so that the ball is tucked underneath the knees. Beginners keep the arms at the sides; advanced place them behind the head.

2. Dig the heels into the ball and contract the abs to bring the knees to the chest.

3. To make it harder, lift the butt off the ground and bring the knees to the chest at the same time, while the arms are behind the head.

4. For the most advanced reverse crunch, do an upper-abdominal crunch simultaneously with the lower-abdominal crunch.

*a*

*b*

# ROMAN CHAIR LEG RAISE

This exercise is a good precursor to hanging leg raises because it gives you low back support and makes it easier for you to complete the movement.

1. Position the body comfortably in a Roman chair. Place the legs in the appropriate position depending on the level of difficulty:
   - Beginner—Bend knees.
   - Intermediate—Raise straight legs to midbody.
   - Advanced—Raise straight legs as high as possible.
2. Tighten the abs and make sure that the low back remains neutral or rounded.
3. Curl the lower body up as high as you can.
4. Hold for 1 to 2 seconds and slowly lower.

*a*

*b*

# HANGING LEG RAISE

The abdominal muscles work only as stabilizers while they isometrically contract to allow the hip flexors to curl the lower body in this exercise, but the hanging leg raise is definitely challenging because the body hangs without support. The abdominals contract concentrically and eccentrically if you are strong enough to pull the feet all the way to the head, though.

1. Hang on to a chin-up bar using an overhand grip with arms straight, shoulder-width apart, or use hanging ab straps. Place the legs in the appropriate position depending on the level of difficulty:
   - Beginner—Bend knees.
   - Intermediate—Raise straight legs to midbody.
   - Advanced—Raise straight legs as high as possible.
2. Tighten the abs and make sure that the low back remains neutral or rounded.
3. Curl the lower body up as high as you can.
4. Hold for 1 to 2 seconds and slowly lower.

*a*

*b*

# WOOD CHOP

This exercise has been adapted for strength-training purposes from the physical therapy world. It uses an upper-body diagonal pattern that is functional for real-life activities. It mimics the ancient chore of chopping wood, something that a 21st-century woman doesn't often have the opportunity to do. But if she did, she would have great abs from pulling the heavy weight down across her body.

1. Stand in between two pulley stacks, closer to the right stack. Make sure the right arm is parallel with the stack and the legs are shoulder-width apart.

2. Position a rope attachment at the top of the stack. Grab the rope from the top position with both hands.

3. Keep the arms extended and overhead, and use the midsection to pull diagonally down on the cable, across the body to the left foot. The movement simulates chopping wood, hence the name.

4. Switch and perform the exercise on the other side after each set.

*a*

*b*

## ABDOMINAL ROTATION

If you are a tennis or softball player, this exercise simulates the tennis stroke and softball swing perfectly. It is also functional in life, whenever the lower body is fixed and you have to twist the upper body.

1. Stand in the middle between two pulley stacks, arms parallel with the stacks.
2. Position a rope attachment at chest height and grasp the rope with extended arms.
3. With legs shoulder-width apart and knees slightly bent, rotate the torso 180 degrees, with the arms completely extended. Use the abdominal muscles to work against the resistance.

*a*

*b*

## TRUNK SIDE RAISE

This exercise challenges the obliques and strengthens the quadratus lumborum muscle of the low back. It is a great lower-body stabilization exercise, because it also incorporates some hip musculature.

1. Lie on your side on a decline or hyperextension bench.
2. Put the arms in the appropriate position for your skill level:
   • Beginner—Place the arms across the chest.
   • Intermediate—Place the hands behind the head.
   • Advanced—Hold a weight plate at chest level.
3. Tighten the abs and maintain a neutral spine.
4. Raise the torso up as high as possible.
5. Hold for 1 or 2 seconds.
6. Slowly lower.
7. Perform all of the repetitions on one side and then switch to the other.

# OVERHEAD THROW-DOWN

This exercise works the abdominals, quadriceps, hamstrings, pectoralis major, deltoids, and latissimus dorsi. It works the front of the body to explosively train the rectus abdominus. To explosively train the obliques, alternate from side to side.

1. With a medicine ball between the hands, raise the arms overhead.
2. Initiate a slight prestretch by moving toward full extension in the ankles, knees, hips, and shoulders.
3. Quickly change direction and slam the medicine ball against the ground.
4. Catch the ball and move rapidly toward the fully extended position to resume the start above.

*a*                    *b*                    *c*

# Low Back Exercises

The low back area tends to get ignored in exercise programs, because the clothes you wear don't usually highlight these muscles as they do, let's say, your abs. You may not look at your low back muscles as much as you do your abs or say that you wish they were more sculpted. It's fairly hard to see them at all—although there are a lot of them, they aren't particularly thick or sturdy. And although they tend to fatigue rapidly, you use them quite a bit for stabilization during other exercises and you need them for postural control throughout the day. Add these exercises to your program and consider adding deadlifts (see chapter 12) also, for a complete regimen to strengthen your low back.

## STABILITY BALL HYPEREXTENSION

When you don't have access to a hyperextension bench, this stability ball variation can come in handy. Remember on this exercise that the larger the ball, the larger the range of motion you can achieve.

1. Lie on the belly on a stability ball. Position the legs straight in back with the toes touching the ground, and place the hands behind the head with the head down.

2. Raise the upper body off the ball and slowly return. If you are a beginner, your range of motion may be smaller than if you are more advanced.

3. To make this exercise more difficult, hold a weight plate behind the head.

*a*

*b*

## PRONE LEG AND ARM EXTENSION

This exercise and its variations are adapted from physical therapy techniques for stabilizing the spine and strengthening the low back in functional diagonal patterns. Use a stability ball size that allows you to have the hands and toes comfortably touching the ground and helping you to balance.

1. Beginners start face down on the floor with the arms at the sides.

2. Tighten the abs and glutes, keep the pelvis down, and then lift one leg off the floor and lower it under control.

3. Progress to raising both legs simultaneously.

4. Intermediates should lie with the belly on a stability ball, arms outstretched over the ball with hands touching the ground, and legs straight back with toes touching the ground.

5. Raise and lower the right arm and left leg simultaneously.

6. Repeat with the left arm and right leg.

7. For a challenge, add hand and ankle weights.

8. Next try lifting both legs up and down together on the stability ball or on a reverse hyper machine.

9. For the superadvanced, just add more weight.

*a*

*b*

# BALL WALKOUT

This is a true all-over core exercise that even gives the entire body a tough workout. Take your cues from yoga and attempt to have the body become a straight plank while balancing on the ball.

1. Get on the knees on the floor with a stability ball touching the front thighs.

2. Extend over the ball until the hands reach the floor.

3. Slowly walk the hands out until you are in position on the ball, according to your strength level:

   • Beginner—Place the thighs on the ball.

   • Intermediate—Place the shins on the ball.

   • Advanced—Place the toes on the ball.

4. Tighten the abs, keep the back flat, keep the legs out straight, hold the head in a neutral position, and put the hands shoulder-width apart on the floor.

5. Hold this isometric pose for 10 seconds and then walk the arms back to return to the starting position.

*a*

*b*

## GOOD MORNING

No exercise emphasizes the tie-in between the low back, glutes, and hamstrings better than the good morning. I personally think it is called good morning because as you rise up from a bent-over position, you are tempted to utter a sarcastic "Good morning!" to the newly awakened muscle fibers in your lower body.

1. Stand with the knees slightly bent and the feet shoulder-width apart. Place a barbell across the upper back.

2. Keeping the abs tight, back flat, and knees slightly bent, inhale and slowly bend down from the hips. The goal is to have the torso parallel to the ground, but limit your range of motion at first and progress slowly. This exercise can make you very sore and if done improperly can result in injury.

3. Return to the starting position and exhale.

*a*                    *b*

# 9

# Pressing and Pulling for Power

A question one commonly asks any person who lifts weights is, How much can you bench? The answer to this question has become such a universal way of determining someone's strength that bench pressing has become almost an obligatory exercise. That many people concentrate on bench pressing is unfortunate, because aside from powerlifting, a sport in which it is a required component, you rarely use the strength gained from it functionally in sports or daily life. It certainly isn't a measure of overall strength; you don't use many muscles to do it. It is far from a total-body movement like a squat, which incorporates the upper body to maintain correct posture and to hold the barbell in place and the lower body to lower and lift the weight. It isn't a good way to measure general strength—especially for women, because our upper bodies are typically weaker in proportion to our lower bodies. We don't usually work on them as guys do. But even though you shouldn't use the bench press to gauge how strong you are, it is still a good exercise for developing upper-body strength and power, which we definitely need. However, you must use bench pressing in combination with other pressing and pulling movements to balance the entire upper-body musculature and shoulder complex.

## Understanding Shoulder Anatomy and Function

The shoulder complex is so named because of both the large area that it covers and the complexity of its anatomy and biomechanics. It includes most of the upper trunk from front to back. If you look at where the muscles involved in upper-body movement originate and attach, the bones that form the entire shoulder complex are the sternum (breastbone), clavicle (collarbone), scapula (shoulder blade), humerus (arm), cervical and thoracic vertebrae (neck and upper spine), parts of the skull, and the ribs (see figure 9.1).

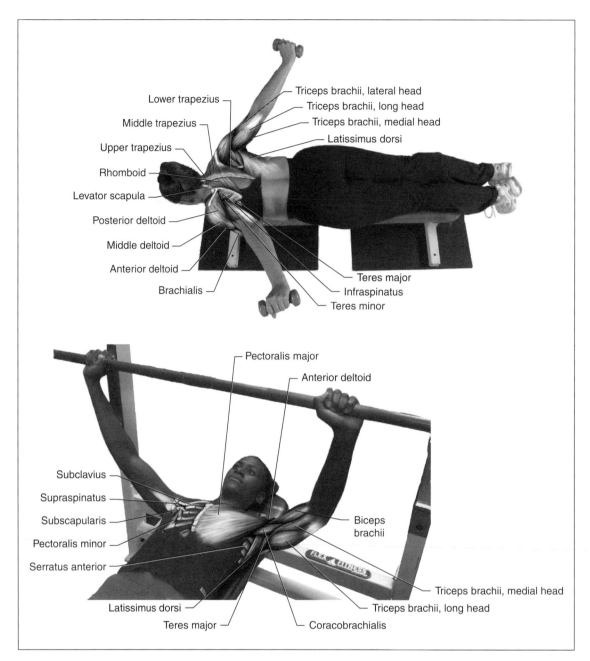

**Figure 9.1** Anatomy of the shoulder complex.

As table 9.1 details, the muscles that are involved in upper-body movement flex (move the arm up), extend (move the arm backward), abduct (move the arm away from the side of the body), adduct (move the arm toward the center of the body), internally or externally rotate the arm, protract (move the shoulder joint forward), retract (move the shoulder joint backward), elevate (move the shoulder joint up) and depress (move the shoulder joint down).

The design of the shoulder joint allows great degrees of freedom. It has the largest range of motion (ROM) of any joint in the body. Because of this mobility, though, it sacrifices some stability. The primary stabilization of the shoulder joint happens as the muscles that surround the entire joint do their job correctly. Without the forces that these muscles produce, the shoulder becomes an unstable joint that is at risk for injury, especially when you perform overhead and

## Table 9.1   Shoulder Muscles and Their Functions

| Muscle | Function |
| --- | --- |
| Upper trapezius | Elevation, upward rotation of scapula |
| Middle trapezius | Retraction of scapula |
| Lower trapezius | Depression, upward rotation of scapula |
| Latissimus dorsi | Extension, hyperextension, internal rotation, and adduction of humerus |
| Teres major | Extension, internal rotation, and adduction of humerus |
| Levator scapula | Elevation and downward rotation of scapula |
| Rhomboids | Retraction and downward rotation of scapula |
| Anterior deltoid | Flexion, horizontal adduction, and internal rotation of humerus |
| Middle deltoid | Abduction of humerus to 90 degrees |
| Posterior deltoid | Extension, horizontal abduction, and external rotation of humerus |
| Coracobrachialis | Flexion and adduction of humerus |
| Supraspinatus (rotator cuff muscle) | Stabilization of head of humerus to initiate abduction and external rotation of humerus |
| Infraspinatus (rotator cuff muscle) | External rotation and extension of humerus |
| Teres minor (rotator cuff muscle) | External rotation and extension of humerus |
| Subscapularis (rotator cuff muscle) | Internal rotation of humerus |
| Pectoralis major | Adduction, horizontal adduction, and internal rotation of humerus<br>Clavicular head: flexion of humerus<br>Sternal head: extension of humerus from a flexed position |
| Pectoralis minor | Protraction, depression, and downward rotation of scapula |
| Subclavius | Stabilization of clavicle |
| Serratus anterior | Protraction and upward rotation of scapula, stabilization of scapula against chest wall |
| Biceps brachii (short head) | Flexion of humerus |
| Triceps brachii (long head) | Extension of humerus, depression and downward rotation of scapula |

rotational movements. The key to having healthy shoulders and super upper-body strength is to balance the upper-body muscles so that they can work synergistically.

The scapula is a flat, triangular bone that has two prominent projections on the top called the acromion process and the coracoid process. You can find your acromion process by following your clavicle out to the end of your shoulder. That bony projection is the acromion process, and the joint located there is the acromioclavicular (AC) joint. Just below and to the inside of the AC joint is the coracoid process. On the outside of the scapula is a slight cavity where the head of the humerus is located. A bony projection on the side of the humerus, called the greater tuberosity, is a site for muscular attachment. The front of the humerus contains a groove where the head of the biceps tendon rests.

Ligaments are strong bands of tissue that connect bones. Many ligaments add degrees of stability to the shoulder, but the coracoacromial ligament is the most talked about because it is the one primarily involved in shoulder impingement (which is discussed in detail later). The coracoacromial ligament connects the acromion process to the coracoid process and makes a roof inside the shoulder. The shoulder capsule is a fibrous but loose sleeve that surrounds the humeral head and is reinforced with ligaments.

The space beneath the acromion is called the subacromial space. The coracoacromial ligament is the roof of the space and the top of the humeral head is the floor. The subacromial space available varies with shoulder movement and steadily decreases as the arm is elevated and as the joint ages. Located inside this space are the subacromial bursa (a small fluid-filled sac that protects tendons from the hard surfaces of bones, allows them to glide smoothly during movement, and provides nutrition), the rotator cuff tendons, and the long head of the biceps tendon.

We live in a sedentary and flexion-biased society. For the majority of the day, we are sitting—whether in the car, at a desk at work, or at home on the couch. We usually do things in front of our body as we lean forward, ever so slightly. Even as you read this book right now, quickly check your posture. Of course, the minute I mentioned posture you probably straightened right up. But before that, more than likely your head was forward, your shoulders were rounded, and your arms were out in front of you. Don't feel bad—such posture is a natural and typical part of our lifestyle. But because of this lifestyle the muscles on the front of our upper body are contracted and shortened and the muscles on our upper back are relaxed and lengthened. Also, such posture reduces the already small space that we have in between the humeral head and the coracoacromial ligament, where all of our rotator cuff tendons and bursa are found, which in turn leads to many common complaints of neck and shoulder pain. When we throw in all of the repetitive motions we do during the day and then add sports and exercise to the mix, we can exacerbate the problem and cause a clinical condition like shoulder impingement. In addition, many sports are flexion-biased and most people concentrate on their fronts (the so-called beach muscles) at the gym—the chest muscles, shoulders, biceps, and abdominal muscles.

Shoulder impingement is the trapping of the rotator cuff tendons, the subacromial bursa, or the biceps tendon in the subacromial space. It progresses in stages and starts with inflammation that is reversible, but that can lead to irreversible thickening of the bursa, tendinitis of the rotator cuff, rotator cuff tears, and bony changes like spurs on the acromion process. Signs and symptoms of shoulder impingement are anterior shoulder pain during movements of flexion, abduction, or rotation; weakness of the rotator cuff muscles; and limited range of motion in the shoulder.

As with many syndromes, the causes of shoulder impingement can be multifactorial (because poor posture increases muscular weakness) and one problem frequently leads to another (because muscular weakness can result in muscular tears). The causative factors can be either intrinsic, pertaining to the muscles of the shoulder joint, or extrinsic, applying to other structures like bones, ligaments, and capsules. Intrinsic factors are muscular weakness, muscular overuse, and muscular degeneration. For example, poor posture contributes to muscular weakness or imbalance, which destabilizes the humerus. This instability can cause the top of the humeral head to bump into the coracoacromial ligament and put pressure on the tendons and bursa in the subacromial space. Muscular overuse that leads to inflammation of tendons also decreases this already small space. In late-stage impingements the constant inflammation leads to degeneration and tendon tears. These problems further weaken the joint and allow excessive movement of the humeral head, which then leads to more trauma.

Extrinsic factors are acromion shape, degeneration of the acromioclavicular joint, and tightness or laxity of the ligaments or the capsule. For example, acromion processes can have three different shapes in different people: flat, curved, or hooked. The hooked acromions are associated with a higher prevalence of rotator cuff tears, because they decrease the subacromial space and can slice at the tendon. Arthritis that causes degenerative spurs to form on the underside of the acromion leaves even less space available for movement without impingement. When the ligaments and capsule of the shoulder are lax, the humerus is unstable. Just as weak muscles do, this instability allows the humeral head to move excessively and damage the rotator cuff tendons and bursa. On the other hand, if the capsule and ligaments are too tight, there won't be enough space available for all of the structures to move without compression.

Finding out what is causing the problem through a physical therapist is crucial for treating the impingement appropriately. A case of tight musculature not letting natural glide occur might mean stretching, whereas a problem caused by joint instability and weak musculature might call for some specific strengthening exercise.

# Building Resilient Shoulders

Shoulder impingement can be treated. You first have to calm down the painful symptoms and then determine why the pain occurred. When your shoulder is in pain, rest, ice, and nonsteroidal anti-inflammatory drugs (NSAIDS) such as ibuprofen can help to decrease the pain and inflammation, but these alone won't solve your problem. Strengthening, increasing flexibility, improving mechanics, maintaining good posture, and using a sound training program are beneficial and may reverse the syndrome. Focus on the reason for the impingement. If it is an overuse syndrome, rest and make alterations to your lifestyle to address that overuse. If muscular weakness or imbalance is the culprit, specific exercises will address strengthening the rotator cuff and other scapular stabilizer muscles. If posture is a problem, upper-back strengthening plus body awareness is the key.

Several exercises can help prehabilitate and rehabilitate the shoulder and help improve posture. Prehabilitate means doing these exercises as preventative medicine before an injury even occurs. Hopefully by doing these exercises, both you and your shoulder joint can bear up under the weight of the world.

## SCAPULAR RETRACTION

Your mother's advice about standing up straight was right. With proper posture, all of the head, neck, and upper-back musculature work together. This harmony leads to a kinetic chain effect that activates your entire body to keep your posture perfect.

1. Stand up tall and squeeze the shoulder blades back.
2. Hold the contraction for 5 seconds as if there is a winning lottery ticket between the shoulder blades.
3. Repeat throughout the day and you'll get posture that a mother will love.

## SCAPTION

Scaption is the plane of motion that the scapula moves in. This motion is important because it helps the shoulder joint achieve healthy mechanics. The scaption exercise primarily works the supraspinatus muscle, part of the rotator cuff. Do this exercise standing in front of a mirror to monitor your form.

1. Hang the arms down by the thighs and supinate both hands to a thumbs-up position.
2. Retract and depress the scapulas as you lift the arms up to shoulder-height at a 45-degree angle from the trunk. The arms should make a Y in front of you. Make sure that the upper trapezius isn't pulling the shoulders into the ears. If it is, work on pulling the shoulders down in order to push the arms up.
3. Perform 2 to 3 sets of 8 reps.

*a*        *b*

From barbell to dumbbell to cable rows, nothing beats a good rhomboid workout for shoulder health. To round out a shoulder health routine, see the many varieties of rows on pages 131 and 133.

## CEILING PUNCH

If your shoulder blades look like chicken wings sticking out from your back, then this exercise is for you. Scapulas wing out when the muscle attached to the underside is weak. This weak musculature could lead to poor posture and shoulder injuries. You'll be using the muscles (serratus and subscapularis) that hold your scapula down on your ribcage wall.

1. Lie flat on the back on a bench.
2. Squeeze the shoulder blades back and bring one arm up to shoulder level.
3. Keep the arm straight and elbow locked while you protract the shoulder to "punch the ceiling."
4. Retract the shoulder to the start position.
5. Repeat with the opposite arm.
6. After you can do 2 to 3 sets of 8 reps with each arm, add a dumbbell.

# Ys, Ts, AND Is

This exercise works the rhomboids and the upper, middle, and lower trapezius muscles. These muscles all insert on the scapula. Proper movement and strength of the scapula is essential for injury prevention and rehabilitation. For the entire routine, make the scapulas do the lifting—the arms are just along for the ride. If you are a beginner, your range of motion for this exercise may be smaller than for a more experienced lifter. Don't worry—you will continue to improve your range of motion as you gain more experience with this exercise.

1. Lie on the belly on a flat bench (or on a stability ball if you are already experienced with this exercise).

2. For the first movement, hang the arms down at the sides, off the bench, and rotate them so that the thumbs are up and leading the way. Squeeze the scapulas together and then lift both arms up toward the head so that you make the letter Y with the arms; slowly lower and repeat.

3. For the next movement, hang the arms down at the sides, off the bench, with the palms down. Squeeze the scapulas and raise the arms out to the side to make the letter T; lower and repeat.

4. For the third movement, start with the arms hanging down at the sides, off the bench, with the thumbs pointing down. Lift the arms backward as close to the body as possible, making the letter I; lower and repeat.

5. Progress slowly with light weights and concentrate on squeezing the scapulas first. Go for 2 to 3 sets of 8 reps for each movement.

a

b

c

## STRAIGHT-ARM LAT PULLDOWN

This exercise uses the lats, but the rhomboids also come into play. When you do the exercise, the humeral head glides down. This gliding reinforces proper shoulder mechanics and prevents injury.

1. Use a straight bar on a high cable.
2. From a standing position, grasp the bar with both arms, slightly wider than shoulder-width, and lock the elbows.
3. Keeping the body upright and the abdominals tight, retract the scapulas and pull the bar down to the thighs.
4. Slowly allow the bar to return to the starting position.
5. Perform 2 to 3 sets of 8 reps.

a

b

## INTERNAL AND EXTERNAL ROTATION

The rotator cuff muscles are responsible for internal and external rotation. They are dynamic muscles, but most of the time we train them quite statically. Of course, if you already have shoulder pathology, then perform these exercises statically, side-lying on a bench with the shoulder held tight to the body. Diagonal patterns are functional for real-life activities and appeal to the muscle's sensory receptors. Perform two external rotation (ER) exercises for every one internal rotation (IR) exercise that you do, to balance a flexion-biased life.

1. Stand in between two pulley stacks, closer to the right stack. The right arm should be parallel with the stack, the legs shoulder-width apart.
2. For internal rotation (IR) of the right shoulder, position a rope attachment at the top of the stack. Grab the rope from the top position with the right hand.
3. Keeping the arm extended and the trunk erect, pull down diagonally on the cable, across the body toward the left hip, for internal rotation of the right arm. Slowly return.
4. For external rotation (ER) of the right shoulder, stand closer to the left stack. Position a rope at the bottom of the stack.
5. Grab the rope and stand up tall. Keep the trunk erect. The right arm should be diagonal across the body.
6. Pull the rope on a diagonal, with arm fully extended, to a fully overhead position.
7. Switch to the left arm and position yourself accordingly (for ER you will pull from the bottom right, for IR you will pull from the top left).
8. Try 2 sets of 8 reps of external rotation exercise and 1 set of internal rotation exercise.

# Developing Symmetrical Shoulders

Attaining safe and symmetrical shoulders requires taking the whole upper body into account during training. The upper-body muscles are intended to work as a unit. When one muscle is pushing, the muscle on the opposite side of the joint should be pulling to keep the shoulder stabilized. If the head of the humerus (which connects at the shoulder joint) is unstable and clunks around inside the joint capsule, the rotator cuff muscles had better help it out or pain and damage can occur. You may decide that improved posture and shoulder health is one of your goals. If so, you should consider adding the pre- and rehabilitation exercises to your overall training program (see chapter 7). And if you are new to strength training, an ounce of prevention can lead to a pound of cure.

Balance between pressing and pulling movements and between elevating and depressing movements should always be a characteristic of training. To help achieve this balance, we have to emphasize upper-back training over chest training. Because we spend most of our lives hunched over a computer keyboard, the steering wheel, or our kitchen counter with poor posture, we need to work the upper-back muscles that have been lazy and stretched out all day. If we train the chest too much, we force our bodies even more into that poor posture. You should also be wary of training your shoulder elevation muscles (upper trapezius and levator scapulae) too much, because they get plenty of work during the day. They are also known as tension muscles or phone muscles. When you are stressed these muscles tense, and when you are doing other things with your hands, these muscles hold your phone securely. Either train the upper back for twice a week and the chest only once, or include more upper-back exercises than chest exercises in your routine. If you train chest and back in the same session, make sure that you end with a back movement (see pulling exercises starting on page 130) to emphasize good posture and reinforce a healthy shoulder joint.

## Pressing for Perfect Pecs and Shoulders

You probably read this far because you thought that I was going to give you a miraculous exercise to increase your bust, right? Unfortunately there isn't one, since breast tissue is just fat. But you can get that fat to look a little perkier by training the muscle underneath it, the pectoral muscle. The pec is a huge muscle with fibers that run from the top of the arm to the bottom of the sternum. The connection with the arm is important, because at that spot the pec comes into contact with the anterior deltoid. These two muscles work together to flex the arm.

## PUSH-UP

Women seldom do enough body-weight lifting, if they do any at all. In theory, you should be able to lift your own body weight before you add weight to your exercise. But this theory isn't exactly true, because you can do many exercises to strengthen individual body parts before you attempt a body-weight lift. I've included both the standard push-up and some variations for those who can't yet do this body-weight exercise.

### Standard

1. Position the hands on the floor, slightly wider than the shoulders. The elbows are bent and the forearms are parallel to the floor.
2. Keep the legs hip-width apart and balance the lower body on the balls of the feet.
3. Form a straight line with the body from the head to the feet and keep the abs tight.
4. Inhale and hold.
5. While exhaling, push the entire body up as a unit until the elbows are straight.
6. Inhale as you slowly lower the body down until the forearms are parallel to the ground.

### Close Grip

A close grip push-up focuses much more on the triceps muscles than the pecs. You bring the hands in close together so that the pec muscles are no longer in a mechanical position to do as much work. The close grip is great as an upper-arm exercise too, because it works the triceps under that wavy skin area on the upper arm. It is also a nice adjunct to a powerlifting routine to help lock out a bench press.

1. Perform the standard push-up with the hands directly underneath the shoulders or touching each other.
2. Instead of letting the elbows angle out slightly during the exercise, keep them close to the body.

a

b

## Legs on Stability Ball

For those who cannot do a conventional push-up, the stability ball will assist you as you get stronger. And for those who can, the balance and stability required on the ball will challenge you. Walk out farther so that the ball travels lower down your body to increase the difficulty. Once your feet are on the stability ball, this exercise is even more difficult than a conventional push-up. If you are really strong, you can try one leg on the ball and one leg in the air.

a

b

1. Start on the knees on the floor with a stability ball touching the front thighs.
2. Extend the body over the ball until the hands reach the floor.
3. Slowly walk the hands out and allow the legs to straighten until the pelvis rests on the ball.
4. Tighten the abs, keep the legs together and straight, and place the hands shoulder-width apart on the floor.
5. Bend the elbows and slowly lower the chest to the ground.
6. Extend the elbows to return to the starting position.

## Hands on Stability Ball

Try this exercise to stimulate your neuromuscular system. Your body is used to doing push-ups on a stable surface, so shake things up a bit, literally, and put the hands on an unstable surface like a stability ball. You can make this exercise even more difficult with one leg on the ground and one in the air.

1. Lie with the chest on top of a stability ball, legs out straight and slightly apart behind you, toes curled under on the floor.
2. Grasp the ball on the sides with an open palm. Keeping the back flat and abs tight, push the chest off the ball.
3. Slowly lower to a light touch on the ball and then repeat.

a

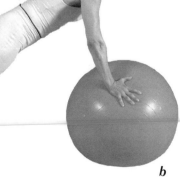

b

## BARBELL BENCH PRESS

The barbell bench press can be done on a flat, incline, or decline bench. The flat bench primarily emphasizes the anterior deltoid, mid-pectoralis, and triceps muscles. The incline bench tends to put more stress on the top portion of the pectoralis and the decline bench tends to put more stress on the lower portion of the pectoralis. Rotate your bench choices to provide variety in your program.

1. Lie on the back on a bench with the knees bent to 90 degrees and the feet firmly on the floor. If the feet do not reach the ground, only then may you put them on the bench. The barbell should be directly over the eyes.

2. Arch the back slightly (such that the back is not completely flat, neutral, or rounded), tighten the abs, and retract the scapulas. Make sure that the gluteal muscles stay in contact with the bench throughout the lift.

3. Grasp the bar with an overhand grip, slightly wider than shoulder-width.

a

4. Press the bar up to release it from the rack, then lock the elbows. Bring the bar into position directly above the neck.

5. Inhale and hold your breath as you lower the bar to the upper chest, just above the nipple line.

6. Reverse directions and forcefully exhale as you push the barbell back up.

b

## DUMBBELL BENCH PRESS

As with the barbell bench press, this exercise can be done on a flat, incline, or decline bench depending on what muscular focus you want (see the descriptions with the barbell bench press). Be sure to rotate the bench choices to provide variety in your program.

1. Grasp dumbbells with an overhand grip and lie on the back on a bench, with the knees bent to 90 degrees and the feet firmly on the floor. If the feet do not reach the ground, only then can you put them on the bench. The shoulder and elbow joints should both be at a 90-degree angle.

2. Arch the back slightly, tighten the abs, and retract the scapulas. Make sure that the glutes stay in contact with the bench throughout the lift. Inhale and hold your breath.

3. Forcefully exhale as you push the dumbbells straight up until the elbows are locked.

4. Inhale as you slowly lower the dumbbells to the starting position.

*a*                                                                          *b*

## STABILITY BALL BENCH PRESS

For this variation you must lower the normal weight you lift in the bench press by 5 to10 pounds. This double-duty exercise works the lower body and core muscles as well as the chest. You can also try a top-hold bench press on a stability ball or flat bench by holding one arm up in the air at all times while the other comes down and up.

1. Sit on top of a stability ball holding the dumbbells.
2. Walk the feet out as you recline back on the ball until only the shoulders are on the ball.
3. Make sure that the glutes and abs are tight and that your body is in a straight line.
4. Perform the dumbbell bench press set.
5. Bring the dumbbells back in close to the chest as you walk the feet back in and curl up.

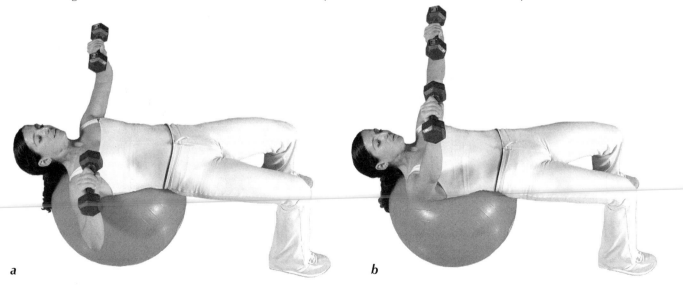

*a*                                                                          *b*

## BARBELL OVERHEAD FRONT PRESS

This exercise is typically used to improve the anterior deltoid shoulder muscles, but it also uses all three triceps heads. It builds shoulder strength for when you need it the most—whenever you reach overhead.

1. Squeeze the shoulder blades back hard and hold them together throughout the entire lift.
2. From a standing position, grasp a barbell slightly wider than shoulder-width using a pronated grip, with the elbows pointed downward and to the front. The bar should rest on hyperextended hands at the clavicle level. In this ready position, inhale.
3. Exhale as you drive the bar overhead until the elbows are fully extended. Keep the bar balanced and under control. Hold for 1 to 2 seconds at the top and squeeze the triceps.
4. Slowly lower the bar to the starting position while inhaling.

a

b

# PUSH PRESS

Use some leg drive in this exercise to power through your overhead weight plateaus. The push press is essentially the same movement as the overhead front press, but you can move more weight with the help of the legs. This exercise is explosive and plyometric.

1. Squeeze the shoulder blades back hard and hold them together throughout the entire lift.

2. From a standing position, grasp a barbell slightly wider than shoulder-width using an overhand grip, with elbows pointed downward and forward. The bar should rest on hyperextended hands at the clavicle level. In this ready position, inhale.

3. Bend the knees slightly and keep the hips and back straight to go down only 3 to 4 inches into a quarter-squat position.

4. From this quarter-squat position, exhale and explosively extend the knees and hips. Use this momentum to drive the bar overhead until the elbows are fully extended. Keep the bar balanced and under control.

5. Slowly lower the bar to the starting position while inhaling.

*a*

*b*

*c*

## POWER JERK

Like the overhead press, this explosive version is the ending part of the clean and jerk. Weightlifters frequently use it as a training tool.

1. From a standing position with the feet hip-width apart, grasp a barbell slightly wider than shoulder-width using an overhand grip, with the elbows pointed downward and forward. Rest the bar on hyperextended hands at the clavicle level. In this ready position, inhale.

*a*

2. Quickly bend the knees as if going into a squat position, but go down only about 3 to 4 inches.

3. Abruptly change direction from this quarter-squat position, exhaling and explosively extending the knees and hips while jumping the feet from hip-width to shoulder-width. Use this momentum to drive the bar overhead until the elbows are fully extended. The jump should occur simultaneously with the overhead arm extension. The feet should reach their final position just as the arms lock out the weight overhead. Keep the bar balanced and under control.

4. Slowly lower the bar to the starting position while inhaling.

5. Return the feet to the starting position.

*b*

*c*

# SPLIT JERK

Primarily an overhead lift, the split jerk also incorporates the entire body to a large degree. Get ready to train the legs when you train the upper body with this exercise.

1. From a standing position with the feet hip-width apart, grasp a barbell slightly wider than shoulder-width using an overhand grip, with elbows pointed downward and forward. Rest the bar on hyperextended hands at the clavicle level. In this ready position, inhale.

2. Quickly bend the knees as if going into a squat position, but go down only about 3 to 4 inches.

3. Abruptly change direction from this quarter-squat position, exhaling and explosively extending the knees and hips while jumping the feet to a split squat position. Use this momentum to drive the bar overhead until the elbows are fully extended. Time the jump so that the feet land in the split squat position while the arms reach full extension. Keep the bar balanced and under control.

4. Push off the front leg and take one step back, then push off the back leg and take one step forward. The feet should be in the starting position.

5. Slowly lower the bar to the starting position while inhaling.

*a*

## DUMBBELL OVERHEAD PRESS

The dumbbell overhead press has several variations. All of these exercises can be performed either seated or standing. With seated exercises you will be able to handle more weight if you lean back against a pad. With a standing or seated unsupported press you'll need more muscles for stabilization, and the extra work will demand lighter weights. All overhead pressing movements require muscles on both sides of the shoulder joint to fire, but they primarily recruit the deltoids. The main exercise, pictured, is the bilateral dumbbell overhead press. I follow that exercise with some good variations to try.

*a*                    *b*

1. Hold one dumbbell in each hand at shoulder height using a pronated grip, with the elbows pointed downward and to the sides. In this ready position, inhale.

2. Exhale as you drive both dumbbells overhead until the elbows are fully extended. Keep the head upright and in a neutral position. At no time should you bend it forward.

3. Slowly lower the dumbbells to the starting position while inhaling.

Try these variations of the dumbbell overhead press.

Alternating unilateral—Set up like a bilateral, except that you raise and lower one dumbbell, then the other.

Unilateral—Do all of your reps on one arm, then the other.

Top hold—Extend both dumbbells overhead. Hold one there while you bring one down and then back up. Hold that dumbbell overhead while you bring the other down and then up.

## Pulling for Precise Back Balance

Pulling movements for the upper body are really the most important movements you can do for your entire body and for your shoulder joint. Because most of our days are spent in flexion, hunched over a computer terminal or the wheel of the car, when we pull the upper body back we can correct the entire body alignment. Although pulling movements are not normally associated with the shoulder, you've seen how the condition of the upper-back muscles can affect shoulder health.

# BARBELL ROW

The barbell row not only works the rhomboids during the row, but also works the core muscles to stabilize the trunk. This exercise can carry over to everyday functioning, such as the act of picking up something from the floor while bending at the hips instead of the      knees.

1. Put a barbell in a rack that is level with the thighs.

2. From a standing position, grasp the barbell with an overhand grip, arms and legs shoulder-width apart, and take it out of the rack.

3. Bend over from the hips with the abs tight and a slight arch in the back. Bend the knees slightly.

4. Retract the scapulas and row the barbell toward the lower chest, keeping the elbows tight to the sides.

5. Slowly return to the starting position. Avoid using momentum with rocking or swinging motions.

*a*                *b*

*a*

*b*

# DUMBBELL ROW

Like the barbell row, the dumbbell row works the rhomboids and core musculature. Beginners should concentrate on form and put the knee and hand on a bench for stability. Angle a bench along a mirror lengthwise so that, with a slight turn of the head, you can see your body. As you progress, increase your ROM and low back involvement by having both feet on the ground and only one hand or no hands on the bench. Eventually you can try putting one knee on a stability ball or stand on one leg and row with the opposite arm.

1. Stand next to the middle of the right side of the bench, with the left leg touching the bench and a dumbbell in the right hand.

2. Start with the abs tight, the low back slightly arched, the head in a neutral position, and the body bent over from the hips.

3. Put the left knee on the bench and allow the left hand to rest on the front of the bench.

4. Start the row by retracting the scapulas and bringing the weight all the way to the chest. Keep the arm close to the trunk of the body.

5. Slowly lower and repeat.

## PULL-UP AND CHIN-UP

Body-weight exercises like the pull-up and chin-up usually prove difficult for women to do, so I've included them. Pull-ups emphasize the lats, since you do them with an overhand grip and the hands wide apart. Because you do chin-ups with an underhand grip and the arms closer together, they also involve the biceps to a great extent. Beginners can use an assistive machine to help perform partial range of movement (ROM) pull-ups and chin-ups. As you become more advanced you can decrease assistance, increase ROM, and slow down the eccentric phase of the movement by adding in stops.

1. Jump up to grasp a pull-up bar with an overhand grip (palms down) slightly wider than shoulder-width for pull-ups, and with an underhand grip (palms up) shoulder-width apart for chin-ups. The closer the hands are, the more the biceps involvement.

2. Start from a full hanging position to work the back muscles throughout a full ROM.

3. Retract the scapulas, arch the back slightly, focus on the lats, and pull the body up, trying to touch the chest to the bar.

4. Slowly lower yourself back down in the eccentric phase.

*a*

*b*

# CABLE ROW

Cables are great because you can isolate muscles and train them in functional patterns. Cable rows are especially functional, because it's common to have to grab something with one arm and pull it toward you. And most of the time it happens on one leg, when you aren't balanced and don't see the need coming. When doing these exercises you have an array of cable attachments that you can use as handles. Some will stress different muscles more than others, and you should try them all so that you can get a feel for the motion. Of course you'll have your favorites, but remember that it's always a good idea to change things up.

1. Set up using a seated position (once you are more advanced you can try the exercise standing on both legs and then standing on one leg).

2. Keep the abs tight, the low back slightly arched, and the entire torso upright.

3. Lean forward from the hips to grasp the handles and return to the upright position.

4. Retract the scapulas and row toward the chest, pulling the handles back as far as possible while keeping the arms close to the body. The pulling or rowing motion should come from the upper back, not the arms or low back. Don't jerk the body backward to complete the movement.

5. Slowly allow the arms to extend to return the handles to the starting upright position. As you become more advanced, you can try using one arm at a time.

a

b

## LAT PULLDOWN

Controversy abounds on whether to perform upper-body presses or pulldowns behind or in front of the neck. The truth is that if there are no preexisting problems and if you follow proper form, behind-the-neck pulldowns are fine. But the excessive external rotation that is required with behind-the-neck exercises is potentially dangerous to the shoulder. It is also possible to sustain neck injury during behind-the-neck presses, if you bend your neck excessively forward. If you decide to do behind the back pulldowns, just lean the entire torso forward so that the bar can clear your head. You may want to mix it up by trying some sets in front and some sets in back of the neck for variety. Maintain pain-free movement and have a spotter watch your form.

1. Start by grasping the lat pulldown bar with an overhand grip slightly wider than shoulder-width.
2. Sit down and position the thighs under the pads, keeping the feet flat on the floor.
3. For pulldowns to the front, lean the torso slightly backward from the hips. For pulldowns to the back, lean the torso slightly forward from the hips.
4. Retract the scapulas and pull the bar down to the upper chest or to the back of the neck, pause, and return. Concentrate on having the upper back pull, not the arms.

*a*

*b*

# 10

# Arming Your Biceps and Triceps

I f I were writing this book for guys, the chapter on arms would be the longest one. Some authors devote entire books to this all-time favorite subject. As soon as someone says, "Make a muscle," guys do not hesitate to roll up their sleeves and flash their biceps. They even have pet names for biceps like guns, cannons, and peaks. But women often find themselves trying to hide their upper arms, feeling they are too flabby. Well, curls are for girls too and triceps training can be terrific. In women's upper bodies, the arms and hands always seem to be the weakest links. It's time to change that and create the strong, sexy arms that say, "We strength train, and we can make a muscle worth looking at, too."

## Understanding Arm Anatomy and Function

The arm consists of the long humerus bone and the forearm bones, the radius and the ulna. The connection between the humerus and forearm bones forms the elbow joint. The metacarpal bones form the wrist, the carpals form the hand, and the phalanges form the fingers and thumbs. Important bony projections on the humerus serve as locations for muscle and ligament attachments and can also be the sites for injury. When the arm is in the anatomical position (palms up), the medial epicondyle is the rounded part of the bone on the inside of the elbow and the lateral epicondyle is the one on the outside. These two sites are attachment points for the medial and lateral collateral ligaments that hold the humerus to the radius and ulna. They are also the points where many wrist and finger flexor and extensor muscles originate. Since many of these muscles attach at the same site, their tendons (which attach muscle to bone) are often referred to in groups: the common extensor tendons (CET) and the common flexor tendons (CFT).

The muscles of the arm can bend (flex) and extend (straighten) the elbow and supinate (rotate the palm up), and pronate (rotate the palm down) the forearm; they can also flex, extend, abduct (bring the body part away from the midline of the body) and adduct (bring the body part toward the midline of the body) the wrist and fingers. The thumb and little finger have their own movement, called opposition, which allows us to hold on to objects. The muscles in the hand are highly specialized and coordinated. Although they are small, they pack a wallop. They can do intricate movements such as playing the piano or typing, and they can perform gross motor movements such as hanging on to a pulldown bar or holding a bag of groceries. Figure 10.1 shows the many muscles and bones of the arm. Table 10.1 describes the functions of these muscles.

Some say that two heads are better than one. If that is true, then three heads will surely crush the competition. In Latin, *biceps* means two heads and *triceps* means three heads. The biceps muscle has two tendons that attach in different places and also two different muscle bellies or heads that arise from these tendons, but these two muscles join together to share a common

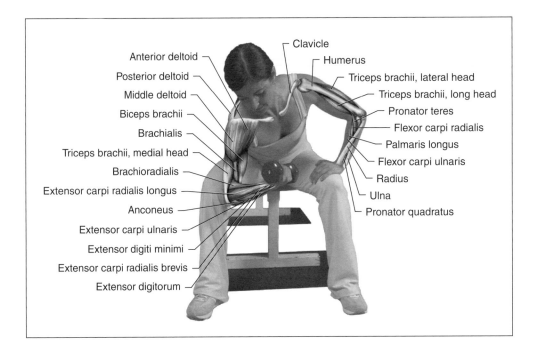

**Figure 10.1**   Muscles and bones of the arm and hand.

## Table 10.1   **Arm Muscles and Their Functions**

| Muscle | Function |
| --- | --- |
| Biceps brachii (long head) | Flexion and supination of elbow |
| Brachialis | Flexion of elbow in all positions, but especially when the forearm is pronated |
| Brachioradialis | Flexion of elbow when the forearm is neutral |
| Triceps brachii and anconeus | Extension of elbow |
| Pronator teres and pronator quadratus | Pronation of forearm |
| Extensor carpi radialis longus Extensor carpi radialis brevis Extensor carpi ulnaris | Extension of wrist |
| Extensor digitorum Extensor digiti minimi | Extension of fingers and thumb |
| Flexor carpi ulnaris Palmaris longus Flexor carpi radialis | Flexion of wrist |

tendon insertion on the forearm. The same is true for the triceps, except that it originates from three tendons and has three different heads that join together for a common tendon insertion on the elbow. This anatomy is nice to know, but how does it affect your training? It should have an impact on the variety of exercises you do. Because of the different origins of the heads, you need to train these muscles using different exercises and angles to emphasize each head.

The tendon of the short head of the biceps muscle attaches on the coracoid process of the scapula and assists with both flexion of the humerus at the shoulder joint and flexion of the elbow. The long head of the biceps tendon travels through the bicipital groove of the humerus and attaches to the top of the scapula at the shoulder joint, but has no action at that joint. It just flexes the elbow and supinates the forearm. Therefore, to work both biceps heads you must not only do elbow flexion and forearm supination exercises (like a standard biceps curl), but also add some humerus flexion to the mix. Usually when we do biceps curls we get in a little bit of humerus flexion anyway. You can add a little extra arm flexion to work on the short head by moving your humerus up slightly as you flex your elbows. So instead of aiming for your chest, you are aiming for your eyes. Realize that any humerus flexion movement you do will involve the biceps short head as well.

All three triceps heads extend the elbow, but the long head that attaches to the bottom of the scapula also helps to extend the humerus. It receives more stress when you bring your arm slightly backward during an exercise, as when you do a one-arm cable pushdown (see page 147) with a reverse grip, in which you get some shoulder extension with the elbow extension. The lateral head of the triceps attaches on the back of the humerus and seems to work hard no matter what elbow extension exercise that you do.

The medial head is buried beneath the lateral head and is equally accentuated during many elbow extension exercises. Of these exercises, the overhead cable extension exercises (see page

## TRAINING AROUND TENNIS ELBOW

Ever had elbow pain that just wouldn't quit and always got worse whenever you had to grip something, type, or do any motion with your hand? If so, you may have had tennis elbow, even if you don't play tennis. Tennis elbow doesn't just occur in tennis players, but was so named because the injury happened to increase as tennis grew in popularity. The medical term is lateral epicondylitis, which refers to an inflammation of the tendons that originate on the lateral epicondyle of the humerus, just next to the elbow joint. It sounds strange that wrist or finger movements might give you pain around your elbow, but it makes anatomical sense. These tendons are the attachment for the wrist and finger extensor muscles. As a matter of fact, they are frequently called the common extensor tendon (CET) because numerous tendons all attach at the same site.

Lateral epicondylitis has been blamed on many factors, but overall it seems to be a result of overuse or what is called a repetitive strain injury. When you overuse the wrist extensor muscles, or if you use improper technique or poor mechanics, injury results. As with any injury, the offending activity needs to be stopped until the tissue can heal. Avoiding gripping or pinching activities, especially with the wrist extended, and wearing a splint or a counterforce brace can calm down the inflammation. Typical conservative treatment involves modalities like ice and ultrasound to decrease inflammation. Stretching and strengthening the wrist and finger flexors and extensors when the acute phase is over and performing nerve and tendon glide exercises are part of a physical therapy protocol. Prevention can be as simple as maintaining good strength in the wrist and finger extensors, improving flexibility, using proper body and sports mechanics, and monitoring repetitive wrist motions and gripping activities. Any exercise that involves gripping a weight (that's most of them), as well as specific gripping exercises like clean holds (see page 150 and the grip-improving exercises that I describe in the hand section of this chapter, can help you maintain good strength in these muscles.

147) tax all three heads the most. They involve full shoulder flexion and may stress the triceps more because you put the muscle on stretch and then force it to perform a contraction.

The bottom line is to vary your exercises from all angles so that you're sure to get the arms you'll be proud to show off in a tank top. The exercises in this chapter, with the many variations offered, will help you reach this goal.

# Biceps Exercises

Biceps exercises are fun to do because you can really see the muscle working. Many people like to train the biceps together with the triceps; although they are both arm movements, they involve muscles on opposite sides of the body that perform entirely different functions. The variety you can add to a training program is endless. You can train the biceps first and then the triceps, or the triceps then the biceps, or you can alternate them, doing first a biceps and then a triceps exercise.

## STANDING BARBELL BICEPS CURL

This curl is a basic and old-time classic biceps exercise that works the long and short heads of the biceps brachii and the brachialis. A standard Olympic bar weighs 45 pounds, but unfortunately that is too much weight for many women. Some gyms have lighter bars that can vary from 5 to 35 pounds so that you can work up to the Olympic bar. When you are finally able to curl that bar and then begin adding weight plates, you'll get a great rush from your newfound strength. You can also use curled bars, which tend to weigh less (anywhere from 25 to 35 pounds) than the straight Olympic barbell. Curled bars are easier on the wrists because they allow them more range of motion, so if you have a wrist problem you might try using them. Regardless, they are great for adding variety to your biceps training (see figure 10.2). The longer Olympic bar will add a dimension of balance and coordination for the upper body.

**Figure 10.2**  Curl bars.

If the temptation to use some body English gets the better of you when doing a curl, then performing barbell curls with the back against a wall throughout the movement will eliminate the urge to swing the weight, thereby helping you focus on working the biceps. It's virtually impossible to cheat and use momentum when your entire spine is pressed against the wall (you may have to walk the feet out from the wall slightly). You may find that you have to decrease the weight that you normally use once you try this curl against a wall. If so, then you have probably been using too many other muscles when you should have been concentrating on your biceps. The other benefit of this variation is that it eliminates the potential for low back injury.

1. Stand erect with an underhand, shoulder-width grip on a barbell or curled bar, with the bar resting on the thighs.

2. Keep the abs tight, the back straight, and the elbows locked at the sides.

3. Inhale and curl the bar up toward the chest until the elbows are completely bent.

4. Squeeze the biceps muscles at the top, pause for 1 second, exhale, and lower the bar back down. Don't lower so far as to release the tension on the muscle at the bottom.

*a*    *b*

## DUMBBELL BICEPS CURL

Because of the variety you can incorporate when using dumbbells, these curls tend to be a favorite. You can curl both at the same time, you can alternate them, and you can include a hold at the top. You can do them standing free, standing against a wall, seated with back support, seated without back support, or seated on an incline bench. Performing curls with dumbbells can also help equalize differences in strength between a dominant and nondominant arm; you can even focus on a weaker arm by training that one only. Using dumbbells can eliminate any wrist pain that may come from curling a straight bar, and you can also use lighter weights than with an Olympic barbell. Variety is the name of the game with dumbbell training, but all dumbbell curls primarily involve the long and short head of the biceps brachii and the brachialis.

### Standing

1. Stand erect holding a dumbbell in each hand, with arms hanging straight down, palms rotated in toward the thighs, and feet shoulder-width apart.

2. Keep the abs tight and the back straight, and avoid swinging the body throughout the movement.

3. Inhale, supinate the palms (turn them up) and curl the dumbbells up toward the chest until the elbows are completely bent.

4. Squeeze the biceps muscles at the top, exhale, and lower the dumbbells back down to the starting position.

5. To do this exercise with alternating arms, fully complete the movement with one arm and then complete the movement with the other.

### Seated Straight or Incline

1. Position a bench with a movable back to a 90-degree angle or incline it to a 30- to 45-degree angle.
2. Sit down holding the dumbbells and let the arms hang straight down by the sides.
3. Keep the abs tight and the back pressed firmly against the back of the bench throughout the movement.
4. Inhale, supinate the hands, and curl the dumbbells up toward the chest until the elbows are completely bent. Pause for 1 second and exhale while slowly lowering to the starting position.
5. To do this exercise with alternating arms, fully complete the movement with one arm and then complete the movement with the other.

a                                                b

### Seated Alternating With Hold

This variation changes the standard biceps curl by using a continuous tension principle lost in modern-day training programs. Continuous tension on the muscle without rest can promote greater strength and hypertrophy gains. For this challenging alternative, you will find that you have to lighten the weight by perhaps 5 or 10 pounds from what you normally curl.

1. Position a bench with a movable back to a 90-degree angle so that you have a back support.
2. Sit down holding the dumbbells and let the arms hang straight down by the sides.
3. Keep the abs tight and the back pressed firmly against the back of the bench.
4. Inhale, supinate the hands, and curl both dumbbells up toward the chest until the elbows are completely bent.
5. Slowly lower the right arm down and curl it back up.
6. Slowly lower the left arm down and curl it back up.
7. One arm is always holding a dumbbell at the top position while the other is curling.

# PREACHER CURL

Feel as if some praying might help you get through your workout? Then this is the perfect exercise for you, because it already puts you in a prayer position—perhaps the reason the exercise is named after a preacher. The benefit of this curl is that having the arms rest on the preacher curl apparatus takes out any extra momentum or body movement and removes most shoulder flexion from the lift. This exercise especially benefits the long head of the biceps brachii.

1. Sit on a preacher bench, placing the back of the upper arms on the pad. Adjust the seat if necessary so that the armpits rest near the top of the pad.
2. Grasp a straight or curled bar with a shoulder-width underhand grip, or dumbbells with an underhand grip.
3. Inhale and curl the barbell or dumbbells up toward the shoulders until the elbows are completely bent.
4. Keep the back of the arms in contact with the bench during the lift.
5. Pause for 1 second, then exhale and lower the barbell or dumbbells back down to the starting position.

a

b

## CONCENTRATION CURL

You don't have to meditate to do this exercise, but you will get full concentration on all of your biceps muscle without a lot of extraneous movement. Having the elbow rest on the thigh also eliminates any unnecessary shoulder flexion during the lift.

1. Sit on the end of a flat bench and grasp a dumbbell with one hand, using an underhand grip.
2. Plant the feet on the ground wider than shoulder-width.
3. Lean forward at the waist and rest the elbow holding the dumbbell on the thigh on the same side, with the arm in full extension.
4. Inhale and curl the dumbbell toward the shoulder.
5. Pause for 1 second and squeeze the biceps, then exhale and lower to the starting position.
6. Complete all of the reps with one arm and then switch arms.

*a*                                          *b*

## HAMMER CURL

The hammer curl is so named because you curl and lower the dumbbell as if you are hammering a nail. You do it with the arm in a neutral position as opposed to the usual supinated (turned-up) position. This position trains the arm muscles from a different angle than usual to emphasize muscles other than the biceps brachii, like the brachioradialis. You can perform the exercise standing, seated upright, or seated at an angle, but most often people do it standing. With standing you involve your core muscles, but you have to make a conscious effort not to swing the weights. When you are seated, you can concentrate on the hammer motion fully since the seat supports you. If you choose to go back on an incline, the greater range of motion and subsequent stretch on the biceps increases the difficulty of the exercise.

1. Stand erect holding a dumbbell in each hand, arms hanging straight down and palms rotated in toward the thighs. To do this curl from a seated position, adjust a bench with a movable back to a 30-, 45-, or 90-degree angle. Sit down holding the dumbbells and let the arms hang straight down by the sides.

3. Keep the abs tight and the back straight (or pressed firmly against the back of the bench if you are seated).

4. Inhale and curl the dumbbells up toward the chest until the elbows are completely bent. Do not supinate or twist the forearm. Pause for 1 second and exhale while slowly lowering to the starting position.

5. To do this exercise with alternating arms, fully complete the movement with one arm and then complete the movement with the other.

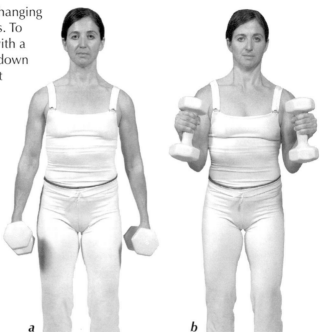

*a*                    *b*

## REVERSE CURL

Change up your routine a bit with this curl variation, in which you curl with the palms down rather than up. You can use a straight bar, a curled bar, or dumbbells, while either standing or sitting. This exercise involves the brachialis and wrist extensors as well as the biceps brachii.

1. Stand erect with an overhand, shoulder-width grip on a barbell or curled bar, with the bar resting on the thighs. If you choose to use dumbbells, stand erect holding a dumbbell in each hand, with arms hanging straight down and palms facing down. Or position a bench with a movable back to a 30-, 45-, or 90-degree angle and sit down holding the dumbbells with a palms-down grip.

2. Keep the abs tight and the back straight and avoid swinging the body throughout the movement.

3. Inhale and curl the barbell or dumbbells up toward the chest until the elbows are completely bent.

4. Pause for 1 second, then exhale and lower the barbell or dumbbells back down to the starting position.

5. To do this exercise with dumbbells and alternating arms, fully complete the movement with one arm and then complete the movement with the other.

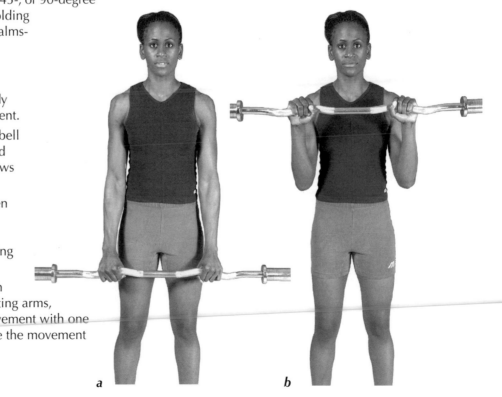

*a*                    *b*

# Triceps Exercises

Use all of these exercises for specific triceps activation, but keep in mind that many pushing exercises from the last chapter like bench presses, push-ups, and overhead presses also work the triceps well.

## DUMBBELL KICKBACK

You see a lot of people in the gym doing the dumbbell kickback for their triceps, and for good reason. You can certainly feel your triceps work on this exercise, especially when you add a squeeze and rotate the palm up when the elbow is fully extended. The benefit of this exercise is how well it isolates the triceps musculature (all heads, especially the long head) so that other muscles don't assist with the movement.

1. Put the right knee on a bench, bend over from the hips while keeping the back straight, and allow the right arm to help support the body by resting it on the bench.

2. Keep the abs tight, the low back slightly arched, the head in a neutral position, and the body bent over from the hips.

3. Bring the left arm up to the side, holding the weight, and bend the elbow to 90 degrees. The elbow should stay glued to the hip for the entire exercise.

4. Kick the lower arm back, straighten the arm into full extension while rotating the palm up, squeeze the triceps, and slowly lower to the starting position.

5. Repeat all of the reps on one side and then switch sides.

*a*

*b*

## OVERHEAD DUMBBELL EXTENSION

Any triceps exercise that you do with the arms overhead seems to put more tension on the muscles, because they start the exercise stretched in a position of maximal range of motion and must then use an entire range of motion to complete the exercise. Watch your form, because it is very easy to help the weight back up using a forward torso lean. This extension works all three brachii heads.

1. Seated on a bench or standing, grasp a dumbbell in an underhand grip, raise the arm overhead, and allow the elbow to bend so that the dumbbell is resting behind the neck. The palm is facing the neck.

2. Keeping the torso erect and the elbow close to the head, extend the arm straight overhead.

3. Squeeze the triceps, pause for 1 second, and slowly lower to the starting position.

4. Perform all reps on one arm before switching to the other.

## LYING FRENCH PRESS

This exercise is frequently called a skull crusher, but don't take its nickname seriously. If you lower the weight under control, you'll keep the beautiful face you were born with. Again, this exercise puts the triceps muscles on stretch and works all three triceps brachii heads.

1. Lie on a flat bench with a straight or curled bar balanced across it just behind the head.

2. Reach back to grasp the bar with the palms up and lift it overhead. The arms should be at a 90-degree angle to the body.

3. Slowly bend the elbows to lower the bar toward the tip of the head, then reverse to full extension.

4. Keep the elbows in tight to the sides of the head throughout the movement.

## CABLE EXERCISES

The cable machine is a versatile piece of equipment for training the triceps brachii muscles. The different ways that you can use cables to work on your triceps are almost too numerous to mention. You can do pushdowns or overhead extensions with a straight bar, angled bar, or rope (see figure 10.3). You can also do unilateral exercises like pronated and supinated pushdowns with a single handle on the cable. With the cable exercises you can vary your grip attachments, hand angles, and movements easily. Try all the variations and rotate them

**Figure 10.3**   Cable bar attachments.

in your training to incorporate variety—keep your triceps always experiencing new things. If you are strict in your movements, you isolate the triceps brachii muscles and get little other muscular assistance.

### Cable Pushdown

1. Stand erect and grasp a bar or rope attached to a high pulley.
2. In the start position, the forearms are just about parallel to the floor.
3. With the upper arms locked into the sides, press the bar or rope down to full extension, squeezing the triceps at the bottom. If using a rope, try to flare the wrists out as well.
4. Return the weight to the starting position under control.

*a*                                    *b*

## One-Arm Cable Pushdown

1. Stand erect and grasp a handle attached to a high pulley with one hand, which is either pronated or supinated. You can vary the grip on different sets or training days. Doing unilateral exercises can improve muscular strength deficits from limb to limb, because the strong arm can't take over the work for the weaker one as it can when you use both arms.

2. In the start position, the forearm is just about parallel to the floor.

3. With the upper arm locked into the side, press the handle down to full extension, squeezing the triceps at the bottom.

4. Return the weight to the starting position under control.

5. Complete all of the reps on one side and then switch.

## Overhead Cable Extension

1. Stand erect and grasp a bar or rope attached to a high pulley with hands shoulder-width apart.

2. Turn around so that the back is facing the weight stack.

3. With the arms overhead, lean forward slightly and allow the elbows to bend to 90 degrees.

4. Keep the elbows in tight to the sides of the head and extend the arms, squeezing the triceps and flaring the wrists out.

5. Slowly return to the starting position.

*a*

*b*

## CLOSE GRIP BENCH PRESS

This exercise is similar to a regular bench press except that, since you place your hands much closer together, it puts the emphasis on your triceps rather than on your chest. The exercise can also help you increase your bench press weight. The exercise primarily uses the medial and lateral heads of the triceps brachii.

*a*

*b*

1. Lie on the back on a bench with the knees bent to 90 degrees and the feet firmly on the floor. If the feet do not reach the ground, only then put them on the bench. The barbell should be directly over the eyes.

2. Arch the back slightly, tighten the abs, and retract the scapulas. Make sure that the glutes stay in contact with the bench throughout the lift.

3. Grasp the bar with an overhand (pronated) grip, less than shoulder-width apart (about 6 to 8 inches).

4. Press the bar up to release it from the rack, then lock the arms directly above the neck.

5. Inhale and hold your breath as you lower the bar to the upper chest, just above the nipple line. Keep the arms close to the sides throughout the lift.

6. Reverse direction and forcefully exhale as you push the barbell back up. Concentrate on extending the elbows fully and forcefully.

# Hand Exercises to Improve Grip

It's great to have strong and shapely arms, but many exercises, strength sports, and daily functional activities require a strong grip as well. Maybe our arms and back are strong enough to do body-weight pull-ups, but we lose our hold on the pull-up bar before we can make any progress. Frequently our legs and low back are strong enough to deadlift some serious weight, but we find that our hands can't hold on to such a heavy weight. Strongwoman events like the farmer's walk (see chapter 13) require a superstrong grip, but often our grip gives way before our true strength is tested. Assistive devices like straps and wraps can take some of the pressure off your grip, but why not train your hand and forearm muscles so that you can lift with hands alone? Not only does it look impressive, but it also saves you some money.

You can use a few tricks of the trade to improve the strength of your grip. Wrap a towel around any handle that you have to grip for any exercise (see figure 10.4). The thickness and size of the towel should increase as your grip strength increases. The towel adds dimension to the handle and forces you to grip even harder to hold on, which in time will strengthen your grip. Using the thick rope attachment on certain exercises like pull-ups and cable pushdowns can also help you strengthen your grip. The instability of the rope challenges your neuromuscular system, and your grip will improve tremendously. You can also simply hang from a thick rope or a pull-up bar. Time yourself and see how long your grip can hold you. If you want to purchase an excellent item for grip training, visit www.ironmind.com and check out the Rolling Thunder Revolving Deadlift Handles. They are thick, rounded handles that rotate and attach to any apparatus with a clip.

**Figure 10.4**  Use a towel to improve the strength of your grip.

## CLEAN HOLD

The clean hold is especially helpful for improving your deadlift and farmer's walk grip, or any grip that you need to hold things at thigh level. It isometrically strengthens your hand muscles—especially the finger flexors—and your shoulder and neck muscles.

1. Set up a barbell in a rack so that the barbell is just above the knees.
2. Place the hands on the barbell using an overhand grip, slightly wider than shoulder-width. Slightly bend the knees, keep the back flat and abs tight, and hold the chest and head up.
3. Extend the knees to lift the bar from the rack to lockout and hold for 30 to 60 seconds.
4. Try not to rest the bar on the thighs or lean backward.
5. Place the bar back down, rest for 1 to 2 minutes, and repeat for 5 reps.

a                                                              b

# Developing Lean, Athletic Legs

The largest muscles in your body are in the front and back of your legs. They are strong and powerful and allow you and whatever excess baggage you have to get where you are going and to do what you need to do. Whether the baggage is groceries, a child hanging on your hip, or a little extra fat, your legs can usually handle the job. However, some of us would prefer to get the job done with legs that both function well and look good; some of us want legs that look good and function still better. Still others grapple with knee pain issues that have plagued them since they were young. You definitely can have lean athletic legs that look great and work great too, even if you've always had problem knees. Learn all about your legs, how squats can help you achieve your aesthetic and functional goals, and how you can eliminate painful knee conditions.

## Understanding Leg Anatomy and Function

The long thigh bone is the femur. It connects to the pelvis to form the hip joint and then extends down to meet the tibia (shin bone) at the knee joint (see figure 11.1). The hip is a ball-and-socket joint where the head of the femur (ball) fits deeply and snugly into the acetabulum (socket) of the pelvis. This perfect fit gives the hip joint a great degree of stability. Because it is such a large and stable joint, it helps dissipate the forces that come from weight-bearing activities. The hip muscles can flex (bring the leg up toward the body), extend (move the leg backward away from the body), abduct (move the leg out to the side of the body), adduct (move the leg toward the midline of the body), and internally and externally rotate the leg.

The knee joint consists of the femur, the tibia, and the patella (kneecap). Patellofemoral refers to the union between the patella and the femur. The primary muscles surrounding the knee joint are the quadriceps muscles on the front of the thigh, the adductor muscles on the inside of the thigh, the hamstring muscles on the back of the thigh, and the tensor fasciae latae and iliotibial band on the outside of the thigh. The patella is located inside the tendon of the rectus femoris muscle, which connects the femur to the tibia. The femur has a concavity or groove where the patella rides up during extension (knee straightening) and down during flexion

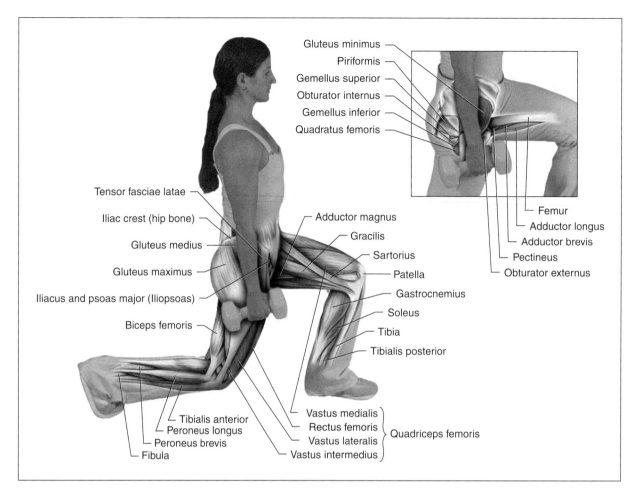

**Figure 11.1**   Anatomy of the leg and hip.

(knee bending). The underside of the patella has many ridges that are covered with protective cartilage. The patella's function is to give the quadriceps muscles increased efficiency and to protect the front of the femur.

The lower-leg bones, the tibia and fibula, also help to form the ankle joint. The tibia sits on top of the talus (an ankle bone), which fits into the calcaneus (heel bone). The fibula forms the lateral malleolus (the bony projection on the outside of your ankle). The lower-leg muscles can act on the ankle and either dorsiflex (bring the toes towards the nose) or plantarflex (point the toes down). They can also act at the foot and either invert (move the foot toward midline) or evert (move the foot away from the body). The foot's bony and muscular anatomy is very similar to that of the hand. There are tarsals, metatarsals, and phalanges, and the muscles can flex, extend, abduct, and adduct the toes. Table 11.1 describes the major muscles of the hip and leg and their functions.

# No Need for Knee Pain

Do your knees hurt when you walk up and down stairs? Do you hate going to the movies because when you sit for too long your knee becomes so stiff that you think it will break when you get up? Are you afraid to squat because you heard that it aggravates knee problems? If you can identify with these situations, then you may be one of the many women who have a

## Table 11.1  Major Muscles of the Hip and Leg and Their Functions

| Muscle | Function |
|---|---|
| Gluteus maximus | Extension, external rotation of hip |
| Gluteus medius and minimus | Abduction, internal rotation of hip |
| Tensor fasciae latae | Maintaining knee extension with gait<br>Assisting abduction, internal rotation of hip |
| Piriformis<br>Gemellus superior<br>Obturator internus<br>Gemellus inferior<br>Obturator externus<br>Quadratus femoris<br>(referred to as the six deep lateral rotators) | External rotation of hip |
| Iliacus and psoas major (iliopsoas) | Flexion, abduction, external rotation of hip |
| Sartorius | Assisting flexion, abduction, external rotation of hip<br>Assisting flexion, internal rotation of knee |
| Quadriceps femoris group<br>Rectus femoris | Flexion of hip<br>Extension of knee |
| Vastus intermedius<br>Vastus medialis<br>Vastus lateralis | Extension of knee |
| Pectineus | Flexion, adduction, internal rotation of hip |
| Adductor longus and brevis | Adduction, flexion, internal rotation of hip |
| Adductor magnus | Adduction, flexion of hip<br>Posterior fibers: extension of hip |
| Gracilis | Adduction of hip<br>Flexion, internal rotation of knee |
| Hamstring group<br>Biceps femoris | Extension of hip<br>Flexion, external rotation of knee |
| Semimembranosus<br>Semitendinosus | Extension of hip<br>Flexion, internal rotation of knee |
| Gastrocnemius | Plantarflexion of ankle<br>Flexion of knee |
| Soleus | Plantarflexion of ankle when knee is flexed |
| Tibialis posterior | Inversion of foot<br>Plantarflexion of ankle |
| Tibialis anterior | Dorsiflexion of ankle<br>Inversion of foot |
| Peroneus tertius | Eversion of foot<br>Dorsiflexion of ankle |
| Peroneus brevis and longus | Eversion of foot<br>Plantarflexion of ankle |

patellofemoral (PF) dysfunction that leads to pain. Women may be predisposed to PF dysfunction if they are overweight, if they have weak or tight musculature, or if they are born with malalignments.

Many theories have been proposed to describe why and how people experience PF pain. The most commonly accepted theory on what causes it is that abnormal patellar tracking (laterally) in the femoral groove increases the stress between the patella and the femur and wears out the cartilage on the underside of the patella. When the cartilage is healthy and the ridges fit into the femur well, the knee is pain-free. However, if the patella and femur do not mesh well together, the cartilage can wear down, predisposing a person to PF pain. Although the cartilage itself has no pain receptors, the bone underneath it does. But the *why* question of PF dysfunction is an individual issue, and cases differ from person to person. In some cases, a congenital malalignment of the lower body may be the culprit. Tight or weak musculature, lax ligaments, overuse, or trauma may also be to blame. Extra body weight that puts increased stress on the knees can contribute. Whatever the whys and hows may be, the signs and symptoms are generally consistent. They include swelling, loss of range of motion, and a sense of instability (feeling that the knee might give way), as well as pain with prolonged sitting, squatting, and walking up and down stairs.

Previously, treatments of PF dysfunction were based on the hypothesis that the vastus medialis muscle could be individually activated and trained to work with little other involvement of the quadriceps muscle group. This muscle could then pull the patella medially (toward the inside of the thigh), more into the femoral groove. Many studies have now shown, however, that such selective treatment is impossible. When you try to selectively strengthen the vastus medialis, you activate the entire quadriceps muscle group, which is actually the desired outcome for treating PF dysfunction. Strengthening the entire quadriceps group may help change the contact areas between the patella and femur and redistribute the pressures. This alteration in turn can relieve painful areas of worn cartilage.

The first course of action with any inflammatory condition, however, is to treat the symptoms with rest and ice. A medical doctor may also prescribe anti-inflammatory medication. Once the painful symptoms abate, you can tackle treating the cause of the problem. Increasing strength and flexibility of the entire lower extremity from the hip to the foot is crucial. Exercises that are safe and effective to start with include backward walking or running, backward stair climbing, lateral step-downs, and bicycling with the seat high and the resistance low. Leg presses and squats can be beneficial too, but you should keep them in the range of 0 to 30 degrees. Likewise, keeping leg extensions at only 90 to 60 degrees decreases the patellofemoral joint reaction (PFJR) forces. However, the rule of thumb should be to perform all exercises pain-free. Proper bracing or taping by a certified athletic trainer or physical therapist can be effective in decreasing pain so that you can strengthen the joint, and it may improve patellar tracking by better positioning the patella in the femoral groove. Orthotics for the feet may be necessary to correct any malalignments.

## TOP FIVE PREVENTIVE AND REHABILITATIVE EXERCISES FOR THE KNEE

1. Backward walking, running, or stair climbing—It's best to do these exercises slowly so that you can emphasize full extension of the knee and the quadriceps muscles. Completing 5 to 10 minutes of any of these activities, from 2 to 4 times a week, should do the trick.

2. Straight-leg raise—Straight-leg raises in all directions (to the front, back, outside, and inside) strengthen the hip muscles that stabilize the leg during movement. Try these exercises lying down or standing up; you can also do them with ankle cuff weights, with a multi-hip machine, or in the pool. Add this exercise to your leg workout program, and after you can do 2 to 3 sets of 8 reps with each leg, add weight.

*a*

*b*

*a*                    *b*

3. Lateral step-down—Stand with one leg sideways on a step about 6 inches high. Slowly bend your knee and lower yourself until the heel of your other foot touches the ground. Straighten your knee to return to the beginning position. The keys to this exercise are keeping all of your body weight on the leg that's on the step and keeping your body upright. Add this step-down to your leg workout program and add weight after you can do 2 to 3 sets of 8 reps with each leg.

4. Wall sit—Remember this punishment for the kids who acted up in gym class? With your back against a wall and your legs shoulder-width apart, walk your legs out from the wall far enough so that when you go into a sitting position, your thighs are parallel to the ground. Bend your knees to a sitting position of not more than 90 degrees, or to the point just before any knee pain occurs. Keeping your arms at your sides (and not on your thighs), hold this position for 10 seconds. Slide up the wall to return to the starting position. Try 10 reps for a great quad burn.

5. Leg press and squat—When rehabilitating, keep leg presses and squats in the range of 0 to 30 degrees. If you can achieve a greater pain-free range of motion, do so to fully strengthen the muscles. The next section covers squats in detail.

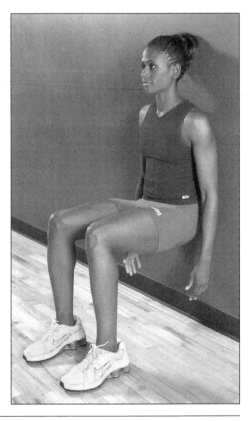

# Why You Should Squat

"I don't squat because it makes my legs and butt too big." "I don't squat because squatting is bad for your knees." I've got a bad back so I can't squat." If you think that these statements are true, then you don't know squat about the squat. One could write an entire book with all of the excuses women give for not performing the squat exercise. Instead of excuses, let's arm you with plenty of information on why you should squat and why squatting may be one of the most important exercises you can do.

In the royal family of leg exercises, squats are the king. They are also the most functional exercise for daily life. Just think about how many times a day you squat: when you sit down in a chair, when you get a file out of the bottom file drawer, and when you squat down to pick something up off the floor, like a bag of groceries or your child (if you lift correctly). Squatting works the largest muscles in your body—the quadriceps (front of thigh), adductors (inside of thigh), gluteals (buttocks), hamstrings (back of thigh), gastrocnemius and soleus complex (calf), and erector spinae (back). Squats can also help you develop flexibility around your hips and calves, when you follow proper form and gradually increase your range of motion. Squats have the added benefit of being a free-weight and weight-bearing exercise. Free weights have many advantages over machines (see chapter 5), and free-weight squats specifically have been shown to improve bone density (see chapters 2 and 7).

If you are an athlete involved in a sport or if you want to be more athletic, squats offer exceptional preparation. The muscles used during squatting are the same muscles used for jumping, sprinting, and running. Squats provide the perfect transfer to the biomechanically similar motions of most ground-based sports. So if you are interested in running faster, lunging for that out-of-reach tennis ball, or jumping up for the perfect volleyball spike, squats should be an essential component of your training program.

Many women rate exercises or exercise programs not on how much they like them or how beneficial they are, but on how many calories they burn. "I need to do 10 more minutes on the stair machine to burn off that mocha latte with chocolate sprinkles," some think. Here's the good news for squatters: Squats burn a ton of calories and stimulate the cardiovascular system. With the additional muscle you'll pack on your legs, your resting metabolic rate will increase even more and allow you to burn some calories by just lounging on the couch. You'll not only burn calories during the squat, but you will also likely burn calories in the 24 hours after your squat workout, because of the intensity and heavy nature of the exercise. Sounds as if you can have your latte and drink it, too!

Squatting has an extra bonus especially for women. It has the potential to increase the bone density of the spine, hips, and legs, which may help prevent osteoporosis. Squats mechanically load the axial skeleton; the spine has to hold the weight upright, and it then distributes that weight to the rest of the body. You've already learned that strong bones can handle more stress and are less likely to fracture. Because the barbell loads weight on your shoulders and spine and your leg muscles work as they never have before, squatting may be the answer to osteoporosis prevention as well.

## The Danger Is Not the Squat

A popular belief is that squatting hurts your knees and puts too much pressure on your back. Actually, it is the lack of squatting and using your leg muscles as they were meant to be used that can harm you. It is more dangerous not to squat than it is to squat, provided that you know the proper mechanics and maintain good form.

Squatting is an everyday occurrence in life, especially for women. Why not make these activities easier on us and on our joints by training our muscles to perform these movements? When the legs are weak and cannot do a sufficient job, the next stress point up the body is the low back. Weak quads and hams can also contribute to injury because of their inability to stabilize and decelerate joints during high-level activities. For example, when you are running to hit a tennis shot or to chase a child on the run and stop short, if your muscles cannot absorb that force, they might tear. Squats are also the best choice for a leg exercise that minimizes joint compression force. Compared to the leg extension machine, squatting allows the patellofemoral forces to be more evenly distributed and dissipated. There is no evidence that squats can cause injuries in women because their bone structure is different than men's. Of course, you can hurt yourself if you aren't careful. If you drop down into your squat too quickly and bounce out of the bottom position, the knee cartilage (menisci) can be squeezed and twisted, resulting in wear and tear and eventual breakdown. Any exercise has the potential to hurt you if you do it improperly. With good form and a gradual increase in intensity, squats can be one of the safest and most functional exercises you'll ever perform.

If you are still skeptical of the squat, follow this line of logic: Women should be afraid of their diets, not of squats. Bigger butts and hips result from too much food, not too much exercise. Ballet dancers get their firm glutes from squatting explosively many times, but they don't have huge butts because of their extremely strict diets and enormous activity levels. So go ahead and squat—your butt will love you for it.

## How to Squat

If you've never squatted before, stand in front of a mirror, start with just your body weight and a stick for the bar, and practice proper form diligently. You may want to have your form evaluated by a qualified person. Even a friend who has read this information can give you good feedback. Start with feet approximately shoulder-width apart and toes pointed slightly outward. Work on keeping your whole foot firmly on the ground while sinking your hips low and in between your heels. Go as low as you can while still maintaining a slight arch in your low back—that is, the back should be slightly arched rather than flat, neutral, or rounded, keeping your upper back as upright as possible, and keeping your head up. Make sure your ascent is straight up and devoid of the twists and turns that can place additional stress on the body. You can progress to holding dumbbells or a variable-weight bar before you try the big Olympic barbell that weighs 45 pounds.

How low should you go? Is a wider stance better? Do twists and turns of the foot help activate different muscles? A lot of topics are controversial when it comes to squatting. When determining how deep to squat, consider that research has shown that quadriceps activity is the greatest when the knee is near full flexion—that means squatting as low as possible. Deep squats are not harmful to the knee—as the knee flexes, although joint compression force increases, the load is more evenly distributed. From a neuromuscular standpoint, full range-of-motion exercises are always the most beneficial because they recruit the most muscles and nerves. The real dangers of going low are failing to practice depth with lighter loads before you attempt the big ones and twisting or bouncing to get up from the bottom position. However, if you already have knee problems or knee pain, you should play it safe and squat no lower than parallel.

Some believe that altering foot position for a squat works different muscles. Many research studies have shown that a foot position wider than shoulder-width might make the buttocks and adductors work a little more, but changes in stance width do not isolate different quadriceps muscles. If you are interested in lifting more weight, like a powerlifter, a wider stance is better. The wider stance increases your base of support and balance and shortens the length you have to go to reach parallel. Ultimately you should position your feet where you are comfortable and stable and can most easily squat.

# BARBELL BACK SQUAT

The barbell back squat is the big mama of the squat, the one that all of the variations originate from. In performing barbell back squats, you center both the barbell and the trunk's center of gravity between the hip and knee. This exercise requires that many joints function and therefore activates many muscles, some even in your upper body and trunk. However, squats primarily stress the quads and glutes.

1. Place a barbell on the squat rack so that it is somewhat even with the collarbone.

2. Grip the bar with a wider than shoulder-width grip and pull the body under the bar so that the bar rests on the upper back.

3. Position the feet comfortably, approximately shoulder-width apart.

4. Inhale and bend the knees and hips to lower the body under control into a squat position.

5. Keep head up, heels on the ground, and back slightly arched.

6. After squatting as deeply as you can, quickly reverse direction and exhale through the sticking point (the most difficult part of the movement). Do not bounce out of the bottom position.

*a*                    *b*

# BARBELL FRONT SQUAT

As the name implies, the barbell rests in front of the body during the front squat. You perform front squats in a more upright position than back squats, and the joint force is more equally distributed between the hip and knee joints. Because the weight load is in the front, this squat emphasizes the quadriceps more than the glutes.

1. From a squat rack, grasp the barbell with an overhand grip at slightly wider than shoulder-width. Stand with the feet approximately shoulder-width apart and the toes pointed slightly outward.

2. With the wrists extended backward, the elbows pointing up, and the arms parallel to the floor, position the bar across the collarbone and the anterior deltoids.

3. Inhale and bend the knees and hips to lower the body under control into a squat position.

4. Keep head up, heels on the ground, and back slightly arched.

5. After squatting as deeply as you can, quickly reverse direction and exhale through the sticking point (the most difficult part of the movement). Do not bounce out of the bottom position.

*a*                    *b*

# ONE-LEG SQUAT

Many think that one-leg squats are harder than the two-leg version because of the balancing that's required. One-leg exercises help eliminate any discrepancies in strength you have from side to side. Your entire lower leg will feel the stress of these squats, from the top of your hip to the bottom of your toe.

1. Stand next to a supportive tall object and grasp it with one hand. If you are a beginner, use the full hand for support; if intermediate, use only touch support—support when you need it. More advanced lifters may keep the hands free and hold weights while performing.

2. Extend the outside leg in front of the body or bend it behind you.

3. Inhale. Slowly bend the inside knee and hip to lower yourself into a squatting position, keeping the upper body straight, the head up, and the back slightly arched. Your center of gravity should be over the middle of the foot.

4. After squatting as deeply as you can, quickly reverse direction and exhale through the sticking point (the most difficult part of the movement). Do not bounce out of the bottom position.

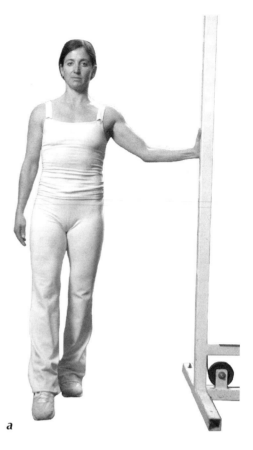

*a*

*b*

## JUMP SQUAT

The jump squat is a plyometric exercise that works the gluteus maximus, quadriceps, hamstrings, spinal erectors, and gastrocnemius. It is a fairly easy movement to perform. When you first start out, perform each repetition slowly, with a brief pause between reps. As you develop more skill, you can perform multiple reps as quickly as possible.

1. Place a barbell behind the neck, resting on the top of the trapezius muscles.

2. Squat to a quarter-squat position and then jump up with the weight as high as you can.

3. Land on the feet and make sure to flex the knees, just as you do in recovering from a jump so that you minimize impact on the joints.

*a*

*b*

*c*

## SUPER SQUAT CIRCUITS

Short on time and equipment and need a quick leg workout? Try combining squats with speed work for fantastic legs and a super butt. Perform 15 reps of body-weight squats and 15 reps of 10-second sprints for 4 to 5 sets. How about 15 reps of barbell squats and 15 reps of jump squats (see page 161) for 4 to 5 sets? Burn out with 15 reps of body-weight squats and 15 reps of walking lunges (see page 80) for 4 to 5 sets. Start with a 3-minute rest between sets and gradually reduce it to 1 minute over a period of 3 to 6 weeks.

# More Multijoint Exercises

When working for lean, athletic legs, you have to consider all of the joints that provide leg movement. The hip, knee, and ankle joints are intricately involved in lower-extremity movement, both functional and athletic. Because of this biomechanical fact, some muscles span more than one joint and are called multijoint muscles. They actually perform different actions at each joint. For example, the rectus femoris is the primary knee extensor at the knee joint, but it also works to flex the hip at the hip joint. The hamstring muscles are primary knee flexors, but because they attach to the pelvis they can also extend the hip.

Multijoint exercises closely simulate the way your body works and plays. For example, if you were to kick a ball, it is unlikely that you would do so from a stationary position, by bending the knee back and extending it to kick the ball. Rather, you would probably run up to the ball to kick it and use some hip extension and flexion for more power. As I discussed in chapter 4, the movement patterns, force application, and velocity of movement of an exercise should mimic those of the activity you are training for in order for you to get the most benefit. You can work your quadriceps muscles when by performing a single-joint leg extension, but that type of exercise will not transfer to your sport performance to the same extent that a dynamic multijoint exercise would.

Likewise as you go about your daily activities, your body just doesn't move one muscle or joint at a time. Walking is a simple example of a multijoint activity. Even though it doesn't look very complicated and most of us do it all of the time, it involves every joint and every muscle in the lower extremities. Many other simple activities that we do everyday, like sitting down, also involve multiple joints and therefore can be trained for by doing multijoint exercises. And keep in mind that because they work more areas at one time than single joint exercises do, multijoint exercises burn more calories and are more time-efficient. In addition to squats, the exercises that follow employ multiple joints and multijoint muscles.

# LEG PRESS

The leg press machine is a valuable tool to incorporate into your strength-training program. You can find many different kinds of leg press machines in gyms, and that gives you an advantage. You can find a machine that is horizontal or one that is vertical, some on which you push a plate down and some on which you push your body up. Many are selectorized weight machines on which you can move a pin to determine the weight; others you can load up with free weights. Leg press machines are valuable for rehabilitating injuries, because you can move light weights and limit ranges of motion.

1. Lie down in a machine, tighten the abs, and press the low back against the support pad.

2. Place the feet shoulder-width apart on the plate.

3. If you are in a free-weight leg press, you must first press out on the plate and extend the legs to release the weight from the locks. Use the lock upright handles to turn the locks out of the way.

4. Grasp the handles on the side of the machine. Inhale.

5. For the free-weight leg press, the first movement is to slowly unlock the knees and bend them to maximum flexion.

6. Exhale and extend the legs to a full lockout position, if you are pain-free.

7. With selectorized equipment, the common starting position is to have the knees in full flexion. From this position you exhale while you extend the legs to a full lockout position, if you are pain-free.

8. Inhale and slowly bend the knees to the starting position.

*a*

*b*

# LUNGE

Nothing makes your muscles sore like a good lunge. So many varieties exist that you will never get bored, and they are hard even without added weight. You can do the standard lunge I will describe first or jazz it up by doing backward lunges, lunges to a step, walking lunges, side lunges, diagonal lunges, or lunges holding dumbbells or a barbell, and still add in twists. Lunges use all of your leg muscles but always seem to hurt the adductors and glutes a bit more. By employing diversity in your lunges you promote function, because life happens in three dimensions. Moreover, you decrease the staleness and boredom that come from doing the same exercise over and over again.

The term *lunge* is somewhat misleading. When performing this exercise, think about dropping your back knee straight down toward the ground to make a 90-degree angle there, instead of lunging forward with the lead leg.

1. Start with an upright posture, abs tight, shoulders back, and arms at the sides. Inhale.
2. Take a large step forward with the right (lead) leg and plant the foot flat on the floor. Allow the left knee to bend slightly.
3. Drop the body down to bend the right knee to about a 90-degree angle, making sure that the knee is directly over the foot.
4. The left knee will bend to a 90-degree angle as the heel rolls off the floor. Keep the knee just above the floor and keep the torso upright.
5. Forcefully exhale and push off the floor with the lead leg.
6. Return to the starting position and switch lead legs.

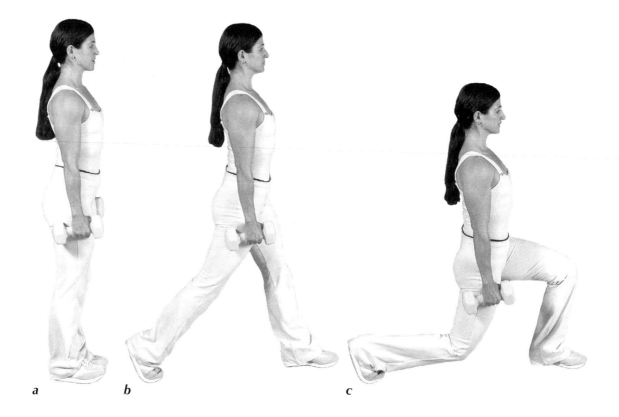

*a*　　　　*b*　　　　　　　　*c*

# STEP-UP

Another type of functional multijoint exercise, the step-up, is as easy to do as its name. But don't let that fool you—you'll work hard and use almost every lower-body muscle that you have. Vary the height of the step to correspond to your strength level, load, and reps. Beginners should use a low step, no weight or light weight, and moderate reps. Intermediate and advanced steppers can increase the height of the step and the amount of the load but shouldn't do lots of reps with a heavy load. How high you step depends on maintaining correct form. Make sure that you can step up and down with good balance and solid strength. Don't hop in order to get on top of the step, and don't allow a significant forward lean. You can do step-ups to the front, side, and back, and you can hold dumbbells or a barbell while performing them.

1. Stand just in front of a box or bench with abs tight, shoulders back, and arms at the sides. Inhale.

2. Step on the box with the right (lead) leg, putting the entire foot on the box.

3. Shift your body weight onto the lead leg and keep the torso upright.

4. Exhale while forcefully extending the hip and knee so that they are straight and bring the left leg up to stand on the box.

5. Inhale and slowly exhale while bending the right knee and hip so that the left leg can return to the floor.

6. Step off the box with the right leg and switch lead legs.

*a*                                    *b*

# Backside Exercises

We already know that squatting will give us a great looking rear, but surely there is more we can do for the back of our thighs. Virtually any multijoint exercise for the legs works your glutes and hamstrings; however, some exercises target these areas more specifically. Keep in mind that the muscles on the back of your leg are intimately connected with your low back. They attach to your pelvis, as does your spine. Tight hamstrings, glutes, or hip rotator muscles may be the culprits in low back pain; the stress of these tight muscles pulling on the pelvis can cause such pain. Also, the piriformis muscle deep in the buttock covers the sciatic nerve, a major nerve that feeds the leg. If this muscle is tight, it may clamp down on that nerve and send shooting pain (sciatica) down the buttocks and the back of the leg. For preventative medicine, make sure that you incorporate flexibility movements and stretching into your routine. Check out the dynamic warm-up in chapter 7.

## BUTT LIFT

Get out of the butt blaster machine and onto a ball. You get to strengthen your glutes by getting them off the floor. You also do double duty by using your core muscles in this exercise.

1. Lie back on a stability ball so that the head, neck, and shoulders are supported by the ball. The knees are fully bent, the abs are tight, and the butt is off the ball. The legs are slightly apart. Arms can rest by the sides.

2. Squeeze the glutes to raise the hips up until the body is in a straight line, like a bridge. The knees should make a 90-degree angle.

3. Hold this position for 3 to 5 seconds, keeping the glutes squeezed and the abs tight.

4. Lower and repeat.

*a*

*b*

# HIP EXTENSION

The hip extension, another stability ball exercise, involves the core muscles as well. You can see how the glutes tie into these core muscles when you make your body as stable as possible during this exercise.

1. Lie flat on the back on the ground, with the heels together on top of the ball. Arms can rest by the sides.
2. Tighten the abs and glutes, dig the heels into the ball, and lift the hips off the floor until the body is in a straight line.
3. Hold this position, keeping the glutes squeezed and the abs tight.
4. To decrease the difficulty, place the ball under the knees rather than under the heels. To increase the difficulty, cross the arms across the chest.

a

b

## STABILITY BALL LEG CURL

Anything that you can do lying on your back doesn't sound too hard, does it? Just try out these stability ball leg curls. Your hamstrings will be screaming for you to stand up.

1. Lie flat on the back on the ground. Place the heels on top of a stability ball. Rest the arms by the sides.
2. Tighten the abs, dig the heels into the ball, bend the knees, and roll the ball toward the butt.
3. Straighten the legs to roll the ball back to the starting position.
4. Make this exercise more challenging by doing a hip extension and holding the hips up while you roll the ball, or by performing the exercise unilaterally.

a

b

# Isolation Exercises

If you have an inherent weakness in your quadriceps or hamstring muscle groups, or if you like to do some machine exercises, you'll want to jump on the leg extension machine for quadriceps work and on the leg curl machine for hamstring work. Although the multijoint exercises produce strong and stable legs and are far superior for overall strengthening, sometimes you need a little extra help. These machines isolate the muscles they are designed to work on and allow them to get an overload without other muscles helping out. I usually don't recommend using machines, but with weakness or injury machines are often a helpful adjunct.

The leg extension machine effectively isolates the quadriceps muscle group. If you have a quadriceps deficiency, then consider adding this exercise to your routine. The leg extension machine is useful for performing slow eccentric contractions (in which the weight is lowering) and for selecting a particular range of motion to train in.

A word of caution, though, for those women who try the leg extension machine and feel pain. There may be a reason why this machine bothers the knees and thus a reason why you shouldn't do them. Seek out professional help to evaluate and remedy the problem. Remember to use isolation exercises as an adjunct to your routine and not as a staple.

To understand why the leg extension machine may be the culprit in knee pain, it helps to understand how the joint works and what kinds of forces it may be susceptible to during daily activities and exercises. The patellofemoral joint reaction (PFJR) force is the result of the amount of knee flexion and the force of the quadriceps muscles creating pressure on the patella against the femur. As the knee flexes, the patella is mostly in contact with the femoral groove. This large contact area can help dissipate compressive forces. However, as the knee extends the patella has minimal contact with the groove. This small contact area cannot disperse compressive forces as effectively. Applying this concept to exercise, we find immense compressive forces when we perform a seated knee extension, because the quadriceps has to generate great force to overcome gravity and lift weight. The compressive forces remain great as the knee extends, and the patella cannot dissipate these forces. As the knee flexes while squatting, on the other hand, the PFJR force does increase but the load is more evenly distributed across the patella as it comes into contact with the femur.

Another reason more women have knee pain in the leg extension machine has to do with the design of the equipment itself. Most machines are designed with the standard male body in mind: 5 feet-10 inches, 180 pounds. Of course the manufacturers try to accommodate all different shapes of people by providing movable backrests and ankle bars. But let's face it—they did not design one especially for you. Your unique body shape may fit with one leg extension machine and not another. You may be trying to force a round peg into a square hole, and that doesn't feel too good on your joints.

## LEG EXTENSION

1. Sit down in a machine, tighten the abs, and press the low back against the support pad.
2. Place the feet behind the roller pad.
3. Make sure that the knee joint is aligned with the axis of the machine. Adjust the back support or roller pad if necessary.
4. Grasp the handles on the sides of the machine. Inhale.
5. Exhale and extend the legs to a full lockout position, if you are pain-free.
6. Hold for 1 to 2 seconds.
7. Slowly lower to the starting position.

*a*

*b*

# LEG CURL

Machine leg curls isolate the hamstring muscles and pull a bit of the glutes into play as well. Keep the abs tight throughout this movement, squeeze the glutes together, and don't use momentum to pull the legs back. The front of your body should be in contact with the pad at all times, and the hips should not kick up.

1. Lie face down on the machine and press the body firmly down. The knees should be slightly off the padding and in line with the axis of the machine.
2. Put the feet underneath the roller pads and adjust if necessary to achieve proper fit.
3. Grasp the handles on the sides of the machine. Inhale.
4. Bend the knees and curl the roller pad toward the buttocks. Curl as far as possible.
5. Hold for 1 to 2 seconds.
6. Exhale while slowly lowering to the starting position.

*a*

*b*

# CALF RAISE

Throughout all of this leg work we have barely mentioned the calves, but that doesn't mean that you haven't been working them. The lower-leg muscles are the pillars that undergird all of these exercises. They are extremely important for your balance and stability, and you shouldn't overlook them. But remember that they are working quite hard during all of your standing exercises, so make sure not to start a hard leg-training session by working your calves—just end it that way. You can do this exercise in a machine, or you can hold dumbbells and hang your heels off the edge of a step.

1. Face the machine, place the forefeet on the footplate, and allow the heels to hang down.
2. Move under the shoulder pads and stand tall, keeping the knees straight and the toes pointed straight ahead. Inhale.
3. Exhale as you extend up on the toes.
4. Hold for 1 to 2 seconds.
5. Slowly lower and repeat.

*a*                              *b*

## TREADMILL CALVES

Incline treadmill walking is challenging enough for your calves, but why not kick it up a notch? Try walking on a supersteep incline while holding heavy dumbbells. Concentrate on clawing at the treadmill with your toes and even try rising up on your toes with each step. Go for 1-minute intervals at first. You don't need a lot to train your calves with this exercise.

# 12

# Deadlifting for Whole-Body Strength

I've organized the previous chapters according to body parts and what exercises you should do for each part. So you'd think that we would have covered it all by now, right? One more exercise needs to be mentioned, however, and it actually deserves its own chapter. You can't categorize it as a low back exercise, although that is typically what people do. If you are performing this exercise correctly, your quads and glutes will get a tremendous workout as well as your low back. Your abs, traps, and upper back will work extremely hard, and you'll be dead on the ground without a good grip. This one exercise—the deadlift—incorporates so many muscles that it is difficult to pigeonhole it.

If you've ever been to a powerlifting meet, then you know that the contest really begins once the bar hits the floor. The weights are loaded on the bar, the deadlifts begin, and that's what separates the record setters from the gym lifters. You don't have to be a record setter, though, to reap the many rewards of the deadlift. But you do need patience, mental focus, and a sound strategy.

Deadlifts are multifunctional exercises used by a variety of people. They are so rewarding that bodybuilders, powerlifters, strongwomen, and other athletes alike all choose to deadlift. Why should anyone be excluded from one of the most beneficial exercises for the entire body? Bodybuilders deadlift because these exercises are excellent for overloading muscles, and they expend an enormous amount of energy. In powerlifting, the deadlift is one of the competition exercises. Strongwoman contests have some sort of extraordinary deadlift event, such as deadlifting a truck. Deadlifting is important for athletes because it requires several large muscle groups to work in a coordinated fashion. Athletes also use this versatile lift to develop explosive strength through the legs, hips, and back. Performing deadlifts will benefit you in any sport that requires jumping, running, lifting an opponent or object, or moving quickly from a stationary spot.

But deadlifts are not just for athletes. Deadlifting, like squatting, is an integral part of life. You may not know you are doing it, but you are deadlifting all day long. Deadlifts are functional movements that carry over to everyday activities outside the gym, such as lifting a heavy box off the ground or picking up the laundry basket. Deadlifts are associated with increases in strength and muscle mass, and no other exercise provides a better way to strengthen the entire body while teaching proper lifting mechanics.

The deadlift effectively involves the entire lower-body musculature and some of the upper-body musculature for stabilization (see figure 12.1). Throughout the movement the erector spinae muscles that run from the back of the head along the entire length of the spine contract isometrically to maintain a flat back, with the help of the abdominal muscles. The latissimus dorsi also contracts isometrically to help hold the shoulder joint upright and keep the arms tightly against the trunk. If your arms drift forward while deadlifting, the weighted bar will change your center of gravity and throw off your balance, leading to missed attempts and injuries. The rhomboids and scapular retractors work at keeping the shoulders back and the chest upright. Wrist and hand muscles help in holding the barbell, and the gastrocnemius and soleus muscles work on stabilization.

The hamstrings and gluteus maximus contract eccentrically while the hips and knees bend to slowly lower the upper body toward the floor. To raise the torso and barbell up, the quadriceps, hamstrings, and gluteal muscles contract concentrically.

The purpose of a deadlift is to lift the weight off the floor with good technique, not to get it up any way you can. Although some deadlifters would argue with this statement, trying to deadlift without good technique is the quickest way to not being able to lift at all. The biggest pitfall that deadlifters stumble into is performing deadlifts with a rounded back. With the back rounded, the load shifts from the hips, glutes, and legs to the low back alone. In addition to stressing the muscles of the low back, this weak mechanical position places stress on the ligaments (which attach bone to bone) and the intervertebral discs (which are shock absorb-

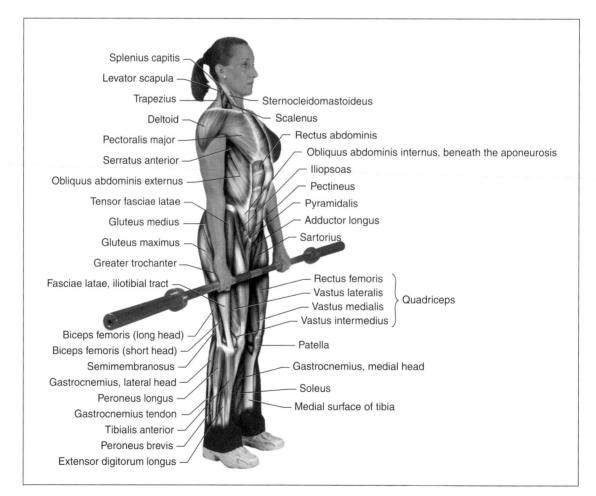

**Figure 12.1**   The muscles involved in executing the deadlift.

ers sandwiched between your vertebrae) in the low back. Although ligaments stretch, they are not like rubber bands. Once overstretched, they do not go back to their previous length. This condition leads to instabilities and back problems down the road. You must be aware of the potential risks involved with this lift. To avoid orthopedic problems, practice the movement and dedicate yourself to learning the proper technique. Perform the deadlift in front of a mirror or with proper supervision until you have it right.

## WARMING UP

As we discussed in chapter 7, a general warm-up increases circulation and heats up the entire body. Some light walking with arm movement or some jumping jacks can do the trick. A general warm-up should last about 5 to 10 minutes. Another good warm-up for lifters is to grab a bar and perform a stiff-leg deadlift, followed by a reverse curl, followed by an overhead press. Try to do this series continuously for 10 to 15 repetitions, without pausing between movements. Don't tire yourself out before the big show; just get the blood flowing to your muscles. After your general warm-up, perform dynamic stretches and then your specific warm-up lifting sets as described in chapter 7.

## CONVENTIONAL DEADLIFT

For beginners and intermediates, starting with light dumbbells is a logical choice. You can work on getting the proper technique with light weights and then progress to heavier dumbbells before moving up to the barbell. However, if you are using dumbbells or a barbell without the standard 45-pound plates on it, realize that you will probably be covering a larger ROM. The 45-pound plates are much larger than dumbbells or any other plates, so you'll be bending down farther with lighter weights. Think of it this way—when you are strong enough to pull 135 pounds (a 45-pound plate on each side of the 45-pound barbell) you won't have to bend as low, because the 45-pound plates are much higher than any of the plates you have been lifting. The heavier weight will actually seem easier.

Deadlift variations derive from this traditional deadlift, but all rely on some simple rules. Follow the instructions for perfect form and execution on every rep.

### Beginner and Intermediate—Dumbbells

1. Set up the dumbbells to the outside of each leg.
2. Position the feet slightly less than shoulder-width apart, flat on the floor, with the toes pointed out slightly.
3. Bend the knees and lower the hips into a deep squat position, with the hips lower than the shoulders.
4. Tighten the back so that it is flat or slightly arched.
5. Grasp the dumbbells with an overhand grip and inhale.
6. Exhale as you pull the weight off the ground, keeping the back flat, the abs tight, the arms straight, the head up, and the weights close to the body.
7. Stand erectly, but don't lean back at the top of the lift.
8. Lower the weight, keeping the back flat by bending first at the hips and then at the knees.
9. Pause and reset the starting position before doing another rep.

a          b

### Intermediate and Advanced—Barbell

1. When you can advance to a barbell, position it on the ground in front of you, lightly touching the shins.
2. Position the feet slightly less than shoulder-width apart, flat on the floor, with the toes pointed out slightly.
3. Bend the knees and lower the hips into a deep squat position, with the hips lower than the shoulders.
4. Tighten the back so that it is flat or slightly arched.
5. Use an overhand grip slightly wider than where the legs touch the bar.
6. Look upward slightly and pull against the bar so that there is no slack in the arms or the bar. Inhale.
7. Exhale and raise up while moving the shoulders and hips as a unit. Keep the bar close to the body throughout the movement.
8. Stand erectly, but don't lean back at the top of the lift.
9. Lower the weight, keeping the back flat by bending first at the hips and then at the knees.
10. Pause and reset the starting position before doing another rep.

*a*                    *b*

## TOP 11 DEADLIFT TRAINING TIPS

1. Always clear an area of at least 4 by 8 feet of loose plates and other items.
2. Don't let the hips kick up before the shoulders start to move; they should come up together.
3. Keep the shoulders in front of the barbell throughout the lift.
4. Keep the arms completely straight throughout the lift.
5. Keep the pull smooth and consistent.
6. Lower the bar with a flat back.
7. Don't bounce the bar off the ground at the end of the lift.
8. Always deadlift with collars on the bar to ensure a balanced bar.
9. Rely on the strong trunk muscles instead of a lifting belt.
10. Make sure that you follow strict form when lifting to failure, because impaired mechanics may increase the risk for injury.
11. Do not perform forced reps or negative-only reps.

## RACK DEADLIFT

The rack deadlift is a partial version of the conventional deadlift. You perform it inside a power rack with pins set so that the bar is located just above the knees. It is an excellent exercise for beginners—you don't have to use a full ROM, and having the rack is like using a spotter. Deadlifts from a racked position emphasize your low back muscles, because you won't be bending as low and thereby incorporating your legs. Use this exercise to help strengthen the low back specifically or if you want to attempt heavier weights than you can lift from the floor.

1. Begin this exercise using a shoulder-width stance with the arms just outside the thighs.
2. Using an overhand grip, bend the knees slightly to grasp the bar. Inhale.
3. Exhale as you pull the weight off the pins, keeping the back flat, the abs tight, the head up, and the weights close to the body.
4. Don't bounce the bar off the pins in the rack when lowering the weight and starting the next rep.

*a*        *b*

## TRAP BAR DEADLIFT

Use the trap bar to reduce stress on your spine and emphasize your quads. Particularly if balance, technique, or the bar hitting the knees is a problem, try the trap bar. You perform this movement as you do the conventional deadlift, except that you stand inside the trap bar.

1. Position yourself inside a trap bar.
2. Bend into a squat to grasp the handles, with the back flat and the abs tight. Inhale.
3. Exhale and raise up while moving the shoulders and hips as a unit.
4. Stand erectly, but don't lean back at the top of the lift.
5. Lower the weight, keeping the back flat by first bending at the hips and then at the knees.
6. Pause and reset the starting position before doing another rep.

*a*        *b*

## SUMO DEADLIFT

This deadlift won't make you look like a sumo wrestler, thank goodness, but it will give you strong legs and a strong low back like a sumo wrestler's. A wide stance with your arms between your legs differentiates this deadlift from the rest. You can go as wide as you want, as long as your feet are firmly on the ground and you are in a stable position. Remember that the wider you go, the more your adductors have to stretch in the bottom position. This movement brings in more thigh muscles like the adductors and quads, rather than the hamstrings, glutes, and low back.

1. Set up in a wide-stance squat position with the hips and feet either neutral or slightly externally rotated. Do not completely externally rotate the legs, as in a ballet plié. Lower the body until the hands grasp the barbell. Inhale.
2. Exhale as you pull the weight off the floor, keeping the back flat, the abs tight, the head up, and the weight close to the body.
3. Slowly lower the weight by bending the knees and dropping the hips.
4. Pause and reset the starting position before doing another rep.

a

b

# STIFF-LEG DEADLIFT

Want to hit your hams and glutes hard? This is the deadlift variation for you. You perform this movement as you do the conventional deadlift, except that the knees are straight. Don't sacrifice form for range of motion. You don't need to do this exercise off the edge of a bench to gain distance. Also, if you round your back to touch the floor, you may never get up. Play it safe, stick with the proper movement, and eventually the flexibility will come.

1. Stand with the feet hip-shoulder-width apart and hold a barbell in both hands with an overhand grip. Inhale.
2. Lean forward from the hips, keeping the head up, the shoulders back, and the chest out.
3. Slightly unlock the knees and, as you lean forward, allow the bar to move out in front of you.
4. Push the hips backward and lean forward until the torso is level to the floor or lower, as long as the back stays flat or arched. Stop the ROM if the back starts to round.
5. Maintain this position and exhale while pulling your torso back into the starting position.

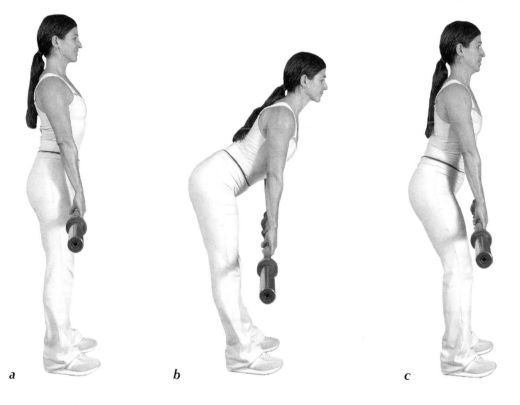

*a*  *b*  *c*

For a change of pace from stiff-leg barbell deadlift, try the movement using dumbbells. You perform stiff-leg dumbbell deadlifts in a manner similar to the barbell version—just keep the dumbbells close to your legs, holding them in an overhand grip. Some people find holding the dumbbells in a parallel fashion on the side of the thighs easier.

## ROMANIAN DEADLIFT

Olympic lifters do this exercise to develop strong hamstrings and glutes. It is just like the stiff-leg deadlift except that you keep the barbell in contact with the legs throughout the lift.

1. Stand with the feet hip-shoulder-width apart and hold a barbell in both hands with an overhand grip. Inhale.
2. Lean forward from the hips, keeping the head up, the shoulders back, and the chest out.
3. Shift the weight toward the heels as the glutes move back.
4. As you lean forward, slide the bar down the thighs to midshin level. Allow the knees to bend slightly.
5. Maintain this position and exhale while pulling the torso back into the starting position.

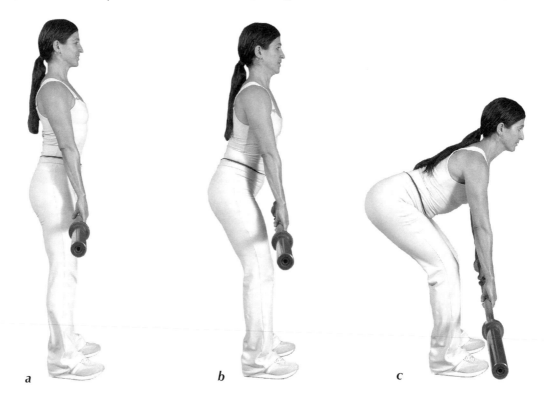

*a*                          *b*                          *c*

In general, you should do compound exercises that use large muscle groups first in a workout (after the warm-up), and do isolation-type exercises that focus on one particular muscle later in the workout. Deadlifts incorporate many muscle groups and joint movements, so you should perform them first. This concept is especially important for beginners. You don't want to be fatigued when you first learn how to do a movement. Deadlifts are typically done on a back workout day, but don't be afraid to use them on a leg workout day or give them a day of their own. Stay with a 5- to 10RM intensity for 3 to 4 sets after your warm-up sets, once a week. You shouldn't have to deadlift more than once a week if you are lifting with the appropriate weight and intensity. Check out chapter 7 to see how well deadlifts can fit into a program.

## USING A HOOK GRIP

Powerlifters use an alternating grip (one palm facing forward, the other backward) when deadlifting to prevent the bar from rolling out of their hands. Yet Olympic weightlifters lift extremely heavy weights with both palms facing backward, or pronated. What's their secret to holding on to the bar so well? They all use a hook grip. The hook grip is more efficient and allows you to lift much more weight without the use of straps. This grip is a little tough to master, but it is well worth the pain. As you grasp the barbell with a pronated grip, the thumbs wrap around the bar first, and then the first two or three fingers on each hand wrap over the thumbs (as opposed to the traditional grip in which the fingers wrap around the bar first and then the thumbs wrap around on top of them). You have more control with the hook grip because two or more fingers are holding on to the thumb, rather than one thumb holding on to two or more fingers. It's a little painful at first, because the thumbs need to stretch quite a bit and the fingers compress them. Start out by lifting lighter weights and let your thumbs adapt. In a short while you will impress all your friends with the weights you can lift without straps.

# 13

# Quenching Your Competitive Fire

Some people are born competitors. Every action they take has an underlying motive of being the best or being first. They compete with themselves and with others, whether the others know it or not. They compete in both their personal and professional lives—they probably would wither up and die without competition. Strength training is an athletic endeavor that can lead you to various formal competitions in weightlifting and powerlifting, as well as to strongwoman contests. Whether or not you eventually decide to match your skill against someone else in a formal competition, you will always be competing with yourself.

The purpose of strength training is to continually lift heavier weights, get stronger, get healthier, and look better. Ultimately, it is always you against the weights. But if your strength training lights a competitive fire within you, go for it. Once you get the competition bug, it can be rewarding to see how you rank among others. You might find that you can outdo the other competitors. In that case, you can progress to more advanced competitions against other strong women. You might also find out that you have a long way to go. You can use that knowledge and experience to fire you up even more in the gym, to strive for increased strength.

Diversity abounds in sports, and it is equally plentiful in the training methods used for each sport. As we learned in the previous chapters, specific training yields specific results, based on the particular exercises you do. If your sport is long-distance running, you won't do very well in a race if you spend the majority of your training time lifting heavy weights in the gym. Likewise, if you are a powerlifter, running marathons won't help you blast heavy weights off your chest. Although strength-related sports are few, they are as different as the many team sports that exist. Because of their differences, their training programs and techniques are different too.

## Olympic Weightlifting

Let's examine an elite-level bodybuilder, a powerlifter, and an Olympic lifter (weightlifter), each weighing the same. The bodybuilder is clearly the most muscular, the powerlifter is usually the strongest, and the weightlifter is usually the most powerful. Participants from each of these sports perform many similar exercises, such as squats and pressing movements.

Why then is the Olympic lifter so much more powerful than the other athletes who also lift weights? One reason is that this type of athlete performs movements in a very explosive fashion. Snatches and clean and jerks form the bulk of the training program for weightlifters, and they are the two lifts used in competitions. These movements are done explosively, meaning that the athlete attempts to move the weights as quickly as possible. The result of this type of training is more power (force × velocity); a fairly high force is required to move an object quickly. With certain Olympic movements, like snatches and cleans, there is a carryover effect from doing explosive lifts that yields increases in jumping and sprinting abilities. This type of training won't guarantee that you will become a better athlete—after all, athletic performance involves a variety of factors. But if you add Olympic lifts or some variation of them to your strength-training program, you can develop the athletic qualities I've mentioned.

In addition, power training is helpful even for those interested in more aesthetic goals. Research suggests that the fast-twitch muscle fibers that are involved in explosive movements are more capable of hypertrophy than slow-twitch fibers. So even if you don't decide to compete in weightlifting, by adding power movements to your training you can have both a buffed body and some of the athletic skills to use it.

You can add explosive movements such as snatches and clean and jerks to most strength-training programs even if you aren't interested in competition just yet. Keep in mind a few pointers to maximize the benefits of performing these movements. The Olympic lifts and their variations require a higher degree of skill than simpler exercises like a barbell curl or a shoulder press. Spend time learning how to do the weightlifting movements with a broomstick first. Once your technique is developed, you can start to progressively add weight.

It's best to do these types of movements first in your workout. If you are learning any new exercise, perform it first so that fatigue from previous movements does not interfere. If you already know how to perform these exercises, then you should still do them first so that you can focus on improving your maximal power while you are fresh. If you are tired or fatigued from other exercises, then you may not be able to perform these explosive movements to the best of your ability.

It takes a long time to perfect weightlifting exercises, and you're not going to make the Olympic team after one workout. Most people add weight too quickly and consequently develop bad habits. Although lifting large weights may seem gratifying, improper technique doesn't allow you to develop power and maximize what you can lift. Those who teach and coach weightlifting start their students out with a broomstick to simulate the barbell, and only when the technique is nailed down does the student graduate to the barbell alone and then to added weights. At first it may help to watch yourself in the mirror so that you can minimize any mistakes in your lifting. As you become better at performing the exercises, try not to rely on the mirror because it will slow you down. Initially you should focus on learning the pulling motion for these exercises. Once you understand the transition that joints such as the knees and hips make throughout the pull, then you can focus on performing the lift more quickly. When you can perform the pulling motion quickly, progress to more advanced movements. If you have access to a coach or to someone familiar with these movements, you can save a tremendous amount of time. Such a person can help correct mistakes in your technique and advise you on when to progress to more advanced movements.

Although there are only two competition lifts, the snatch and the clean and jerk, weightlifters do other explosive exercises to get the most out of their training. Besides those exercises that follow, many do the split jerk (page 129), the push press (page 127), and the power jerk (page 128).

# SNATCH PULL

The snatch pull is a good training tool for learning the first part of the snatch. You simply extend the hips, knees, and ankles without catching the weight overhead. This exercise works the gluteus maximus, quadriceps, and spinal erectors, and to a smaller extent the trapezius, deltoids, and biceps brachii.

1. Position a weighted barbell on the ground. Squat down and grasp the barbell with the hands in a pronated position using a hook grip (fingers covering thumb—see page 183), spaced apart much wider than shoulder-width. If you are using a barbell only or light weights, start with the barbell at midshin level.

2. Pull against the bar so that the arms are straight and the low back is flat or slightly arched. You will lean forward slightly, but distribute your weight evenly on the feet. Inhale.

3. Lift the bar off the floor by forcefully extending the knees and hips. Keep the shoulders in front of the bar and keep the bar close to the shins. Do not let the hips rise faster than the shoulders.

4. Just after the bar passes the knees, drive the hips forward and bend the knees so that the thighs are under the bar.

5. Explosively extend the knees, hips, and ankles as you shrug the shoulders, keeping the arms straight. Simultaneously exhale.

6. Lower the bar to the ground in the reverse order of that you lifted it in.

a

b

c

*a*

*b*

## SNATCH

One of the competition lifts, the snatch requires that you explosively lift the weight off the floor to an overhead position in one continuous movement. It works the gluteus maximus, hamstrings, quadriceps, gastrocnemius, soleus, and spinal erector muscles primarily, with a smaller emphasis on the trapezius, deltoids, biceps brachii, and triceps brachii.

Focus on jumping with the weight. Relax the arms so that initially they are straight and so that the momentum from the bar moving upward is timed with bending the arms. Don't forget to bend the knees after the bar passes them (the bar should be around the upper third of the thigh when the knee bend occurs).

1. Position a weighted barbell on the ground. Squat down and grasp the barbell with the hands in a pronated position using a hook grip (fingers covering thumb—see page 183), spaced apart much wider than shoulder-width. If you are using a barbell only or light weights, start with the barbell at midshin level.

2. Pull against the bar so that the arms are straight and the low back is flat or slightly arched. You will lean forward slightly, but your weight should be evenly distributed on the feet. Inhale.

3. Lift the bar off the floor by forcefully extending the hips and knees. Keep the shoulders in front of the bar and keep the bar close to the shins. Do not let the hips rise faster than the shoulders.

*c*

*d*

4. Just after the bar passes the knees, drive the hips forward and bend the knees so that the thighs are under the bar.

5. Explosively extend the knees, hips, and ankles as you shrug the shoulders, keeping the arms straight, and then flex the elbows to pull the body under the bar as you raise the bar overhead.

6. Simultaneously jump, shuffle the feet out laterally, and pull the body underneath the bar. You'll catch the weight in an overhead squat position with elbows fully extended, bar slightly behind the head, abs tight, back arched, and feet flat.

7. Exhale as you stand up out of the deep overhead squat position.

8. Return the bar to the starting position. If you are using rubber weights, you can just guide the bar down as it free-falls to the floor. Remove the hands after the bar passes the knees so that it doesn't bounce up and hit you. If you don't have access to rubber weights, you can lower the bar to the thighs and then resume the starting position from there. Be careful not to let it fall too fast or you will bruise the thighs.

## CLEAN PULL

The clean pull is a good training tool for learning the first part of the clean and jerk. You extend the hips, knees, and ankles without racking in the weight. This exercise works the gluteus maximus, quadriceps, and spinal erectors, and to a smaller extent the trapezius, deltoids, and biceps brachii.

1. Position a barbell on the ground. Squat down and grasp the barbell with the hands in a pronated position using a hook grip (fingers covering thumb), spaced slightly wider than shoulder-width.

2. Pull against the bar so that the arms are straight and the low back is flat or slightly arched. You will lean forward slightly, but your weight should be evenly distributed on the feet. Inhale.

3. Lift the bar off the floor by forcefully extending the knees and hips. Keep the shoulders in front of the bar and keep the bar close to the shins. Do not let the hips rise faster than the shoulders.

4. Just after the bar passes the knees, drive the hips forward and bend the knees so that the thighs are under the bar.

5. Explosively extend the knees, hips, and ankles as you shrug the shoulders, keeping the arms straight. Simultaneously exhale.

6. Lower the bar to the ground in the reverse order of that you lifted it in.

Refer also to the split jerk (on page 129). The split jerk is a training tool for teaching the second part of the clean and jerk. It works the deltoids and triceps primarily, and the quadriceps and gluteus maximus to a lesser degree.

*a*

*b*

*a*

*b*

*c*

## CLEAN AND JERK

The clean and jerk is the second weightlifting competition lift, and it also works the gluteus maximus, hamstrings, quadriceps, gastrocnemius, soleus, and spinal erector muscles primarily, with a secondary focus on the trapezius, deltoids, biceps brachii, and triceps brachii. During the clean phase, you lift the barbell from the floor to the shoulders and rack it on the clavicle in one continuous motion. (This phase can be done as its own exercise – the power clean.) During the second part of the lift, called the jerk, you lift the bar overhead with a combined effort of the legs and arms.

1. Position a weighted barbell on the ground. Squat down and grasp the barbell with the hands in a pronated position using a hook grip (fingers covering thumb), spaced slightly wider than shoulder-width. If you are using a barbell only or light weights, start with the barbell at midshin level.

2. Pull against the bar so that the arms are straight and the low back is flat or slightly arched. You will lean forward slightly, but your weight should be evenly distributed on the feet. Inhale.

3. Lift the bar off the floor by forcefully extending the knees and hips. Keep the shoulders in front of the bar and keep the bar close to the shins. Do not let the hips rise faster than the shoulders.

4. Just after the bar passes the knees, drive the hips forward and bend the knees so that the thighs are under the bar.

5. Extend the hips and knees again and elevate the heels.

6. Shrug the shoulders, keeping the arms straight, and then flex the elbows to pull the body under the bar as you raise it.

7. Simultaneously, jump the feet from hip-width to shoulder-width, and pull the body underneath the bar.

8. Catch the bar and rack it on the clavicles and anterior shoulders while you are in a deep squat position. Keep the head up and the torso tight, and exhale as you stand up.

9. To jerk the weight overhead, slightly bend and extend the knees and forcefully extend the weight overhead while the legs split and land, first the back foot, then the front foot.

10. Push off the front leg and take one step back. Push off the back leg and take one step forward. The feet should be in the starting position.

11. Slowly lower the weight back down to the clavicle.

12. Lower the bar slowly to the thighs while bending the knees and hips to cushion the impact of the bar. If you are using rubber weights, you can just guide the bar down as it free-falls to the floor. Remove the hands after the bar passes the knees so that it doesn't bounce up and hit you. If you don't have access to rubber weights, you can lower the bar to the thighs and then resume the starting position from there. Be careful not to let it fall too fast or you will bruise the thighs.

*d*

*e*

# Powerlifting

Powerlifting should really be called strength lifting or force lifting, because although it requires quite high levels of strength, it requires only low levels of power. Remember that strength is the maximal amount of force a muscle or muscle group can generate at a specified velocity. Also, strength movements are slow compared to other movements because it takes time to generate maximal force. Because power movements exert force at a high speed, lighter resistances have to be used than with pure strength movements. So what we have is a sport that was incorrectly named. Powerlifting competitions are composed of three lifts: the squat, the bench press, and the deadlift. Each competitor gets three attempts to achieve her best lift in each exercise. Rest time between the lifts will vary according to the organization's rules and how many people are competing. The heaviest weight the competitor reaches is recorded, and the overall meet winner is the one with the highest total of weight for all three lifts. Awards may also be given to the winners of each individual lift.

Despite its name, powerlifting requires more strength than power.

A powerlifter needs to become a triple threat in the squat, bench press, and deadlift to rack up serious points. But she can also supersucceed at one lift and merely do well on the others, and still win a competition. Although powerlifting burns calories and increases muscular mass, 1RM lifts in general are not going to make you particularly lean. In fact the more you weigh, the more weight you can push around, and the less distance you have to push it. Therefore, powerlifters frequently try to gain extra weight to improve their performance.

If you are interested in strength training and love to shop, powerlifting just may be the sport for you. You'll need to buy many accessories that are essential in powerlifting. Belts, wraps, straps, shirts, suits, gloves—you just can't have enough training equipment if you are a powerlifter. There is no doubt about the efficacy of these tools for helping to increase a 1RM, though.

Another technique that powerlifters use extensively is called the Valsalva maneuver. Doing the Valsalva maneuver not only helps you achieve a high 1RM, but also protects the low back musculature if you tighten your abdominal muscles at the same time. This maneuver increases intra-abdominal and intrathoracic pressure when you exhale with the glottis (the opening at the back of the tongue) closed. It is frequently described as bearing down, as if you are giving birth or trying to pass something else. Be aware that this technique briefly increases blood pressure and heart rate; therefore, only healthy people who have no history of cardiovascular disease should use it. Sometimes the Valsalva maneuver is performed unknowingly throughout many lifts.

The competition lifts are the squat, bench press, and deadlift, but you can incorporate many other exercises in powerlifting training to increase strength and maintain joint integrity. When training for powerlifting competitions, a lifter doesn't do only the competition lifts. Many accessory muscles contribute to the stability and integrity of the joints involved in these lifts. Exercises that are popular in a powerlifting routine are called assistive exercises and include most of the basic exercises for individual body parts that are listed in chapters 8 through 11. You will find detailed descriptions of the squat in chapter 11, the bench press in chapter 9, and the deadlift in chapter 12. But powerlifting squats, bench presses, and deadlifts differ slightly from the standards, so the powerlifting specifics are outlined as follows:

**Squat**—Powerlifting squats can be different from traditional squats (shown on page 159). One technique that powerlifters employ has the bar traveling the least distance in order to maximize the weight lifted. With this technique powerlifters take the widest leg stance possible to make the regulation bend in the knee come sooner than if their legs were shoulder-width apart. This technique causes the powerlifter to lean forward much more than in a traditional squat and transfers a lot of the load to the low back, glutes and hamstrings.

**Bench press**—The powerlifting bench press includes a pause on the chest with the bar. The bar must come to a complete stop and touch your chest before you explode up. A wider

© Dennis Light/Light Photographic

grip and an excessively arched back shorten the distance that the bar must travel to touch the chest. During the lift, the glutes and shoulders must maintain contact with the bench or the lift is disqualified.

**Deadlift**—You have to be careful with deadlifts, because if you don't maintain strict form it is easy to get injured. In the process of competition, when the weights get heavier and heavier and the pressure to perform becomes intense, the temptation is to lift the bar up any way possible, including such dangerous practices as lifting with a rounded back, bouncing the weight off the floor, and twisting the body. There are two competition styles of deadlifts: conventional and sumo (see pages 178 and 180). Both are described in chapter 12. Following the logic of a wide-stance powerlifting squat, if you sumo deadlift, you shorten the distance that the bar has to travel. You need to practice both techniques to determine which one is right for you.

## ISOMETRICS AND POWERLIFTING

Although they don't strengthen muscles through a full range of motion, isometrics can strengthen isolated ranges of motion that are weak. For example, if you can bench press a certain weight but have trouble locking it out at the top, then an isometric exercise concentrating on that range is beneficial. But if you are trying to move a (seemingly) immovable object like a vehicle, then the sticking point is going to be at the start of the movement. You would perform an isometric move in which your elbows are bent as opposed to almost straight.

Isometrics call on every muscle fiber to respond, so they are very fatiguing. Put them in at the end of a workout session so you don't get injured by your tired muscles. Isometrics are very safe because if you fail with the weight, the only thing that falls from exhaustion is the body part you are training. You can do isometrics against anything that would be immovable for you—superheavy weights with barbells, dumbbells, or machines; a Smith machine; or the wall.

*Barbell Bench Press Isometrics*

1. Set up in a rack that has adjustable pins for the barbell to rest on or use a Smith machine (barbell that travels on tracks).
2. Set the barbell at the beginning of the sticking point (the point at which you have difficulty pushing through or completing a movement for a full lockout).
3. Load the bar with enough weight that you couldn't budge it if you and your girlfriend were lifting it or keep the bar locked into the Smith machine hooks.
4. Lie down on the bench, grasp the barbell, and get into the bench press position.
5. Push up against the bar and hold the effort for 10 seconds. Repeat 10 times.

*Vehicle Push Isometrics*

1. Pretend the wall is the back of the vehicle you are pushing.
2. Get into the stance, feet shoulder-width apart, knees bent, elbows bent, and hands on the wall.
3. Lean into the wall and push, holding the push for 10 seconds. Repeat 10 times.
4. You can also try a split-stance, with one foot in front of the other. Repeat 5 times with the right foot in front and 5 times with the left foot in front.

# Strongwoman Contests

Although *strong* is in the name, strongwoman competitions are a combination of speed, power, strength, and endurance. Many of the events require you to lift a large amount of weight and either carry it, hold it, push it, or pull it for a set distance or time. Most competitions are one day long and involve five to six events, the sixth event being reserved for the finalists only. But every competition is different—some are even two days long, with the preliminaries on one day and the finals on the next. If you are serious about competing, it is best to check with the contest promoter to confirm which events it will include and what their order will be before you design your training schedule. Some of the events typical of a strongwoman competition are the yoke walk, tire flip, sled drag, keg lift and load, farmer's walk, stone lift and load, log press, iron cross, Conan's wheel, vehicle push or pull, and a combination of events in a medley.

Strongwoman events are extremely physically and mentally challenging because they are not typical things that people do to strength train—especially not most women. But if you decide to incorporate some strongwoman training into your program or even decide to compete, it will be well worth it. You will get to enjoy the outdoors while training instead of being stuck inside a dark gym. Your body composition will change favorably, because strongwoman training burns an enormous amount of calories and works every muscle in your body. You will conquer your boredom with the standard strength-training protocols, and your confidence will soar when you can see in concrete terms how strong you are. In addition, strongwoman training is an extremely efficient use of our precious time. Lifting, pushing, and pulling weighted objects works the majority of our muscles, and doing intense exercises in short bursts of time challenges our cardiovascular system—quite a bang for our fitness buck.

Detractors of strongwoman training claim that it has a high risk for injury. It's true that the exercises are extreme and do seem crazy. But with a suitable strength base, appropriate form, necessary auxiliary exercises, sufficient rest, and proper nutrition, a strongwoman training program can be quite safe. You don't need an extensive background in strength training before you begin a strongwoman program, but you do need a base of strength and conditioning before embarking on this advanced sport. The strength-training beginner program in chapter 7 is an excellent start. Some of the more common strongwoman exercises follow.

## VEHICLE PUSH

The initial push against a heavy vehicle that is at a dead stop is tough but once you get started, the faster you push the vehicle, the faster the wheels roll and the easier it gets.

1. Measure out a 100-foot flat course.
2. Set up at the back of the vehicle with arms extended and palms on the rear bumper. Your feet are shoulder-width apart, knees slightly bent. Have a friend put the vehicle in neutral, steer, and time you.
3. Lean in hard to the vehicle to start the push.
4. Switch over to a normal running pattern (i.e., one foot then the other).
5. Keep the head up and the arms straight so that you can transfer more leg and hip drive into pushing the truck.
6. Stay low and move in a straight line.

7. When you've hit 100 feet, have your friend brake the vehicle as you run to the front of it. Now you get to push it backward while you sit on the bumper. Extend the arms back so that the hands rest on the bumper.

8. Extend the legs one at a time to push the vehicle backward. If you feel the quads on fire, you are doing it right.

Photo courtesy of the author

## FARMER'S WALK

You don't need the standard farmer's walk implements—long metal cylinders or pipes with handles on the top and room to add weights on either side—to do this exercise, because dumbbells work just fine. But if you are entering a competition, try to find out exactly what they are using because dumbbells and actual farmer's walk implements are designed quite differently, and the weight distribution difference is significant. The farmer's walk competitions vary in the amount of weight held per hand, the amount of distance traveled, and the type of course (straight or with a turn).

1. Measure out a 100- and a 300-foot course. You can use a standard track, an empty parking lot in the back of the gym, or a street in front of your house.

2. On the light speed day (see table 13.1c on page 209), use the weight that you would normally lift for a biceps curl. Set up in a deadlift position with the dumbbells or implements on either side of the legs. Grasp the dumbbell or implement in each hand, deadlift it up, and sprint 300 yards. Rest for 1 to 2 minutes and repeat for 2 to 4 reps.

3. On the heavy strength day, use double the weight in dumbbells or implements that you did for the light speed day. Grasp a dumbbell or implement in each hand and walk fast for 100 yards. Rest for 1 to 2 minutes and repeat for 2 to 4 reps.

4. Try to keep your walks at 30 seconds and under. When you have achieved this speed, increase the weights.

## KEG RUN

Keg events are popular because it is easy to get a used keg, make sure it's empty, and pour water or sand in it to add weight. This event is a great conditioning drill to get you into strongwoman shape.

1. Set up a 100-foot course.
2. Position a 30- to 50-pound keg upright on the ground. Bend down to grip it with one hand high on the top and one hand low on the bottom.
3. Deadlift it to chest height and start running until you reach the end of the course. Put the keg down, run back to the starting point, and run back to pick up the keg.
4. Repeat running with the keg 5 times.

Photo courtesy of the author

## TIRE FLIP

Tires are also easy to acquire because after they are used, they usually end up in junkyards. Tire companies pay a lot of money to have used tires recycled, so they are more than willing to give them to you for free.

1. Set up a 100-foot course.
2. Start with the tire upright on its side, as it looks when it is on a vehicle.
3. Begin by using a split stance with the dominant leg in front and forcefully push the tire down. Use the push to gain some extra ground.
4. Squat down in a sumo deadlift stance, with the hands in between the legs. Reach the hands underneath the tire and try to position them between the treads.
5. Inhale, lean the chest into the tire, and forcefully stand up, bringing the tire up with you as you exhale. You can either use a knee to keep the tire moving upward or shuffle both feet to the side and drop down as if going into a power clean position
6. As the momentum keeps the tire moving upward, quickly change the hand position so that you are pushing against the tire to flip it over.
7. Quickly push the tire over and down and begin again. Make sure that you flip the tire over the finish line and not up to the finish line, because in competition the tire has to cross the line.

# Sample Programs for Competition

Throughout the years, competitors and experts have toiled to perfect competition workouts to maximize performance. The training programs shown in table 13.1, *a* through *c*, barely skim the surface when it comes to the variety and diversity of training programs that are available or that you can design. These programs are presented as a starting block and an introduction—use them as a baseline. If you are interested in adding diversity to your strength-training program even without competitive goals, and if you then decide to continue in the sport, search out mentors who can guide you and do the research to become an expert yourself. There are many wonderful resources to help you if you want to be competitive. For the sport of weightlifting visit www.usaweightlifting.org, for powerlifting go to www.usapowerlifting.com, and for strongwoman check out www.nastrongman.com. As you advance in your sport, you will find the training and competition programs that work best for you.

The strongwoman training program (table 13.1*c*) consists of one strength day for lower body and upper body and one hypertrophy and conditioning day for the entire body. The third day of the program is a strongwoman event day. Squat jumps and track-and-field drills like skips, hops, cariocas, and side shuffling are excellent and dynamic warm-ups for strongwoman feats. As you get closer to a competition, restrict your training to events only and try to simulate the actual competition.

## Table 13.1a Sample 10-Week Weightlifting Program

| Week | Day | Exercise | Weight | Reps | Sets | Time (sec) |
|------|-----|----------|--------|------|------|------------|
| 1 | Monday | Power clean (the first phase of the clean and jerk) | 75% 1RM | 2 | 6 | 120 |
| | | Snatch | 80% 1RM | 2 | 6 | 120 |
| | | Snatch pull | 80% 1RM | 2 | 6 | 120 |
| | | Barbell front squat | 80% 1RM | 2 | 6 | 120 |
| | | Hanging leg raise | Submax | 9 | 3 | 60 |
| | Wednesday | Barbell overhead press | 80% 1RM | 2 | 6 | 120 |
| | | Lat pulldown | 80% 1RM | 2 | 6 | 120 |
| | | Bench press | Submax | 9 | 3 | 60 |
| | | Cable row | Submax | 9 | 3 | 60 |
| | | Cable push-down | Submax | 9 | 3 | 60 |
| | | Dumbbell biceps curl | Submax | 9 | 3 | 60 |
| | Friday | Power snatch | 75% 1RM | 2 | 6 | 120 |
| | | Clean and jerk | 80% 1RM | 2 | 6 | 120 |
| | | Clean pull | 80% 1RM | 2 | 6 | 120 |
| | | Barbell back squat | 80% 1RM | 2 | 6 | 120 |
| | | Stability ball straight crunch (with weight) | Submax | 9 | 3 | 60 |
| 2 | Monday | Power clean | 75% 1RM | 3 | 6 | 120 |
| | | Snatch | 80% 1RM | 3 | 6 | 120 |
| | | Snatch pull | 80% 1RM | 3 | 6 | 120 |
| | | Barbell front squat | 80% 1RM | 3 | 6 | 120 |
| | | Hanging leg raise | Submax | 9 | 3 | 60 |
| | Wednesday | Barbell overhead press | 80% 1RM | 3 | 6 | 120 |
| | | Lat pulldown | 80% 1RM | 3 | 6 | 120 |
| | | Bench press | Submax | 9 | 3 | 60 |
| | | Cable row | Submax | 9 | 3 | 60 |
| | | Cable push-down | Submax | 9 | 3 | 60 |
| | | Dumbbell biceps curl | Submax | 9 | 3 | 60 |
| | Friday | Power snatch | 75% 1RM | 3 | 6 | 120 |
| | | Clean and jerk | 80% 1RM | 3 | 6 | 120 |
| | | Clean pull | 80% 1RM | 3 | 6 | 120 |
| | | Barbell back squat | 80% 1RM | 3 | 6 | 120 |
| | | Stability ball straight crunch (with weight) | Submax | 9 | 3 | 60 |
| 3 | Monday | Power clean | 75% 1RM | 4 | 6 | 120 |
| | | Snatch | 80% 1RM | 4 | 6 | 120 |
| | | Snatch pull | 80% 1RM | 4 | 6 | 120 |
| | | Barbell front squat | 80% 1RM | 4 | 6 | 120 |
| | | Hanging leg raise | Submax | 9 | 3 | 60 |
| | Wednesday | Barbell overhead press | 80% 1RM | 4 | 6 | 120 |
| | | Lat pulldown | 80% 1RM | 4 | 6 | 120 |
| | | Bench press | Submax | 9 | 3 | 60 |

| Week | Day | Exercise | Weight | Reps | Sets | Time (sec) |
|------|-----|----------|--------|------|------|------------|
|  |  | Cable row | Submax | 9 | 3 | 60 |
|  |  | Cable push-down | Submax | 9 | 3 | 60 |
|  |  | Dumbbell biceps curl | Submax | 9 | 3 | 60 |
|  | Friday | Power snatch | 75% 1RM | 4 | 6 | 120 |
|  |  | Clean and jerk | 80% 1RM | 4 | 6 | 120 |
|  |  | Clean pull | 80% 1RM | 4 | 6 | 120 |
|  |  | Barbell back squat | 80% 1RM | 4 | 6 | 120 |
|  |  | Stability ball straight crunch (with weight) | Submax | 9 | 3 | 60 |
| 4 | Monday | Power clean | 75% 1RM | 5 | 6 | 120 |
|  |  | Snatch | 80% 1RM | 5 | 6 | 120 |
|  |  | Snatch pull | 80% 1RM | 5 | 6 | 120 |
|  |  | Barbell front squat | 80% 1RM | 5 | 6 | 120 |
|  |  | Hanging leg raise | Submax | 6 | 3 | 60 |
|  | Wednesday | Barbell overhead press | 80% 1RM | 5 | 6 | 120 |
|  |  | Lat pulldown | 80% 1RM | 5 | 6 | 120 |
|  |  | Bench press | Submax | 6 | 3 | 60 |
|  |  | Cable row | Submax | 6 | 3 | 60 |
|  |  | Cable push-down | Submax | 6 | 3 | 60 |
|  |  | Dumbbell biceps curl | Submax | 6 | 3 | 60 |
|  | Friday | Power snatch | 75% 1RM | 5 | 6 | 120 |
|  |  | Clean and jerk | 80% 1RM | 5 | 6 | 120 |
|  |  | Clean pull | 80% 1RM | 5 | 6 | 120 |
|  |  | Barbell back squat | 80% 1RM | 5 | 6 | 120 |
|  |  | Stability ball straight crunch (with weight) | Submax | 6 | 3 | 60 |
| 5 | Monday | Power clean | 75% 1RM | 6 | 6 | 120 |
|  |  | Snatch | 80% 1RM | 6 | 6 | 120 |
|  |  | Snatch pull | 80% 1RM | 6 | 6 | 120 |
|  |  | Barbell front squat | 80% 1RM | 6 | 6 | 120 |
|  |  | Hanging leg raise | Submax | 6 | 3 | 60 |
|  | Wednesday | Barbell overhead press | 80% 1RM | 6 | 6 | 120 |
|  |  | Lat pulldown | 80% 1RM | 6 | 6 | 120 |
|  |  | Bench press | Submax | 6 | 3 | 60 |
|  |  | Cable row | Submax | 6 | 3 | 60 |
|  |  | Cable push-down | Submax | 6 | 3 | 60 |
|  |  | Dumbbell biceps curl | Submax | 6 | 3 | 60 |
|  | Friday | Power snatch | 75% 1RM | 6 | 6 | 120 |
|  |  | Clean and jerk | 80% 1RM | 6 | 6 | 120 |
|  |  | Clean pull | 80% 1RM | 6 | 6 | 120 |
|  |  | Barbell back squat | 80% 1RM | 6 | 6 | 120 |
|  |  | Stability ball straight crunch (with weight) | Submax | 6 | 3 | 60 |

*(continued)*

Table 13.1a **Sample 10-Week Weightlifting Program** *(continued)*

| Week | Day | Exercise | Weight | Reps | Sets | Time (sec) |
|------|-----|----------|--------|------|------|------------|
| 6 | Monday | Power clean | 80% 1RM | 5 | 5 | 120 |
| | | Snatch | 85% 1RM | 5 | 5 | 120 |
| | | Snatch pull | 85% 1RM | 5 | 5 | 120 |
| | | Barbell front squat | 85% 1RM | 5 | 5 | 120 |
| | | Hanging leg raise | Submax | 6 | 3 | 60 |
| | Wednesday | Barbell overhead press | 85% 1RM | 5 | 5 | 120 |
| | | Lat pulldown | 85% 1RM | 5 | 5 | 120 |
| | | Bench press | Submax | 6 | 3 | 60 |
| | | Cable row | Submax | 6 | 3 | 60 |
| | | Cable push-down | Submax | 6 | 3 | 60 |
| | | Dumbbell biceps curl | Submax | 6 | 3 | 60 |
| | Friday | Power snatch | 80% 1RM | 5 | 5 | 120 |
| | | Clean and jerk | 85% 1RM | 5 | 5 | 120 |
| | | Clean pull | 85% 1RM | 5 | 5 | 120 |
| | | Barbell back squat | 85% 1RM | 5 | 5 | 120 |
| | | Stability ball straight crunch (with weight) | Submax | 6 | 3 | 60 |
| 7 | Monday | Power clean | 85% 1RM | 4 | 4 | 120 |
| | | Snatch | 90% 1RM | 4 | 4 | 120 |
| | | Snatch pull | 90% 1RM | 4 | 4 | 120 |
| | | Barbell front squat | 90% 1RM | 4 | 4 | 120 |
| | | Hanging leg raise | Submax | 3 | 3 | 60 |
| | Wednesday | Barbell overhead press | 90% 1RM | 4 | 4 | 120 |
| | | Lat pulldown | 90% 1RM | 4 | 4 | 120 |
| | | Bench press | Submax | 3 | 3 | 60 |
| | | Cable row | Submax | 3 | 3 | 60 |
| | | Cable push-down | Submax | 3 | 3 | 60 |
| | | Dumbbell biceps curl | Submax | 3 | 3 | 60 |
| | Friday | Power snatch | 85% 1RM | 4 | 4 | 120 |
| | | Clean and jerk | 90% 1RM | 4 | 4 | 120 |
| | | Clean pull | 90% 1RM | 4 | 4 | 120 |
| | | Barbell back squat | 90% 1RM | 4 | 4 | 120 |
| | | Stability ball straight crunch (with weight) | Submax | 3 | 3 | 60 |
| 8 | Monday | Power clean | Work up to new max power clean | | | 120 |
| | | Snatch | 95% 1RM | 3 | 3 | 120 |
| | | Snatch pull | 95% 1RM | 3 | 3 | 120 |
| | | Barbell front squat | 95% 1RM | 3 | 3 | 120 |
| | | Hanging leg raise | Submax | 3 | 3 | 60 |
| | Wednesday | Barbell overhead press | 95% 1RM | 3 | 3 | 120 |
| | | Lat pulldown | 95% 1RM | 3 | 3 | 120 |
| | | Bench press | Submax | 3 | 3 | 60 |
| | | Cable row | Submax | 3 | 3 | 60 |
| | | Cable push-down | Submax | 3 | 3 | 60 |
| | | Dumbbell biceps curl | Submax | 3 | 3 | 60 |

| Week | Day | Exercise | Weight | Reps | Sets | Time (sec) |
|------|-----|----------|--------|------|------|------------|
| | Friday | Power snatch | Work up to new max power snatch | | | 120 |
| | | Clean and jerk | 95% 1RM | 3 | 3 | 120 |
| | | Clean pull | 95% 1RM | 3 | 3 | 120 |
| | | Barbell back squat | 95% 1RM | 3 | 3 | 120 |
| | | Stability ball straight crunch (with weight) | Submax | 3 | 3 | 60 |
| 9 | Monday | Power clean | 90% 1RM | 2 | 2 | 120 |
| | | Snatch | 100% 1RM | 2 | 2 | 120 |
| | | Snatch pull | 100% 1RM | 2 | 2 | 120 |
| | | Barbell front squat | 100% 1RM | 2 | 2 | 120 |
| | | Hanging leg raise | Submax | 3 | 3 | 60 |
| | Wednesday | Barbell overhead press | 100% 1RM | 2 | 2 | 120 |
| | | Lat pulldown | 100% 1RM | 2 | 2 | 120 |
| | | Bench press | Submax | 3 | 3 | 60 |
| | | Cable row | Submax | 3 | 3 | 60 |
| | | Pushdown | Submax | 3 | 3 | 60 |
| | | Dumbbell biceps curl | Submax | 3 | 3 | 60 |
| | Friday | Power snatch | 90% 1RM | 2 | 2 | 120 |
| | | Clean and jerk | 100% 1RM | 2 | 2 | 120 |
| | | Clean pull | 100% 1RM | 2 | 2 | 120 |
| | | Barbell back squat | 100% 1RM | 2 | 2 | 120 |
| | | Stability ball straight crunch (with weight) | Submax | 3 | 3 | 60 |
| 10 | Wednesday | Snatch | 80% 1RM | 2 | 6 | 120 |
| | | Clean and jerk | 80% 1RM | 2 | 6 | 120 |
| | Saturday or Sunday | Snatch | Bar | 5 | 1 | 120 |
| | | | 50% 1RM | 3 | 1 | 120 |
| | | | 60% 1RM | 3 | 1 | 120 |
| | | | 70% 1RM | 2 | 1 | 120 |
| | | | 80% 1RM | 2 | 1 | 120 |
| | | | 90% 1RM | 1 | 1 | 120 |
| | | | 95% 1RM | 1 | 1 | 120 |
| | | | 100% 1RM | 1st attempt | | 120 |
| | | | 105% 1RM | 2nd attempt | | 120 |
| | | | 110% 1RM | 3rd attempt | | 120 |
| | | Clean and jerk | Bar | 5 | 1 | 120 |
| | | | 50% 1RM | 3 | 1 | 120 |
| | | | 60% 1RM | 3 | 1 | 120 |
| | | | 70% 1RM | 2 | 1 | 120 |
| | | | 80% 1RM | 2 | 1 | 120 |
| | | | 90% 1RM | 1 | 1 | 120 |
| | | | 95% 1RM | 1 | 1 | 120 |
| | | | 100% 1RM | 1st attempt | | 120 |
| | | | 105% 1RM | 2nd attempt | | 120 |
| | | | 110% 1RM | 3rd attempt | | 120 |

## Table 13.1b Sample 10-Week Powerlifting Program

| Week | Day | Exercise | Weight | Reps | Sets | Rest time between sets (sec) |
|------|-----|----------|--------|------|------|------------------------------|
| 1 | Tues. | Barbell back squat | 80% 1RM | 2 | 6 | 120 |
| | | Deadlift | 80% 1RM | 3 | 6 | 120 |
| | | Lunge | Submax | 12 | 3 | 60 |
| | | Leg curl | Submax | 12 | 3 | 60 |
| | | Hanging leg raise | Submax | 12 | 3 | 60 |
| | | Stability ball straight crunch with weight | Submax | 12 | 3 | 60 |
| | Wed. | Bench press | 80% 1RM | 2 | 6 | 120 |
| | | Barbell overhead press | 80% 1RM | 3 | 6 | 120 |
| | | Lat pulldown | Submax | 12 | 3 | 60 |
| | | Cable row | Submax | 12 | 3 | 60 |
| | | Cable push-down | Submax | 12 | 3 | 60 |
| | | Dumbbell biceps curl | Submax | 12 | 3 | 60 |
| | Sat. | Barbell back squat | 80% 1RM | 3 | 6 | 120 |
| | | Leg press | Max | 9 | 3 | 120 |
| | | Good morning | Submax | 9 | 3 | 60 |
| | | Leg extension | Max | 9 | 3 | 60 |
| | | Hanging leg raise | Max | 9 | 3 | 60 |
| | | Stability ball straight crunch with weight | Max | 9 | 3 | 60 |
| | Sun. | Bench press | 80% 1RM | 3 | 6 | 120 |
| | | Barbell bench press (incline) | 80% 1RM | 3 | 6 | 120 |
| | | Chin-up | Max | 9 | 3 | 60 |
| | | Dumbbell row | Max | 9 | 3 | 60 |
| | | Close-grip bench press | Max | 9 | 3 | 60 |
| | | Barbell curl | Max | 9 | 3 | 60 |
| 2 | Tues. | Barbell back squat | 80% 1RM | 2 | 6 | 120 |
| | | Deadlift | 80% 1RM | 4 | 6 | 120 |
| | | Lunge | Submax | 12 | 3 | 60 |
| | | Leg curl | Submax | 12 | 3 | 60 |
| | | Hanging leg raise | Submax | 12 | 3 | 60 |
| | | Stability ball straight crunch with weight | Submax | 12 | 3 | 60 |
| | Wed. | Bench press | 80% 1RM | 2 | 6 | 120 |
| | | Barbell overhead press | 80% 1RM | 4 | 6 | 120 |
| | | Lat pulldown | Submax | 12 | 3 | 60 |
| | | Cable row | Submax | 12 | 3 | 60 |
| | | Cable push-down | Submax | 12 | 3 | 60 |
| | | Dumbbell biceps curl | Submax | 12 | 3 | 60 |
| | Sat. | Barbell back squat | 80% 1RM | 4 | 6 | 120 |
| | | Leg press | Max | 9 | 3 | 120 |
| | | Good morning | Submax | 9 | 3 | 60 |
| | | Leg extension | Max | 9 | 3 | 60 |

| Week | Day | Exercise | Weight | Reps | Sets | Rest time between sets (sec) |
|------|-----|----------|--------|------|------|------------------------------|
| | | Hanging leg raise | Max | 9 | 3 | 60 |
| | | Stability ball straight crunch with weight | Max | 9 | 3 | 60 |
| | Sun. | Bench press | 80% 1RM | 4 | 6 | 120 |
| | | Barbell bench press (incline) | 80% 1RM | 4 | 6 | 120 |
| | | Chin-up | Max | 9 | 3 | 60 |
| | | Dumbbell row | Max | 9 | 3 | 60 |
| | | Close-grip bench press | Max | 9 | 3 | 60 |
| | | Barbell curl | Max | 9 | 3 | 60 |
| 3 | Tues. | Barbell back squat | 80% 1RM | 2 | 6 | 120 |
| | | Deadlift | 80% 1RM | 5 | 6 | 120 |
| | | Lunge | Submax | 12 | 3 | 60 |
| | | Leg curl | Submax | 12 | 3 | 60 |
| | | Hanging leg raise | Submax | 12 | 3 | 60 |
| | | Stability ball straight crunch with weight | Submax | 12 | 3 | 60 |
| | Wed. | Bench press | 80% 1RM | 2 | 6 | 120 |
| | | Barbell overhead press | 80% 1RM | 5 | 6 | 120 |
| | | Lat pulldown | Submax | 12 | 3 | 60 |
| | | Cable row | Submax | 12 | 3 | 60 |
| | | Cable push-down | Submax | 12 | 3 | 60 |
| | | Dumbbell biceps curl | Submax | 12 | 3 | 60 |
| | Sat. | Barbell back squat | 80% 1RM | 5 | 6 | 120 |
| | | Leg press | Max | 9 | 3 | 120 |
| | | Good morning | Submax | 9 | 3 | 60 |
| | | Leg extension | Max | 9 | 3 | 60 |
| | | Hanging leg raise | Max | 9 | 3 | 60 |
| | | Stability ball straight crunch with weight | Max | 9 | 3 | 60 |
| | Sun. | Bench press | 80% 1RM | 5 | 6 | 120 |
| | | Barbell bench press (incline) | 80% 1RM | 5 | 6 | 120 |
| | | Chin-up | Max | 9 | 3 | 60 |
| | | Dumbbell row | Max | 9 | 3 | 60 |
| | | Close-grip bench press | Max | 9 | 3 | 60 |
| | | Barbell curl | Max | 9 | 3 | 60 |
| 4 | Tues. | Barbell back squat | 80% 1RM | 2 | 6 | 120 |
| | | Deadlift | 80% 1RM | 6 | 6 | 120 |
| | | Lunge | Submax | 9 | 3 | 60 |
| | | Leg curl | Submax | 9 | 3 | 60 |
| | | Hanging leg raise | Submax | 9 | 3 | 60 |
| | | Stability ball straight crunch with weight | Submax | 9 | 3 | 60 |

*(continued)*

Table 13.1b **Sample 10-Week Powerlifting Program** *(continued)*

| Week | Day | Exercise | Weight | Reps | Sets | Rest time between sets (sec) |
|---|---|---|---|---|---|---|
| | Wed. | Bench press | 80% 1RM | 2 | 6 | 120 |
| | | Barbell overhead press | 80% 1RM | 6 | 6 | 120 |
| | | Lat pulldown | Submax | 9 | 3 | 60 |
| | | Cable row | Submax | 9 | 3 | 60 |
| | | Cable push-down | Submax | 9 | 3 | 60 |
| | | Dumbbell biceps curl | Submax | 9 | 3 | 60 |
| | Sat. | Barbell back squat | 80% 1RM | 6 | 6 | 120 |
| | | Leg press | Max | 6 | 3 | 120 |
| | | Good morning | Submax | 6 | 3 | 60 |
| | | Leg extension | Max | 6 | 3 | 60 |
| | | Hanging leg raise | Max | 6 | 3 | 60 |
| | | Stability ball straight crunch with weight | Max | 6 | 3 | 60 |
| | Sun. | Bench press | 80% 1RM | 6 | 6 | 120 |
| | | Barbell bench press (incline) | 80% 1RM | 6 | 6 | 120 |
| | | Chin-up | Max | 6 | 3 | 60 |
| | | Dumbbell row | Max | 6 | 3 | 60 |
| | | Close-grip bench press | Max | 6 | 3 | 60 |
| | | Barbell curl | Max | 6 | 3 | 60 |
| 5 | Tues. | Barbell back squat | 80% 1RM | 2 | 6 | 120 |
| | | Deadlift | 85% 1RM | 5 | 5 | 120 |
| | | Lunge | Submax | 9 | 3 | 60 |
| | | Leg curl | Submax | 9 | 3 | 60 |
| | | Hanging leg raise | Submax | 9 | 3 | 60 |
| | | Stability ball straight crunch with weight | Submax | 9 | 3 | 60 |
| | Wed. | Bench press | 80% 1RM | 2 | 6 | 120 |
| | | Barbell overhead press | 85% 1RM | 5 | 5 | 120 |
| | | Lat pulldown | Submax | 9 | 3 | 60 |
| | | Cable row | Submax | 9 | 3 | 60 |
| | | Cable push-down | Submax | 9 | 3 | 60 |
| | | Dumbbell biceps curl | Submax | 9 | 3 | 60 |
| | Sat. | Barbell back squat | 85% 1RM | 5 | 5 | 120 |
| | | Leg press | Max | 6 | 3 | 120 |
| | | Good morning | Submax | 6 | 3 | 60 |
| | | Leg extension | Max | 6 | 3 | 60 |
| | | Hanging leg raise | Max | 6 | 3 | 60 |
| | | Stability ball straight crunch with weight | Max | 6 | 3 | 60 |
| | Sun. | Bench press | 85% 1RM | 5 | 5 | 120 |
| | | Barbell bench press (incline) | 85% 1RM | 5 | 5 | 120 |
| | | Chin-up | Max | 6 | 3 | 60 |

| Week | Day | Exercise | Weight | Reps | Sets | Rest time between sets (sec) |
|------|-----|----------|--------|------|------|------------------------------|
| | | Dumbbell row | Max | 6 | 3 | 60 |
| | | Close-grip bench press | Max | 6 | 3 | 60 |
| | | Barbell curl | Max | 6 | 3 | 60 |
| 6 | Tues. | Barbell back squat | 80% 1RM | 2 | 6 | 120 |
| | | Deadlift | 90% 1RM | 4 | 4 | 120 |
| | | Lunge | Submax | 9 | 3 | 60 |
| | | Leg curl | Submax | 9 | 3 | 60 |
| | | Hanging leg raise | Submax | 9 | 3 | 60 |
| | | Stability ball straight crunch with weight | Submax | 9 | 3 | 60 |
| | Wed. | Bench press | 80% 1RM | 2 | 6 | 120 |
| | | Barbell overhead press | 90% 1RM | 4 | 4 | 120 |
| | | Lat pulldown | Submax | 9 | 3 | 60 |
| | | Cable row | Submax | 9 | 3 | 60 |
| | | Cable push-down | Submax | 9 | 3 | 60 |
| | | Dumbbell biceps curl | Submax | 9 | 3 | 60 |
| | Sat. | Barbell back squat | 90% 1RM | 4 | 4 | 120 |
| | | Leg press | Max | 6 | 3 | 120 |
| | | Good morning | Submax | 6 | 3 | 60 |
| | | Leg extension | Max | 6 | 3 | 60 |
| | | Hanging leg raise | Max | 6 | 3 | 60 |
| | | Stability ball straight crunch with weight | Max | 6 | 3 | 60 |
| | Sun. | Bench press | 90% 1RM | 4 | 4 | 120 |
| | | Barbell bench press (incline) | 90% 1RM | 4 | 4 | 120 |
| | | Chin-up | Max | 6 | 3 | 60 |
| | | Dumbbell row | Max | 6 | 3 | 60 |
| | | Close-grip bench press | Max | 6 | 3 | 60 |
| | | Barbell curl | Max | 6 | 3 | 60 |
| 7 | Tues. | Barbell back squat | 80% 1RM | 2 | 6 | 120 |
| | | Deadlift | 90% 1RM | 4 | 4 | 120 |
| | | Lunge | Submax | 6 | 3 | 60 |
| | | Leg curl | Submax | 6 | 3 | 60 |
| | | Hanging leg raise | Submax | 6 | 3 | 60 |
| | | Stability ball straight crunch with weight | Submax | 6 | 3 | 60 |
| | Wed. | Bench press | 80% 1RM | 2 | 6 | 120 |
| | | Barbell overhead press | 90% 1RM | 4 | 4 | 120 |
| | | Lat pulldown | Submax | 6 | 3 | 60 |
| | | Cable row | Submax | 6 | 3 | 60 |
| | | Cable push-down | Submax | 6 | 3 | 60 |
| | | Dumbbell biceps curl | Submax | 6 | 3 | 60 |

*(continued)*

Table 13.1b **Sample 10-Week Powerlifting Program** *(continued)*

| Week | Day | Exercise | Weight | Reps | Sets | Rest time between sets (sec) |
|---|---|---|---|---|---|---|
| | Sat. | Barbell back squat | 90% 1RM | 4 | 4 | 120 |
| | | Leg press | Max | 3 | 3 | 120 |
| | | Good morning | Submax | 3 | 3 | 60 |
| | | Leg extension | Max | 3 | 3 | 60 |
| | | Hanging leg raise | Max | 3 | 3 | 60 |
| | | Stability ball straight crunch with weight | Max | 3 | 3 | 60 |
| | Sun. | Bench press | 90% 1RM | 4 | 4 | 120 |
| | | Barbell bench press (incline) | 90% 1RM | 4 | 4 | 120 |
| | | Chin-up | Max | 3 | 3 | 60 |
| | | Dumbbell row | Max | 3 | 3 | 60 |
| | | Close-grip bench press | Max | 3 | 3 | 60 |
| | | Barbell curl | Max | 3 | 3 | 60 |
| 8 | Tues. | Barbell back squat | 80% 1RM | 2 | 6 | 120 |
| | | Deadlift | 95% 1RM | 3 | 3 | 120 |
| | | Lunge | Submax | 6 | 3 | 60 |
| | | Leg curl | Submax | 6 | 3 | 60 |
| | | Hanging leg raise | Submax | 6 | 3 | 60 |
| | | Stability ball straight crunch with weight | Submax | 6 | 3 | 60 |
| | Wed. | Bench press | 80% 1RM | 2 | 6 | 120 |
| | | Barbell overhead press | 95% 1RM | 3 | 3 | 120 |
| | | Lat pulldown | Submax | 6 | 3 | 60 |
| | | Cable row | Submax | 6 | 3 | 60 |
| | | Cable push-down | Submax | 6 | 3 | 60 |
| | | Dumbbell biceps curl | Submax | 6 | 3 | 60 |
| | Sat. | Barbell back squat | 95% 1RM | 3 | 3 | 120 |
| | | Leg press | Max | 3 | 3 | 120 |
| | | Good morning | Submax | 3 | 3 | 60 |
| | | Leg extension | Max | 3 | 3 | 60 |
| | | Hanging leg raise | Max | 3 | 3 | 60 |
| | | Stability ball straight crunch with weight | Max | 3 | 3 | 60 |
| | Sun. | Bench press | 95% 1RM | 3 | 3 | 120 |
| | | Barbell bench press (incline) | 95% 1RM | 3 | 3 | 120 |
| | | Chin-up | Max | 3 | 3 | 60 |
| | | Dumbbell row | Max | 3 | 3 | 60 |
| | | Close-grip bench press | Max | 3 | 3 | 60 |
| | | Barbell curl | Max | 3 | 3 | 60 |
| 9 | Tues. | Barbell back squat | 80% 1RM | 2 | 6 | 120 |
| | | Deadlift | 100% 1RM | 2 | 2 | 120 |
| | | Lunge | Submax | 6 | 3 | 60 |

| Week | Day | Exercise | Weight | Reps | Sets | Rest time between sets (sec) |
|------|-----|----------|--------|------|------|------------------------------|
| | | Leg curl | Submax | 6 | 3 | 60 |
| | | Hanging leg raise | Submax | 6 | 3 | 60 |
| | | Stability ball straight crunch with weight | Submax | 6 | 3 | 60 |
| | Wed. | Bench press | 80% 1RM | 2 | 6 | 120 |
| | | Barbell overhead press | 100% 1RM | 2 | 2 | 120 |
| | | Lat pulldown | Submax | 6 | 3 | 60 |
| | | Cable row | Submax | 6 | 3 | 60 |
| | | Cable push-down | Submax | 6 | 3 | 60 |
| | | Dumbbell biceps curl | Submax | 6 | 3 | 60 |
| | Sat. | Barbell back squat | 100% 1RM | 2 | 2 | 120 |
| | | Leg press | Max | 3 | 3 | 120 |
| | | Good morning | Submax | 3 | 3 | 60 |
| | | Leg extension | Max | 3 | 3 | 60 |
| | | Hanging leg raise | Max | 3 | 3 | 60 |
| | | Stability ball straight crunch with weight | Max | 3 | 3 | 60 |
| | Sun. | Bench press | 100% 1RM | 2 | 2 | 120 |
| | | Barbell bench press (incline) | 100% 1RM | 2 | 2 | 120 |
| | | Chin-up | Max | 3 | 3 | 60 |
| | | Dumbbell row | Max | 3 | 3 | 60 |
| | | Close-grip bench press | Max | 3 | 3 | 60 |
| | | Barbell curl | Max | 3 | 3 | 60 |
| 10 | Wed. | Barbell back squat | 80% 1RM | 2 | 6 | 120 |
| | | Bench press | 80% 1RM | 2 | 6 | 120 |
| | | Deadlift | 80% 1RM | 2 | 6 | 120 |
| Contest | Saturday or Sunday | Barbell back squat | Bar | 5 | 1 | 120 |
| | | | 50% 1RM | 3 | 1 | 120 |
| | | | 60% 1RM | 3 | 1 | 120 |
| | | | 70% 1RM | 2 | 1 | 120 |
| | | | 80% 1RM | 2 | 1 | 120 |
| | | | 90% 1RM | 1 | 1 | 120 |
| | | | 95% 1RM | 1 | 1 | 120 |
| | | | 100% 1RM | 1st attempt | | 120 |
| | | | 105% 1RM | 2nd attempt | | 120 |
| | | | 110% 1RM | 3rd attempt | | 120 |
| | | Bench press | Bar | | 5 | 120 |
| | | | 50% 1RM | | 3 | 120 |
| | | | 60% 1RM | | 3 | 120 |
| | | | 70% 1RM | | 2 | 120 |
| | | | 80% 1RM | | 2 | 120 |
| | | | 90% 1RM | | 1 | 120 |

*(continued)*

Table 13.1b **Sample 10-Week Powerlifting Program** *(continued)*

| Week | Day | Exercise | Weight | Reps | Sets | Rest time between sets (sec) |
|------|-----|----------|--------|------|------|-------------------------------|
|      |     |          | 95% 1RM |     | 1 | 120 |
|      |     |          | 100% 1RM | 1st attempt | | 120 |
|      |     |          | 105% 1RM | 2nd attempt | | 120 |
|      |     |          | 110% 1RM | 3rd attempt | | 120 |
|      |     | Deadlift | Bar |     | 5 | 120 |
|      |     |          | 50% 1RM |     | 3 | 120 |
|      |     |          | 60% 1RM |     | 3 | 120 |
|      |     |          | 70% 1RM |     | 2 | 120 |
|      |     |          | 80% 1RM |     | 2 | 120 |
|      |     |          | 90% 1RM |     | 1 | 120 |
|      |     |          | 95% 1RM |     | 1 | 120 |
|      |     |          | 100% 1RM | 1st attempt | | 120 |
|      |     |          | 105% 1RM | 2nd attempt | | 120 |
|      |     |          | 110% 1RM | 3rd attempt | | 120 |

## Table 13.1c   Weekly Strongwoman Training Program

| Day | General info | Exercises |
|-----|--------------|-----------|
| 1 | Rest 2 to 3 min between supersets. Perform 3 × 5 of each exercise. High-intensity day—lift 85 to 95% 1RM. | Squat supersetted with stability ball straight crunch<br>Deadlift supersetted with stability ball reverse crunch<br>Lunge supersetted with stability ball diagonal crunch |
| 2 | Rest 2 to 3 min between supersets. Perform 3 × 5 of each exercise. High-intensity day—lift 85 to 95% 1RM. | Bench press supersetted with barbell row<br>Barbell overhead press supersetted with lat pulldown<br>Abdominal rotation<br>Clean hold (3 × 30-sec holds; rest for 2 min) |
| 3 | Rest | |
| 4 | Warm up with squat jumps and track and field drills like skips, hops, cariocas, and side shuffling.<br>Then do 2-3 sets of each exercise with 3 min between sets. | Vehicle push for 100 ft forward and backward<br>Keg run for 100 ft<br>Farmer's walk for 100 ft<br>Tire flip |
| 5 | Rest | |
| 6 | Finish each exercise before beginning the next.<br>Take only 1-min rest between sets and 2-min rest between exercises.<br>Perform 3 to 4 × 10 of each exercise<br>Low- to moderate-intensity day—65 to 75% 1RM. | Clean pull<br>Step-up<br>Push-up<br>Pull-up<br>Barbell curl<br>Triceps pushdown<br>Wood chop |
| 7 | Rest | |

# Appendix

## Percent Body Fat Estimated From Height (inches) and Circumference Value (CV)[a]

| | Height in inches | | | | | | | | | | | | | | | | | | | |
|------|------|------|------|------|------|------|------|------|------|------|------|------|------|------|------|------|------|------|------|------|
| CV | 58.0 | 58.5 | 59.0 | 59.5 | 60.0 | 60.5 | 61.0 | 61.5 | 62.0 | 62.5 | 63.0 | 63.5 | 64.0 | 64.5 | 65.0 | 65.5 | 66.0 | 66.5 | 67.0 | 67.5 |
| 34.5 | 1 | 0 | - | - | - | - | - | - | - | - | - | - | - | - | - | - | - | - | - | - |
| 35.0 | 2 | 1 | 1 | 1 | 0 | - | - | - | - | - | - | - | - | - | - | - | - | - | - | - |
| 35.5 | 3 | 2 | 2 | 2 | 1 | 1 | 0 | 0 | - | - | - | - | - | - | - | - | - | - | - | - |
| 36.0 | 4 | 3 | 3 | 3 | 2 | 2 | 1 | 1 | 1 | 0 | 0 | - | - | - | - | - | - | - | - | - |
| 36.5 | 5 | 4 | 4 | 4 | 3 | 3 | 2 | 2 | 2 | 1 | 1 | 1 | 0 | - | - | - | - | - | - | - |
| 37.0 | 6 | 5 | 5 | 4 | 4 | 4 | 3 | 3 | 3 | 2 | 2 | 2 | 1 | 1 | 1 | 0 | - | - | - | - |
| 37.5 | 7 | 6 | 6 | 5 | 5 | 5 | 4 | 4 | 4 | 3 | 3 | 3 | 2 | 2 | 2 | 1 | 1 | 1 | 0 | - |
| 38.0 | 7 | 7 | 7 | 6 | 6 | 6 | 5 | 5 | 5 | 4 | 4 | 3 | 3 | 3 | 2 | 2 | 2 | 1 | 1 | 1 |
| 38.5 | 8 | 8 | 8 | 7 | 7 | 7 | 6 | 6 | 5 | 5 | 5 | 4 | 4 | 4 | 3 | 3 | 3 | 2 | 2 | 2 |
| 39.0 | 9 | 9 | 9 | 8 | 8 | 7 | 7 | 7 | 6 | 6 | 6 | 5 | 5 | 5 | 4 | 4 | 4 | 3 | 3 | 3 |
| 39.5 | 10 | 10 | 9 | 9 | 9 | 8 | 8 | 8 | 7 | 7 | 7 | 6 | 6 | 6 | 5 | 5 | 5 | 4 | 4 | 4 |
| 40.0 | 11 | 11 | 10 | 10 | 10 | 9 | 9 | 8 | 8 | 8 | 7 | 7 | 7 | 6 | 6 | 6 | 5 | 5 | 5 | 4 |
| 40.5 | 12 | 12 | 11 | 11 | 10 | 10 | 10 | 9 | 9 | 9 | 8 | 8 | 8 | 7 | 7 | 7 | 6 | 6 | 6 | 5 |
| 41.0 | 13 | 12 | 12 | 12 | 11 | 11 | 11 | 10 | 10 | 10 | 9 | 9 | 8 | 8 | 8 | 7 | 7 | 7 | 6 | 6 |
| 41.5 | 14 | 13 | 13 | 13 | 12 | 12 | 11 | 11 | 11 | 10 | 10 | 10 | 9 | 9 | 9 | 8 | 8 | 8 | 7 | 7 |
| 42.0 | 14 | 14 | 14 | 13 | 13 | 13 | 12 | 12 | 12 | 11 | 11 | 10 | 10 | 10 | 9 | 9 | 9 | 8 | 8 | 8 |
| 42.5 | 15 | 15 | 15 | 14 | 14 | 13 | 13 | 13 | 12 | 12 | 12 | 11 | 11 | 11 | 10 | 10 | 10 | 9 | 9 | 9 |
| 43.0 | 16 | 16 | 15 | 15 | 15 | 14 | 14 | 14 | 13 | 13 | 12 | 12 | 12 | 11 | 11 | 11 | 10 | 10 | 10 | 9 |
| 43.5 | 17 | 17 | 16 | 16 | 15 | 15 | 15 | 14 | 14 | 14 | 13 | 13 | 13 | 12 | 12 | 12 | 11 | 11 | 11 | 10 |
| 44.0 | 18 | 17 | 17 | 17 | 16 | 16 | 16 | 15 | 15 | 14 | 14 | 13 | 13 | 13 | 13 | 12 | 12 | 12 | 11 | 11 |
| 44.5 | 19 | 18 | 18 | 17 | 17 | 17 | 16 | 16 | 16 | 15 | 15 | 14 | 14 | 14 | 14 | 13 | 13 | 13 | 12 | 12 |
| 45.0 | 19 | 19 | 19 | 18 | 18 | 17 | 17 | 17 | 16 | 16 | 16 | 15 | 15 | 15 | 14 | 14 | 14 | 13 | 13 | 13 |
| 45.5 | 20 | 20 | 19 | 19 | 19 | 18 | 18 | 18 | 17 | 17 | 16 | 16 | 16 | 15 | 15 | 15 | 14 | 14 | 14 | 13 |
| 46.0 | 21 | 20 | 20 | 20 | 19 | 19 | 19 | 18 | 18 | 18 | 17 | 17 | 17 | 16 | 16 | 16 | 15 | 15 | 15 | 14 |
| 46.5 | 22 | 21 | 21 | 20 | 20 | 20 | 19 | 19 | 19 | 18 | 18 | 18 | 17 | 17 | 17 | 16 | 16 | 16 | 15 | 15 |
| 47.0 | 22 | 22 | 22 | 21 | 21 | 20 | 20 | 20 | 19 | 19 | 19 | 18 | 18 | 18 | 17 | 17 | 17 | 16 | 16 | 16 |
| 47.5 | 23 | 23 | 22 | 22 | 22 | 21 | 21 | 21 | 20 | 20 | 19 | 19 | 19 | 18 | 18 | 18 | 17 | 17 | 17 | 16 |
| 48.0 | 24 | 23 | 23 | 23 | 22 | 22 | 22 | 21 | 21 | 21 | 20 | 20 | 20 | 19 | 19 | 18 | 18 | 18 | 18 | 17 |
| 48.5 | 25 | 24 | 24 | 23 | 23 | 23 | 22 | 22 | 22 | 21 | 21 | 21 | 20 | 20 | 20 | 19 | 19 | 19 | 18 | 18 |
| 49.0 | 25 | 25 | 25 | 24 | 24 | 23 | 23 | 23 | 22 | 22 | 22 | 21 | 21 | 21 | 20 | 20 | 20 | 19 | 19 | 19 |
| 49.5 | 26 | 26 | 25 | 25 | 24 | 24 | 24 | 23 | 23 | 23 | 22 | 22 | 22 | 21 | 21 | 21 | 20 | 20 | 20 | 19 |
| 50.0 | 27 | 26 | 26 | 26 | 25 | 25 | 24 | 24 | 24 | 23 | 23 | 23 | 22 | 22 | 22 | 21 | 21 | 21 | 20 | 20 |
| 50.5 | 27 | 27 | 27 | 26 | 26 | 26 | 25 | 25 | 24 | 24 | 24 | 23 | 23 | 23 | 22 | 22 | 22 | 21 | 21 | 21 |
| 51.0 | 28 | 28 | 27 | 27 | 27 | 26 | 26 | 25 | 25 | 25 | 24 | 24 | 24 | 23 | 23 | 23 | 22 | 22 | 22 | 21 |
| 51.5 | 29 | 28 | 28 | 28 | 27 | 27 | 26 | 26 | 26 | 25 | 25 | 25 | 24 | 24 | 24 | 23 | 23 | 23 | 22 | 22 |
| 52.0 | 29 | 29 | 29 | 28 | 28 | 28 | 27 | 27 | 27 | 26 | 26 | 25 | 25 | 25 | 24 | 24 | 24 | 23 | 23 | 23 |
| 52.5 | 30 | 30 | 29 | 29 | 29 | 28 | 28 | 28 | 27 | 27 | 26 | 26 | 26 | 25 | 25 | 25 | 24 | 24 | 24 | 23 |
| 53.0 | 31 | 30 | 30 | 30 | 29 | 29 | 29 | 28 | 28 | 27 | 27 | 27 | 26 | 26 | 26 | 25 | 25 | 25 | 24 | 24 |
| 53.5 | 31 | 31 | 31 | 30 | 30 | 30 | 29 | 29 | 28 | 28 | 28 | 27 | 27 | 27 | 26 | 26 | 26 | 25 | 25 | 25 |
| 54.0 | 32 | 32 | 31 | 31 | 31 | 30 | 30 | 30 | 29 | 29 | 28 | 28 | 28 | 27 | 27 | 26 | 26 | 26 | 26 | 25 |
| 54.5 | 33 | 32 | 32 | 32 | 31 | 31 | 31 | 30 | 30 | 29 | 29 | 29 | 28 | 28 | 28 | 27 | 27 | 27 | 26 | 26 |

| | Height in inches | | | | | | | | | | | | | | | | | | | |
|---|---|---|---|---|---|---|---|---|---|---|---|---|---|---|---|---|---|---|---|---|
| CV | 68.0 | 68.5 | 69.0 | 69.5 | 70.0 | 70.5 | 71.0 | 71.5 | 72.0 | 72.5 | 73.0 | 73.5 | 74.0 | 74.5 | 75.0 | 75.5 | 76.0 | 76.5 | 77.0 | 77.5 |
| 34.5 | - | - | - | - | - | - | - | - | - | - | - | - | - | - | - | - | - | - | - | - |
| 35.0 | - | - | - | - | - | - | - | - | - | - | - | - | - | - | - | - | - | - | - | - |
| 35.5 | - | - | - | - | - | - | - | - | - | - | - | - | - | - | - | - | - | - | - | - |
| 36.0 | - | - | - | - | - | - | - | - | - | - | - | - | - | - | - | - | - | - | - | - |
| 36.5 | - | - | - | - | - | - | - | - | - | - | - | - | - | - | - | - | - | - | - | - |
| 37.0 | - | - | - | - | - | - | - | - | - | - | - | - | - | - | - | - | - | - | - | - |
| 37.5 | - | - | - | - | - | - | - | - | - | - | - | - | - | - | - | - | - | - | - | - |
| 38.0 | 0 | 0 | - | - | - | - | - | - | - | - | - | - | - | - | - | - | - | - | - | - |
| 38.5 | 1 | 1 | 1 | 0 | 0 | - | - | - | - | - | - | - | - | - | - | - | - | - | - | - |
| 39.0 | 2 | 2 | 2 | 1 | 1 | 1 | 0 | 0 | - | - | - | - | - | - | - | - | - | - | - | - |
| 39.5 | 3 | 3 | 3 | 2 | 2 | 2 | 1 | 1 | 1 | 0 | 0 | - | - | - | - | - | - | - | - | - |
| 40.0 | 4 | 4 | 3 | 3 | 3 | 3 | 2 | 2 | 2 | 1 | 1 | 1 | 0 | 0 | - | - | - | - | - | - |
| 40.5 | 5 | 5 | 4 | 4 | 4 | 3 | 3 | 3 | 2 | 2 | 2 | 2 | 1 | 1 | 1 | 0 | 0 | - | - | - |
| 41.0 | 6 | 5 | 5 | 5 | 5 | 4 | 4 | 4 | 3 | 3 | 3 | 2 | 2 | 2 | 2 | 1 | 1 | 1 | 0 | 0 |
| 41.5 | 7 | 6 | 6 | 6 | 5 | 5 | 5 | 4 | 4 | 4 | 4 | 3 | 3 | 3 | 2 | 2 | 2 | 2 | 1 | 1 |
| 42.0 | 8 | 7 | 7 | 7 | 6 | 6 | 6 | 5 | 5 | 5 | 4 | 4 | 4 | 4 | 3 | 3 | 3 | 2 | 2 | 2 |
| 42.5 | 8 | 8 | 8 | 7 | 7 | 7 | 6 | 6 | 6 | 6 | 5 | 5 | 5 | 4 | 4 | 4 | 3 | 3 | 3 | 3 |
| 43.0 | 9 | 9 | 9 | 8 | 8 | 8 | 7 | 7 | 7 | 6 | 6 | 6 | 5 | 5 | 5 | 5 | 4 | 4 | 4 | 3 |
| 43.5 | 10 | 10 | 9 | 9 | 9 | 8 | 8 | 8 | 7 | 7 | 7 | 7 | 6 | 6 | 5 | 5 | 5 | 5 | 5 | 4 |
| 44.0 | 11 | 10 | 10 | 10 | 9 | 9 | 9 | 9 | 8 | 8 | 8 | 7 | 7 | 6 | 6 | 6 | 6 | 6 | 5 | 5 |
| 44.5 | 12 | 11 | 11 | 11 | 10 | 10 | 10 | 9 | 9 | 9 | 8 | 8 | 8 | 8 | 7 | 7 | 7 | 6 | 6 | 6 |
| 45.0 | 12 | 12 | 12 | 11 | 11 | 11 | 10 | 10 | 10 | 10 | 9 | 9 | 9 | 8 | 8 | 8 | 7 | 7 | 7 | 7 |
| 45.5 | 13 | 13 | 12 | 12 | 12 | 12 | 11 | 11 | 11 | 10 | 10 | 10 | 9 | 9 | 9 | 9 | 8 | 8 | 8 | 7 |
| 46.0 | 14 | 14 | 13 | 13 | 13 | 12 | 12 | 12 | 11 | 11 | 11 | 10 | 10 | 10 | 10 | 9 | 9 | 9 | 8 | 8 |
| 46.5 | 15 | 14 | 14 | 14 | 13 | 13 | 13 | 12 | 12 | 12 | 12 | 11 | 11 | 11 | 10 | 10 | 10 | 9 | 9 | 9 |
| 47.0 | 15 | 15 | 15 | 14 | 14 | 14 | 13 | 13 | 13 | 13 | 12 | 12 | 12 | 11 | 11 | 11 | 11 | 10 | 10 | 10 |
| 47.5 | 16 | 16 | 15 | 15 | 15 | 15 | 14 | 14 | 14 | 13 | 13 | 13 | 12 | 12 | 12 | 12 | 11 | 11 | 11 | 10 |
| 48.0 | 17 | 17 | 16 | 16 | 16 | 15 | 15 | 15 | 14 | 14 | 14 | 13 | 13 | 13 | 13 | 12 | 12 | 12 | 11 | 11 |
| 48.5 | 18 | 17 | 17 | 17 | 16 | 16 | 16 | 15 | 15 | 15 | 14 | 14 | 14 | 14 | 13 | 13 | 13 | 12 | 12 | 12 |
| 49.0 | 18 | 18 | 18 | 17 | 17 | 17 | 16 | 16 | 16 | 15 | 15 | 15 | 15 | 14 | 14 | 14 | 13 | 13 | 13 | 13 |
| 49.5 | 19 | 19 | 18 | 18 | 18 | 17 | 17 | 17 | 17 | 16 | 16 | 16 | 15 | 15 | 15 | 14 | 14 | 14 | 14 | 13 |
| 50.0 | 20 | 19 | 19 | 19 | 18 | 18 | 18 | 18 | 17 | 17 | 17 | 16 | 16 | 16 | 15 | 15 | 15 | 15 | 14 | 14 |
| 50.5 | 20 | 20 | 20 | 19 | 19 | 19 | 19 | 18 | 18 | 18 | 17 | 17 | 17 | 16 | 16 | 16 | 16 | 15 | 15 | 15 |
| 51.0 | 21 | 21 | 20 | 20 | 20 | 20 | 19 | 19 | 19 | 18 | 18 | 18 | 17 | 17 | 17 | 17 | 16 | 16 | 16 | 15 |
| 51.5 | 22 | 21 | 21 | 21 | 21 | 20 | 20 | 20 | 19 | 19 | 19 | 18 | 18 | 18 | 17 | 17 | 17 | 17 | 16 | 16 |
| 52.0 | 22 | 22 | 22 | 22 | 21 | 21 | 21 | 20 | 20 | 20 | 19 | 19 | 19 | 18 | 18 | 18 | 18 | 17 | 17 | 17 |
| 52.5 | 23 | 23 | 22 | 22 | 22 | 22 | 21 | 21 | 21 | 20 | 20 | 20 | 19 | 19 | 19 | 19 | 18 | 18 | 18 | 17 |
| 53.0 | 24 | 23 | 23 | 23 | 23 | 22 | 22 | 22 | 21 | 21 | 21 | 20 | 20 | 20 | 20 | 19 | 19 | 19 | 18 | 18 |
| 53.5 | 24 | 24 | 24 | 23 | 23 | 23 | 23 | 22 | 22 | 22 | 21 | 21 | 21 | 20 | 20 | 20 | 20 | 19 | 19 | 19 |
| 54.0 | 25 | 25 | 24 | 24 | 24 | 24 | 23 | 23 | 23 | 22 | 22 | 22 | 21 | 21 | 21 | 21 | 20 | 20 | 20 | 19 |
| 54.5 | 26 | 25 | 25 | 25 | 24 | 24 | 24 | 24 | 23 | 23 | 23 | 22 | 22 | 22 | 21 | 21 | 21 | 21 | 20 | 20 |

(continued)

*(continued)*

**Height in inches**

| CV | 58.0 | 58.5 | 59.0 | 59.5 | 60.0 | 60.5 | 61.0 | 61.5 | 62.0 | 62.5 | 63.0 | 63.5 | 64.0 | 64.5 | 65.0 | 65.5 | 66.0 | 66.5 | 67.0 | 67.5 |
|---|---|---|---|---|---|---|---|---|---|---|---|---|---|---|---|---|---|---|---|---|
| 55.0 | 33 | 33 | 33 | 32 | 32 | 32 | 31 | 31 | 30 | 30 | 30 | 29 | 29 | 29 | 28 | 28 | 28 | 27 | 27 | 27 |
| 55.5 | 34 | 34 | 33 | 33 | 33 | 32 | 32 | 31 | 31 | 31 | 30 | 30 | 30 | 29 | 29 | 29 | 28 | 28 | 28 | 27 |
| 56.0 | 35 | 34 | 34 | 33 | 33 | 33 | 32 | 32 | 32 | 31 | 31 | 31 | 30 | 30 | 30 | 29 | 29 | 29 | 28 | 28 |
| 56.5 | 35 | 35 | 34 | 34 | 34 | 33 | 33 | 33 | 32 | 32 | 32 | 31 | 31 | 31 | 30 | 30 | 30 | 29 | 29 | 29 |
| 57.0 | 36 | 35 | 35 | 35 | 34 | 34 | 34 | 33 | 33 | 33 | 32 | 32 | 32 | 31 | 31 | 31 | 30 | 30 | 30 | 29 |
| 57.5 | 36 | 36 | 36 | 35 | 35 | 35 | 34 | 34 | 34 | 33 | 33 | 32 | 32 | 32 | 31 | 31 | 31 | 30 | 30 | 30 |
| 58.0 | 37 | 37 | 36 | 36 | 36 | 35 | 35 | 35 | 34 | 34 | 33 | 33 | 33 | 32 | 32 | 32 | 31 | 31 | 31 | 30 |
| 58.5 | 38 | 37 | 37 | 37 | 36 | 36 | 35 | 35 | 35 | 34 | 34 | 34 | 33 | 33 | 33 | 32 | 32 | 32 | 31 | 31 |
| 59.0 | 38 | 38 | 38 | 37 | 37 | 36 | 36 | 36 | 35 | 35 | 35 | 34 | 34 | 34 | 33 | 33 | 33 | 32 | 32 | 32 |
| 59.5 | 39 | 38 | 38 | 38 | 37 | 37 | 37 | 36 | 36 | 36 | 35 | 35 | 35 | 34 | 34 | 34 | 33 | 33 | 33 | 32 |
| 60.0 | 39 | 39 | 39 | 38 | 38 | 38 | 37 | 37 | 37 | 36 | 36 | 35 | 35 | 35 | 34 | 34 | 34 | 33 | 33 | 33 |
| 60.5 | 40 | 40 | 39 | 39 | 39 | 38 | 38 | 37 | 37 | 37 | 36 | 36 | 36 | 35 | 35 | 35 | 34 | 34 | 34 | 33 |
| 61.0 | 41 | 40 | 40 | 39 | 39 | 39 | 38 | 38 | 38 | 37 | 37 | 37 | 36 | 36 | 36 | 35 | 35 | 35 | 34 | 34 |
| 61.5 | 41 | 41 | 40 | 40 | 40 | 39 | 39 | 39 | 38 | 38 | 38 | 37 | 37 | 37 | 36 | 36 | 36 | 35 | 35 | 35 |
| 62.0 | 42 | 41 | 41 | 41 | 40 | 40 | 40 | 39 | 39 | 38 | 38 | 38 | 37 | 37 | 37 | 36 | 36 | 36 | 35 | 35 |
| 62.5 | 42 | 42 | 42 | 41 | 41 | 40 | 40 | 40 | 39 | 39 | 39 | 38 | 38 | 38 | 37 | 37 | 37 | 36 | 36 | 36 |
| 63.0 | 43 | 42 | 42 | 42 | 41 | 41 | 41 | 40 | 40 | 40 | 39 | 39 | 39 | 38 | 38 | 38 | 37 | 37 | 37 | 36 |
| 63.5 | 43 | 43 | 43 | 42 | 42 | 42 | 41 | 41 | 40 | 40 | 40 | 39 | 39 | 39 | 38 | 38 | 38 | 37 | 37 | 37 |
| 64.0 | 44 | 44 | 43 | 43 | 42 | 42 | 42 | 41 | 41 | 41 | 40 | 40 | 40 | 39 | 39 | 39 | 38 | 38 | 38 | 37 |
| 64.5 | 45 | 44 | 44 | 43 | 43 | 43 | 42 | 42 | 42 | 41 | 41 | 41 | 40 | 40 | 40 | 39 | 39 | 39 | 38 | 38 |
| 65.0 |  | 45 | 44 | 44 | 44 | 43 | 43 | 42 | 42 | 42 | 41 | 41 | 41 | 40 | 40 | 40 | 39 | 39 | 39 | 38 |
| 65.5 |  |  | 45 | 44 | 44 | 44 | 43 | 43 | 43 | 42 | 42 | 42 | 41 | 41 | 41 | 40 | 40 | 40 | 39 | 39 |
| 66.0 |  |  |  |  | 45 | 44 | 44 | 44 | 43 | 43 | 43 | 42 | 42 | 41 | 41 | 41 | 40 | 40 | 40 | 39 |
| 66.5 |  |  |  |  |  | 45 | 44 | 44 | 44 | 43 | 43 | 43 | 42 | 42 | 42 | 41 | 41 | 41 | 40 | 40 |
| 67.0 |  |  |  |  |  |  | 45 | 45 | 44 | 44 | 44 | 43 | 43 | 43 | 42 | 42 | 42 | 41 | 41 | 41 |
| 67.5 |  |  |  |  |  |  |  |  | 45 | 44 | 44 | 44 | 43 | 43 | 43 | 42 | 42 | 42 | 41 | 41 |
| 68.0 |  |  |  |  |  |  |  |  |  | 45 | 45 | 44 | 44 | 44 | 43 | 43 | 43 | 42 | 42 | 42 |
| 68.5 |  |  |  |  |  |  |  |  |  |  |  | 45 | 44 | 44 | 44 | 43 | 43 | 43 | 42 | 42 |
| 69.0 |  |  |  |  |  |  |  |  |  |  |  |  | 45 | 45 | 44 | 44 | 44 | 43 | 43 | 43 |
| 69.5 |  |  |  |  |  |  |  |  |  |  |  |  |  |  | 45 | 44 | 44 | 44 | 43 | 43 |
| 70.0 |  |  |  |  |  |  |  |  |  |  |  |  |  |  |  | 45 | 45 | 44 | 44 | 44 |
| 70.5 |  |  |  |  |  |  |  |  |  |  |  |  |  |  |  |  |  | 45 | 44 | 44 |
| 71.0 |  |  |  |  |  |  |  |  |  |  |  |  |  |  |  |  |  |  | 45 | 45 |
| 71.5 |  |  |  |  |  |  |  |  |  |  |  |  |  |  |  |  |  |  |  |  |
| 72.0 |  |  |  |  |  |  |  |  |  |  |  |  |  |  |  |  |  |  |  |  |
| 72.5 |  |  |  |  |  |  |  |  |  |  |  |  |  |  |  |  |  |  |  |  |
| 73.0 |  |  |  |  |  |  |  |  |  |  |  |  |  |  |  |  |  |  |  |  |
| 73.5 |  |  |  |  |  |  |  |  |  |  |  |  |  |  |  |  |  |  |  |  |
| 74.0 |  |  |  |  |  |  |  |  |  |  |  |  |  |  |  |  |  |  |  |  |
| 74.5 |  |  |  |  |  |  |  |  |  |  |  |  |  |  |  |  |  |  |  |  |
| 75.0 |  |  |  |  |  |  |  |  |  |  |  |  |  |  |  |  |  |  |  |  |
| 75.5 |  |  |  |  |  |  |  |  |  |  |  |  |  |  |  |  |  |  |  |  |

| Height in inches | | | | | | | | | | | | | | | | | | | | |
|---|---|---|---|---|---|---|---|---|---|---|---|---|---|---|---|---|---|---|---|---|
| CV | 68.0 | 68.5 | 69.0 | 69.5 | 70.0 | 70.5 | 71.0 | 71.5 | 72.0 | 72.5 | 73.0 | 73.5 | 74.0 | 74.5 | 75.0 | 75.5 | 76.0 | 76.5 | 77.0 | 77.5 |
| 55.0 | 26 | 26 | 26 | 25 | 25 | 25 | 24 | 24 | 24 | 24 | 23 | 23 | 23 | 22 | 22 | 22 | 22 | 21 | 21 | 21 |
| 55.5 | 27 | 27 | 26 | 26 | 26 | 25 | 25 | 25 | 25 | 24 | 24 | 24 | 23 | 23 | 23 | 22 | 22 | 22 | 22 | 21 |
| 56.0 | 28 | 27 | 27 | 27 | 26 | 26 | 26 | 25 | 25 | 25 | 25 | 24 | 24 | 24 | 23 | 23 | 23 | 22 | 22 | 22 |
| 56.5 | 28 | 28 | 28 | 27 | 27 | 27 | 26 | 26 | 26 | 25 | 25 | 25 | 25 | 24 | 24 | 24 | 23 | 23 | 23 | 23 |
| 57.0 | 29 | 29 | 28 | 28 | 28 | 27 | 27 | 27 | 26 | 26 | 26 | 25 | 25 | 25 | 25 | 24 | 24 | 24 | 23 | 23 |
| 57.5 | 30 | 29 | 29 | 29 | 28 | 28 | 28 | 27 | 27 | 27 | 26 | 26 | 26 | 26 | 25 | 25 | 25 | 24 | 24 | 24 |
| 58.0 | 30 | 30 | 29 | 29 | 29 | 29 | 28 | 28 | 28 | 27 | 27 | 27 | 26 | 26 | 26 | 26 | 25 | 25 | 25 | 24 |
| 58.5 | 31 | 30 | 30 | 30 | 29 | 29 | 29 | 29 | 28 | 28 | 28 | 27 | 27 | 27 | 26 | 26 | 26 | 26 | 25 | 25 |
| 59.0 | 31 | 31 | 31 | 30 | 30 | 30 | 29 | 29 | 29 | 28 | 28 | 28 | 28 | 27 | 27 | 27 | 26 | 26 | 26 | 26 |
| 59.5 | 32 | 32 | 31 | 31 | 31 | 30 | 30 | 30 | 29 | 29 | 29 | 28 | 28 | 28 | 28 | 27 | 27 | 27 | 26 | 26 |
| 60.0 | 32 | 32 | 32 | 32 | 31 | 31 | 31 | 30 | 30 | 30 | 29 | 29 | 29 | 28 | 28 | 28 | 28 | 27 | 27 | 27 |
| 60.5 | 33 | 33 | 32 | 32 | 32 | 31 | 31 | 31 | 31 | 30 | 30 | 30 | 29 | 29 | 29 | 28 | 28 | 28 | 28 | 27 |
| 61.0 | 34 | 33 | 33 | 33 | 32 | 32 | 32 | 31 | 31 | 31 | 31 | 30 | 30 | 30 | 29 | 29 | 29 | 28 | 28 | 28 |
| 61.5 | 34 | 34 | 34 | 33 | 33 | 33 | 32 | 32 | 32 | 31 | 31 | 31 | 31 | 30 | 30 | 30 | 29 | 29 | 29 | 28 |
| 62.0 | 35 | 34 | 34 | 34 | 34 | 33 | 33 | 33 | 32 | 32 | 32 | 31 | 31 | 31 | 30 | 30 | 30 | 30 | 29 | 29 |
| 62.5 | 35 | 35 | 35 | 34 | 34 | 34 | 33 | 33 | 33 | 33 | 32 | 32 | 32 | 31 | 31 | 31 | 30 | 30 | 30 | 30 |
| 63.0 | 36 | 36 | 35 | 35 | 35 | 34 | 34 | 34 | 33 | 33 | 33 | 32 | 32 | 32 | 32 | 31 | 31 | 31 | 30 | 30 |
| 63.5 | 36 | 36 | 36 | 35 | 35 | 35 | 35 | 34 | 34 | 34 | 33 | 33 | 33 | 32 | 32 | 32 | 32 | 31 | 31 | 31 |
| 64.0 | 37 | 37 | 36 | 36 | 36 | 35 | 35 | 35 | 35 | 34 | 34 | 34 | 33 | 33 | 33 | 32 | 32 | 32 | 32 | 31 |
| 64.5 | 38 | 37 | 37 | 37 | 36 | 36 | 36 | 35 | 35 | 35 | 34 | 34 | 34 | 34 | 33 | 33 | 33 | 32 | 32 | 32 |
| 65.0 | 38 | 38 | 37 | 37 | 37 | 37 | 36 | 36 | 36 | 35 | 35 | 35 | 34 | 34 | 34 | 34 | 33 | 32 | 33 | 32 |
| 65.5 | 39 | 38 | 38 | 38 | 37 | 37 | 37 | 36 | 36 | 36 | 36 | 35 | 35 | 35 | 34 | 34 | 34 | 33 | 33 | 33 |
| 66.0 | 39 | 39 | 39 | 38 | 38 | 38 | 37 | 37 | 37 | 36 | 36 | 36 | 35 | 35 | 35 | 35 | 34 | 34 | 34 | 33 |
| 66.5 | 40 | 39 | 39 | 39 | 38 | 38 | 38 | 37 | 37 | 37 | 37 | 36 | 36 | 36 | 35 | 35 | 35 | 35 | 34 | 34 |
| 67.0 | 40 | 40 | 40 | 39 | 39 | 39 | 38 | 38 | 38 | 37 | 37 | 37 | 37 | 36 | 36 | 36 | 35 | 35 | 35 | 34 |
| 67.5 | 41 | 40 | 40 | 40 | 39 | 39 | 39 | 39 | 38 | 38 | 38 | 37 | 37 | 37 | 36 | 36 | 36 | 36 | 35 | 35 |
| 68.0 | 41 | 41 | 41 | 40 | 40 | 40 | 39 | 39 | 39 | 38 | 38 | 38 | 38 | 37 | 37 | 37 | 36 | 36 | 36 | 36 |
| 68.5 | 42 | 41 | 41 | 41 | 40 | 40 | 40 | 40 | 39 | 39 | 39 | 38 | 38 | 38 | 37 | 37 | 37 | 37 | 36 | 36 |
| 69.0 | 42 | 42 | 42 | 41 | 41 | 41 | 40 | 40 | 40 | 39 | 39 | 39 | 39 | 38 | 38 | 38 | 37 | 37 | 37 | 37 |
| 69.5 | 43 | 42 | 42 | 42 | 42 | 41 | 41 | 41 | 40 | 40 | 40 | 39 | 39 | 39 | 38 | 38 | 38 | 38 | 37 | 37 |
| 70.0 | 43 | 43 | 43 | 42 | 42 | 42 | 41 | 41 | 41 | 40 | 40 | 40 | 40 | 39 | 39 | 39 | 38 | 38 | 38 | 38 |
| 70.5 | 44 | 43 | 43 | 43 | 43 | 42 | 42 | 42 | 41 | 41 | 41 | 40 | 40 | 40 | 39 | 39 | 39 | 39 | 38 | 38 |
| 71.0 | 44 | 44 | 44 | 43 | 43 | 43 | 42 | 42 | 42 | 41 | 41 | 41 | 41 | 40 | 40 | 40 | 39 | 39 | 39 | 39 |
| 71.5 | 45 | 44 | 44 | 44 | 43 | 43 | 43 | 43 | 42 | 42 | 42 | 41 | 41 | 41 | 40 | 40 | 40 | 40 | 39 | 39 |
| 72.0 |  | 45 | 45 | 44 | 44 | 44 | 43 | 43 | 43 | 42 | 42 | 42 | 42 | 41 | 41 | 41 | 40 | 40 | 40 | 40 |
| 72.5 |  |  | 45 | 44 | 44 | 44 | 44 | 43 | 43 | 43 | 42 | 42 | 42 | 41 | 41 | 41 | 41 | 40 | 40 |  |
| 73.0 |  |  |  | 45 | 45 | 44 | 44 | 44 | 43 | 43 | 43 | 43 | 42 | 42 | 42 | 41 | 41 | 41 | 40 |  |
| 73.5 |  |  |  |  |  | 45 | 44 | 44 | 44 | 44 | 43 | 43 | 43 | 42 | 42 | 42 | 42 | 41 | 41 |  |
| 74.0 |  |  |  |  |  | 45 | 45 | 44 | 44 | 44 | 43 | 43 | 43 | 43 | 42 | 42 | 42 | 41 |  |  |
| 74.5 |  |  |  |  |  |  |  | 45 | 45 | 44 | 44 | 44 | 43 | 43 | 43 | 42 | 42 | 42 |  |  |
| 75.0 |  |  |  |  |  |  |  |  |  | 45 | 44 | 44 | 44 | 44 | 43 | 43 | 43 | 42 |  |  |
| 75.5 |  |  |  |  |  |  |  |  |  |  | 45 | 45 | 44 | 44 | 44 | 43 | 43 | 43 |  |  |

[a]CV = Upper abdominal girth + hip girth - neck girth

Source: *Exercise physiology laboratory manual*, 2nd ed. Gene Adams, 1994.

# Strength-Training Glossary

**aerobic muscle fibers**—Type I muscle fibers used for muscular endurance.

**agonist**—The muscle initiating a desired movement.

**anaerobic muscle fibers**—Type II muscles fibers used for strength and power.

**antagonist**—The opposing muscle in a contraction, located on the opposite side of the joint.

**ATP**—Adenosine triphosphate; the energy for muscle activity.

**basal metabolic rate (BMR)**—The amount of energy that the body needs for normal physiological functioning while we are awake.

**concentric contraction**—A shortening and contracting of the muscle.

**delayed-onset muscle soreness (DOMS)**—The scientific term for the muscle soreness you feel after a weight-training session.

**eccentric contraction**—A lengthening and contracting of the muscle.

**estimated energy requirement (EER)**—The dietary energy intake predicted to maintain energy balance consistent with good health in healthy, normal-weight individuals of a defined age, gender, weight, height, and level of physical activity.

**fat-free mass (FFM)**—The portion of muscle, bone, and organ weight that contains no fat.

**fat mass (FM)**—Total body fat, which includes essential fat and storage fat.

**frequency**—The number of training sessions completed in a certain time period.

**functional training**—Training that utilizes specific exercises that mimic sports or life movements.

**hyperplasia**—The splitting of muscle fibers to make more muscle fibers.

**hypertrophy**—An enlargement of the muscle fiber.

**intensity**—The level of difficulty of an exercise, relating to load. It can be measured by a percentage of the RM, with 1RM (100 percent RM) being the highest intensity

**interval training**—The division of a training period into work and rest intervals.

**isometric contraction**—A contraction of the muscle without joint movement.

**isotonic contraction**—A contraction that involves a concentric phase, in which the weight is lifted and the muscle is shortened, and an eccentric phase, in which the weight is slowly lowered and the muscle is lengthened under tension.

**lean body mass (LBM**—The amount of fat-free and some essential fat mass.

**load**—The amount of weight assigned to an exercise set.

**metabolic training**—Classically, training an athlete's body at particular work and rest intervals that closely mimic those the athlete encounters during her sport. It comes at a high metabolic cost to the body, and it is now also associated with interval training.

**muscular endurance**—The ability to do submaximal muscular contractions with high repetitions, low intensity, high volume, and little recovery between sets.

**one-repetition maximum (1RM)**—The most weight that can be lifted with perfect technique one time.

**osteoporosis**—Porous bone; low bone mass that leads to structural deterioration of bone tissue and bone fragility and that can result in fractures.

**plyometrics**—Exercise that employs the stretch-shortening cycle; quick, powerful movements preceded by a prestretch of the muscles.

**power**—The exertion of force at a high speed.

**repetition**—The number of times an exercise is performed.

**repetition maximum (RM)**—The most weight that can be lifted for a specific number of repetitions.

**resting metabolic rate (RMR)**—A rate that includes the basal metabolic rate plus the amount of energy we use when we are sleeping and waking up from sleep.

**set**—A group of repetitions.

**strength**—The ability to exert force.

**thermic effect of food (TEF)**—The energy (calories) required for the processes of chewing, digestion, and absorption.

**total daily energy expenditure (TDEE)**—A combination of the resting metabolic rate, physical activity, and the thermic effect of food (TEF).

**Type I muscle fibers (aerobic)**—Slow-twitch muscle fibers that are fatigue resistant. They are used for cardiovascular and muscular endurance work.

**Type II muscle fibers (anaerobic)**—Fast-twitch muscle fibers that fatigue quickly and that hypertrophy more than Type I fibers. They are used for short bursts of strength and power.

**volume**—The total amount of weight lifted in an entire training session (sets × repetitions).

# References and Resources

Adams, Gene. *Exercise Physiology Laboratory Manual.* 2nd ed. Wm. C. Brown Communications, Inc. USA, 1994.

Baechle, Thomas R., and Roger W. Earle, ed. *Essentials of Strength Training and Conditioning.* 2nd ed. Champaign, IL: Human Kinetics, 2000.

Bompa, Tudor O. *Periodization: Theory and Methodology of Training.* 4th ed. Champaign, IL: Human Kinetics, 1999.

Bompa, Tudor O., and Lorenzo J. Cornacchia. *Serious Strength Training.* Champaign, IL: Human Kinetics, 1998.

Costa, D. Margaret, and Sharon R. Guthrie, ed. *Woman and Sport: Interdisciplinary Perspectives.* Champaign, IL: Human Kinetics, 1994.

Fleck, Steven J., and William J. Kraemer. *Designing Resistance Training Programs.* 2nd ed. Champaign, IL: Human Kinetics, 1997.

Goldenberg, Lorne, and Peter Twist. *Strength Ball Training.* Champaign, IL: Human Kinetics, 2002.

Siff, Mel C., and Yuri V. Verkhoshansky. *Supertraining.* 4th ed. Denver: Supertraining International, 1999.


International Federation of Strength Athletes: www.ifsastrongestman.com

International Powerlifting Federation: www.powerlifting-ipf.com

International Weightlifting Federation: www.iwf.net

NASA Powerlifting: www.nasa-sports.com

National Osteoporosis Foundation's website at www.nof.org

North American Strongman Society: www.nastrongman.com

Supertraining group: http://health.groups.yahoo.com/group/supertraining

United States All-Round Weightlifting Federation: www.usawa.com

USA Powerlifting: www.usapowerlifting.com

USA Weightlifting: www.usaweightlifting.org


www.alwyncosgrove.com

www.davedraper.com

www.loriincledon.com

www.rachelcosgrove.com

www.thomasincledon.com

# Index

# About the Author

**Lori Incledon** serves as vice president of Human Performance Specialists, Inc. For more than 10 years she has been involved in personal training, sport-specific conditioning, physical therapy, athletic training, and injury prevention. She specializes in women's personal training, placing an emphasis on strength training.

Previously, Incledon was the head strength and conditioning specialist at Cypress Bay High School and St. Thomas Aquinas High School in Fort Lauderdale, Florida (where she was also the head athletic trainer). She initiated the strength and conditioning program for the then-new Cypress Bay, and during her time at St. Thomas she assisted in sending a majority of their sports teams to state competitions.

Incledon has a BS in public relations from the University of Florida, and an AS as a physical therapist assistant. She holds a National Athletic Trainers' Association certification in athletic training, and she is a certified strength and conditioning specialist and a certified personal trainer through the National Strength and Conditioning Association. Additionally, she is licensed in the states of Florida and Arizona as a physical therapist assistant and as an athletic trainer.

She is an active lecturer and rehabilitation consultant to high school, collegiate, and professional sports teams. Her freelance articles appear in *Muscle & Fitness*, *Muscle & Fitness Hers*, and on numerous Internet sites.

Incledon lives in Chandler, Arizona.

# More advice for training and fueling the female body!

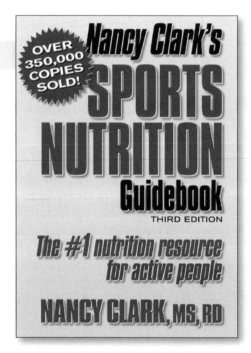